FRENCH ENTRÉE 10
THE SOUTH
OF FRANCE

A Gatwick Guide

D1003975

FRENCH ENTRÉE 10
THE SOUTH OF FRANCE

Peter King and Patricia Fenn

Quiller Press

First published 1992 by Quiller Press Ltd
46 Lillie Road, London SW6 1TN

Line drawings: Emma Macleod-Johnstone
Area maps: Paul Emra
Design and production in association with
Book Production Consultants, Cambridge

ISBN 1 870948 55 6

Photoset by Rowland Phototypesetting Ltd
Bury St Edmunds, Suffolk
Printed in Great Britain by
Cox and Wyman Ltd, Reading, Berks.

**For a full list of the *French Entrée* Series and related titles, please see
the last pages of this book**

Contents

Notes on using the book – and an appeal

1 The area maps are to help the reader to find the place he wishes to visit on his own map. Each place is given a reference on the relevant area map, but they are not designed to replace a good touring map.

2 A number in brackets at the beginning of a telephone number is the area dialling code, used when making calls from outside the area.

3 o.o.s. stands for 'out of season'. Other abbreviations such as f for francs, are standard.

4 L, M or S in the margin stand for 'L' = Luxury, 'S' = Simple and 'M' for those in between.

5 H stands for Hotel and R for Restaurant in combination with 4 above, ie (H)S, (R)L etc.

6 stc means service and taxes are included (*service et taxes compris*).

7 The ➤ symbol means the establishment fulfils exceptionally well at least one of the author's criteria of comfort, welcome and cuisine – see also page 41.

8 P. stands for parking, Ⓣ for Tourist Office and Ⓜ for market day. ᴘᴠ indicates a perched village (see p. 26).

9 Credit cards: *A* = Access, *AE* = American Express, *V* = Visa, *DC* = Diners Club, *EC* is Eurocard and *CB* = Carte Bleue.

10 Prices represent a room for two people, except for demi-pension, which is per head.

11 The numbers with the addresses, eg. 62000, are the postal codes, which should be used in all correspondence.

Author's appeal
In order to keep *French Entrée* up to date I need all the latest information I can get on establishments listed in the guide. If you have any comments on these or any other details that might supplement my own researching I should be most grateful if you would pass them on.

Please include the name and address of establishment, date and duration of visit. Also please state if you will allow your name to be used.

**Patricia Fenn,
c/o Quiller Press
46 Lillie Road
London SW6 1TN**

FOREWORD

On May 17 1936 a de Havilland DH-86 took off from London's Gatwick Airport bound for Paris and a place in aviation history. The passengers, paying the princely sum of four pounds and five shillings (including return first-class rail fare from London), were embarked on the first international scheduled service from an airport which had once been a racecourse and was destined to become one of the busiest international airports in the world.

Not surprisingly Gatwick has maintained its strong links with France. It now has routes to 17 cities, with eight airlines operating 204 flights a week between them – there are 12 flights a day to Paris alone, which remains Gatwick's most popular destination.

It therefore seems most fitting that Gatwick Airport Ltd should support this latest *French Entrée* guide which, we are sure, will prove a vital part of the travel tool-kit for those bound for the South of France – perhaps through Gatwick, which has scheduled routes to the region through Perpignan, Montpellier and Nice.

Air travel has developed in leaps and bounds since that first flight in 1936, opening up the world, broadening horizons and making it possible for those even on limited budgets to travel abroad. It is also still one of the most exciting ways to travel.

The role of an airport like Gatwick, and its 'sister' airports within BAA, is to help make that journey by air pleasant and trouble-free – working with the airlines and other airport-based companies to provide the best possible service, from the time passengers arrive and check in to the time they are airborne. With nearly 20 million passengers a year, Gatwick has plenty of experience and gets lots of practice.

We like travellers to feel that their holiday really starts when they arrive at the airport – and we are confident that, armed with a copy of *French Entrée*, the rest of their trip is sure to be a success.

Allan Munds
Managing Director,
Gatwick Airport Ltd.

ENTRÉE TO THE ENTRÉES

I thought I knew the South of France well. It was there that I had had my first ever foreign holiday. There had been subsequent regular family holidays in hotels, villas, boats and caravans. We had numerous friends who lived in the area. We would sneak down whenever an excuse beckoned for a fix of sunshine, wine and roses. It was not until I read Peter's manuscript that I realised that my knowledge barely scratched the surface. He made me ache to explore those perched villages, to experience the festivals and to share in the unique southern way of life that still exists a few miles away from the fleshpots, so surprisingly intact, and withstanding the onslaught of international tourism.

I was reluctant to delegate the writing of a *French Entrée* to anyone else. These books have been my babies – nine of them, with faults and credits attributable to no one else – bringing enormous gratification which I was not anxious to share. But whereas research on Normandy and the Pas de Calais for previous guides was but a short hop away, that on the South of France would involve more planning, more effort and especially more time. I realise now too that it also involves more local knowledge than I had or could hope to acquire in a short time.

Peter was the ideal collaborator. He lives in Valbonne, works in Monaco, and communicates vividly his love of his home ground. Apart from the entries on Le Lavandou, Port Grimaud, Menton, Cannes, Bormes-les Mimosas, and part of Antibes – places I know particularly well – all the work has been his. It has been an illumination to edit his research. I know that both faithful *Entrée* readers and new devotees will enjoy and profit from his accounts as much as I have.

How many of the bodies sardined on the beaches have even heard of the Grand Canyon de Verdon, let alone taken time off from tanning to explore it? This book will be of no interest to them. Rather it is for those with a mind open enough to conceive that one holiday – or one day for that matter – could encompass a walk along the Croisette, a swim in the Med, a discovery of a mediaeval village, a mountain climb, an evening fashion promenade, and dinner at a bistro under the stars.

Accept the gloss and the glitter by all means – it was invented here, after all – but don't be fooled into the popular misconception that there's where the Riviera begins and ends. Disprove the fallacy that it's all crowds and concrete. Visit it in spring or autumn, as early as Easter, as late as October, when the French shudder at the thought of outdoor exposure, and you will find empty beaches and, if you're lucky, water that is warm by British standards. If you have to stick to school holidays, avoid the coast and make for the hills.

Remember that the Riviera was developed early simply because it was the most beautiful coastline in Europe. It still is and there's a lot of it about between the tower blocks. Resorts like Villefranche, Beaulieu and Menton were built at a time of prosperity, when embellishment and extravagance were the pattern, and their architecture and style are correspondingly infinitely more attractive than a new custom-built holiday centre can ever be. Antibes, St-Tropez and Cannes have fishing village ancestry and still benefit from their picturesque natural harbours and fleets of working fishing boats – but it's fun to gawp at their beautiful people too. Every day there's a free peepshow outside the casino in Monte Carlo, among the cafés in St-Trop, along the Croisette in Cannes, by the marina in Antibes. Who needs television?

Most holidaymakers will want to explore the legendary coastline, at least a few kilometres either side of their lodging place. The choice is vast. So vast that a limit had to be placed on the western extremity. Lovely Le Lavandou seemed to be the appropriate full stop, before the holiday atmosphere gives way to Toulon and Marseille. Personally, I would have liked to include some of the less fashionable little ports like Bandol and Cassis beyond Toulon, but, as usual, time and space ran out, and these will have to wait for further editions. Beyond the barrier of the autoroute at Marseille the character of the Camargue and the new holiday town developments are so utterly incompatible with the character of the rest of this territory that there was little temptation to investigate their possibilities.

We had plenty to be getting on with. The obvious eastern limit was the Italian border and the charmingly old-fashioned Anglophile **Menton**. The contrasts of the region become immediately evident from the proximity of Menton's unfashionable, somewhat staid image to that of its unlikely neighbour, scintillating **Monte Carlo**. The Caps **Martin**, **d'Ail** and **Ferrat** break away from the busy coast roads and offer comparative calm; **Beaulieu** reverts to Edwardian decorum; **Villefranche** combines traditional fishing-harbour charm with café animation, before the sweep of **Nice**'s incomparable Bay of Angels. **Antibes** has it all ways – intriguing explorable old walled town next to jet-set modern marina. After cosmopolitan **Cannes**, Queen of the Riviera, the main roads and most of the traffic cut inland to avoid the Esterel massif, leaving behind a succession of little-known resorts, Le Trayas, Anthéor and Agay, backed by those extraordinary red mountains of the Esterel, so unlike anything else on the Riviera. From bustling **St-Raphaël**, going its own very French way, impervious to the Riviera hype, the beaches of **Fréjus**, St-Aygulf and Les Issambres are more family-orientated, less expensive, more camp-prone; **Ste-Maxime** is good for everyday shopping, chalk and cheese from its unrepentantly over-the-top neighbour just across the bay, **St-Tropez**.

Satellite beaches, renowned for their fine sands and fine bosoms, spread all round the headland, which escaped wholesale development until comparatively recently; the new villas still being built there are mostly upmarket holiday homes, and there are few hotels. Cavalaire and its bay I find rather dull, but between here and **Le Lavandou** it is still possible to find little coves and beaches unaffected by tourist influx. This is a stretch that the French are determined to keep to themselves. Le Rayol in particular does not take kindly to foreign invasion, and has a clubby atmosphere for its regular visitors. **Le Lavandou**, one erstwhile fishing village which has adapted to the 90s more or less gracefully, is a particular personal favourite.

All this I knew. I was familiar too with some of the interior, from sorties into the hills for picnics, wet day drives, alternatives to steamy days on the beaches. I had visited the obvious tourist attractions – Grasse, Vence, Mougins and a few of the smaller perched villages; I had even explored some of the gorges and Lac St-Cassien, and marvelled that their outstanding beauty was not better known. But I had no idea about the variety and richness of all the other scenery and villages just behind the coastal strip that Peter, from his in-depth local knowledge, has described. He has sold me the passionate desire to explore them. If nobody else benefits from this book, I emphatically shall.

For hotels and restaurants this is not an easy area to cover. Many of the most famous and expensive hotels in the world are sited here, but finding recommendable examples for the more budget-conscious is not at all the same as with Normandy for example, where the problem is which of the many worthy contestants to leave out. I am frankly amazed at what Peter has unearthed. In spite of protestations that the Riviera is not all mega-bucks, I never expected to be able to include so many wholesome little inns and bistros as he has dug out.

If there are omissions in *FE10* it is those of the 'L' grade establishments, which are so thick on the ground that anyone can find them without much help. Locals like Peter tend not to use them; not only because of their cost, but because many of them are more geared to the seriously rich international set than to the holidaymaker feeling like an odd splurge (i.e. the typical *FE* reader).

Similarly, in common with the previous *Entrées*, chain hotels don't feature here. Practical though they may be, they need no description from me to paint the picture. Once you've seen one in Boulogne or Burgundy you can guess what its clone in Provence will have to offer.

As regular *French Entrée* readers will well know, the restaurants and hotels are graded into 'L' for Luxury, 'M' for Medium and 'S' for Simple. We could have left it at that, but decided for the moment to continue the practice of quoting actual prices, correct at the time of going to press (helpful for the reader, hell for me!). Very approximately: 'L' hotels cost over 600f; 'M' between 300 and 600, and 'S' less than 300f (always for a double room). 'L' restaurants will set you back more than 250f per meal without wine; 'M' between 100 and 250f, and 'S' less than 100f. *French Entrées* deliberately do not stick to one price band, believing that the same reader will have need of several ('S' with the family, 'L' with the secretary).

The arrows are awarded for outstanding characteristics – good cooking, good value, good location, comfort, welcome.

Patricia Fenn.

INTRODUCTION

So you have arrived in the South of France – one of the great playgrounds of the world! You can find a clean and comfortable room for 60 francs or you can have a more luxurious one for 2,500 francs. You can enjoy a three-course meal for 48 francs or a grander six-course meal for 600 francs.

You can see Khashoggi's £60 million yacht (which may still be on sale when you arrive, should you be interested), and you can see the villa that Andrew Lloyd-Webber paid £13.5 million for and spends one or two weeks a year in. Or you can see the topless and bottomless beaches which don't cost anything.

You can try breaking the bank at Monte Carlo; you can attend the Cannes Film Festival and rub shoulders with the stars; you can watch the Monaco Grand Prix; you can see the world's top tennis players, golfers and soccer players – and you can see the finest entertainers from Frank Sinatra to Dire Straits to Placido Domingo to the Bolshoi Ballet.

You may want to visit the island where the Man in the Iron Mask was imprisoned or you might like to stay in the former home of the Marquis de Sade. You may prefer to see the village which Picasso turned into a pottery centre and the studio which is just as Renoir left it. You can see the landscapes that the Impressionists painted, and the paintings; or you can see a bullfight or a performance of Shakespeare in English by moonlight.

All of these – and much more – can be enjoyed and in a sensuous climate of warm days and velvety nights. The South of France is a rich man's playground, to be sure – the wealthy and the famous come here in numbers – but there is so much that can be relished on even the thinnest wallet. One of the joys of a warm region is that so many pleasures are outdoors – strolls through the picturesque mediaeval villages, picnics on the beach, people-watching from a sidewalk café, seeing para-gliders, water-skiers, balloonists, yacht and power-boat races, the Monte Carlo Rally, the gaily-costumed Provençal festivals, wandering around the many ports which bristle with boats of all sizes and descriptions and from all nations, observing the portrait painters, the artists, the animal acts, the mimers, the acrobats, the musicians, spotting celebrities trying to look inconspicuous and Mary Smith from Clapham trying to look as if she is waiting for Roger Vadim . . . all of these and so much more provide days of free entertainment.

The expression 'South of France' is an elastic one which means different things to different people. For the purposes of this book, it covers:–

- the coastal strip from Hyères east to the Italian border
- inland as far as there is any place of interest. This means a strip approximately 35 km wide.

The Highlights

If you don't have enough time to enjoy everything in this guide – and you would need years to do that -- the following list suggests some highlights for a holiday in the South of France.

Monaco – especially the Palace, the port, the Casino and the shopping areas.

The Perched Villages – see as many as you can.

Villefranche-sur-Mer – take the walk along the water-front.

Nice – especially the old town, the promenade des Anglais, and some of the museums.

Saint-Tropez – especially the port and the beaches.

Lac Sainte-Croix and the Gorges du Verdon.

Gorges du Loup.

Èze – the village.

Maeght Museum in Saint-Paul-de-Vence – unique among museums.

Roquebrune-Cap-Martin – especially the château and the old village around it.

Drive along the wine road – Lorgues, Taradeau and Vidauban. Sample and buy.

Haut Cagnes – the château.

Vallée des Merveilles – especially the rock engravings.

Antibes – especially the port and the old town.

Picnics – at least one on the beach, one in the Massif des Maures, one in the Haut Var (perhaps on a lake or a stream).

Grateful thanks are due to a number of people who made valuable suggestions and recommendations during the preparation of this guide. Among them are:

Richard Barnes
Molly Brown
Andrew Dickens
Daevid Fortune
Diana Fowler
Michael Freeland
John Greaves
Jacqueline Jones
Duncan Larkin

Gordon and Dorothy Lucas
Renée Mazziotta
Donaleta Robinson
Sheila Smith
John and Margaret van Thiel
Alan West
Ron and Anneke Wood
Murray and Myra Wrobel

Peter King
November 1991

ENGLISH SPOKEN HERE

More English is spoken on the Côte d'Azur than anywhere else in France. There are over 100,000 permanent residents whose native language is English and about another 100,000 who speak English as a second language. Add to these three million English-speaking visitors every year and you can be sure that you will not have a problem making yourself understood no matter how little French you speak. And speak a little you should – even the worst effort will stamp you as a tryer. The French are certainly trying – most supermarkets have their aisle signs in English as well as French now, and many checkers wear flag-badges identifying the languages spoken, and the majority of these speak English. In the department stores, there are many salespersons who have recently learned or are now learning English.

The Regional Commission of Tourism for the Côte d'Azur has a special phone number – 92.96.06.06 – which answers questions in English only on matters of accommodation, leisure activities and tourist services.

Radio: You can listen to Radio Riviera broadcasting in English from Monte Carlo 24 hours a day on 106.3 and 106.5. The BBC World Service can be received in many areas on 108.0. Radio Riviera has an excellent information service on what is happening and going to happen on the Côte d'Azur.

Television: Monte Carlo television transmits a programme in English every Sunday night at 8 p.m. This is a magazine programme on people and events.

Newspapers: English newspapers are on sale daily on many news-stands, and this applies equally to villages way up in Provence. The *International Herald-Tribune* is now published daily in Marseille and is on the news-stands every day.

Magazines: The *Riviera Reporter* is an English-language magazine published every two months. It is free and available at over 50 pick-up points, including the Nice airport and shops and stores selling British products, and restaurants with British owners. It is a mine of valuable information and although its primary appeal is to the resident, it is useful for the visitor too.

Banks: Many British and American banks have branches in several cities along the Riviera. These include Lloyds, Barclays, NatWest, Grindlays, Citibank, Republic-National and Chase Manhattan. However, don't expect the same service you get back home. In the South of France, none of these is interested in small accounts or passing trade, so the most any of them will do may be to cash a cheque for you.

Hospitals: Sunnybank Anglo-American Hospital is considered by long-time Riviera residents as an indispensable institution, and visitors should know about it in case they are unfortunate enough to need medical services while they are here.

It is principally a convalescent hospital but has an out-patients' dispensary, and facilities include an X-ray machine and a heart machine. The nurses all speak (and most are) English and are very sympathetic and highly qualified. Doctors are available on immediate call. The phone number is 93.68.26.96, and the hospital is located at 133 avenue du Petit Juas in Cannes (just off boulevard Carnot, the main N–S street).

Clubs: British and American clubs hold monthly lunches and you will always be welcome as a guest. Some organise visits too. The American Club of the Riviera is on 93.71.87.26; the American International Club is on 93.38.18.30; and the British Association has branches in Nice, Cannes, Menton and Monaco.

Libraries: There are libraries which carry hardback and paperback books in English, both fiction and non-fiction. Temporary membership is available for visitors. They are located at:

Nice – The English-American Library
rue de la Buffa *or* rue de France
(in the grounds of Holy Trinity Church)
Open Tuesday to Saturday 10–11 a.m.
and 3–5 p.m.

Monaco – St Paul's Church Library
Avenue de Grande Bretagne
Open Wednesday 10–11 a.m. and
5–6.30 p.m.; Saturday 10–11.30 a.m.

Cannes – English Library
4 rue du Général Ferie
Open Tuesday 10–12 a.m. and
Friday 3–5 p.m.

Menton – English Library
St John's Church
Avenue Verdun
Open Tuesday and Saturday 9.30–
11.30 a.m.

St-Raphaël – St John's Church
Avenue Paul Doumer
Check current hours of opening

Diplomatic Represen- tation:	Should you get into difficulties and need the advice of a consul, the nearest British Consulate is in Marseille on 91.53.43.32, but the Honorary Consul, Ronnie Challoner, is most helpful and can be found at 2 rue du Congres in Nice.

The US Consulate is at 31 rue Maréchal Joffre in Nice on 93.68.14.40.

English and American Food: If you're on the Côte d'Azur and you suddenly find that you can't exist a minute longer without baked beans or corned beef or HP sauce or British bangers or tacos or chilli beans or grits – don't despair. More and more supermarkets are carrying these and other foreign foods but the two speciality houses are Ashley's in the Galerie du Port in Antibes, and Mr Brian at 7 avenue Berceau in Monaco. Both are well practised at nourishing those who are homesick for items that French cuisine omits.

Churches: Those in need of spiritual sustenance have a number of English churches available:

Beaulieu-sur-Mer – St Michael's, 11 chemin des Myrtes
Cannes – Holy Trinity, rue du Canada
Menton – St John's, avenue Carnot
Monaco – St Paul's, avenue de Grande Bretagne
Nice – Holy Trinity, rue de France
St-Raphaël – St John the Evangelist, avenue Paul Doumer
Valbonne – St Mark's, Garbejaire
Vence – St Hugh's, 21 avenue de la Résistance

Drama: The Monaco Drama Group presents a play-reading in English twice a month on Tuesday nights. It is in the Green Room in the Stade Louis II in Monaco. Call 93.78.45.34 for information.

The group also puts on full stage presentations at the Princess Grace Theatre in Monaco twice a year. These are highly acclaimed, professional-quality entertainment.

Pubs: There are several English gathering places with dart-boards, live music, fish and chips and similar, for the nostalgic:

Flashman's, 7 avenue Princess Alice, Monaco
Ship and Castle, 42 quai de Sanbarani, Monaco Fontvielle
Scarlett O'Hara's, 22 rue Droite, Nice (Irish, really!)
The Queen's Legs, Valbonne village
The King's Head, Roquebrune

Bookshops: Several shops sell books in English – hardback and paperback, fiction and non-fiction, guide books, reference books, etc:

Cannes	– The Cannes English Bookshop
	11 Bivouac Napoléon
	93.99.40.08
Monaco	– Scruples
	9 rue Princess Caroline
	93.50.43.52
Nice	– Cat's Whiskers
	26 rue Lamartine
	93.80.02.66
	The Riviera Bookshop
	10 rue Chauvin
	93.85.84.61
	Sophia Antipolis
	26 rue de la Haute Vigne
	Garbejaire (next to the Mairie Annexe)
	93.65.41.78
Valbonne	– The English Reading Centre
	Rue Aléxis Julien
	93.40.21.42

Films: The Sporting Club in the place du Casino in Monaco shows films in English on Mondays and Thursdays. Call 93.31.81.08 for programme information.

The Mercury Cinema in Cannes (on the place Garibaldi) shows films in English but days and times vary. Call 93.55.32.31.

The Olympia Cinema on rue d'Antibes in Cannes has been remodelled as a multi-screen cinema, one, and sometimes two, of which show in English. Call 93.39.13.93.

Always look for 'VO' meaning *Version Originale*, which refers to the sound-track. Be careful because this does not always mean English – if it is an Italian film then the dialogue will be in Italian.

EATING IN THE SOUTH OF FRANCE
by Patricia Fenn

The Côte d'Azur, alas, is not the place to savour the
flavour of regional cooking. Too many chefs there bow to
current food fads and think it cleverer to aim at nouvelle
cuisine than reproduce the traditional *cuisine de terroir*. Of
the few coastal recipes that survive, *bouillabaisse* is
probably the best-known, offered in restaurants, as a token
of local allegiance, in many forms, ranging from sublime
to unspeakably awful; for a real taste of the warm south
you must head for a modest country restaurant, still
faithful to time-honoured local traditions.

Once into the hills, away from the fumes and credit cards,
the flavour of Provence is all around. Predominant are
the herbs. Lavender and rosemary, thyme and winter
savoury, bay and juniper, all contribute to the airborne
perfume. Orange- and lemon-zest, garlic, honeysuckle and
broom, mimosa, almond blossom and lime play their part
in the heady blend. The peasants stick fragrant twigs or peel
into the bottles of their home-produced olive oil and
vinegars, to produce a flavoured nectar fit for the shelves
of Fortnum's. Provençal bees are happy bees with all that
variety of nectar there for the sucking, and flower-flavoured
Provençal honey, makes one of the best take-home buys.

The rest of France does not rate Provençal cuisine very
highly. For bourgeois appreciation, it is too rustic, too
limited; for us foreigners, on the other hand, it is what we
mean when we talk about 'French food'. By that we mean
garlic, olives, herbs and oil, and pronounced flavours
exploding in the mouth, warm-weather light-hearted
holiday food, colourful and light, unlike the heavy pale
creamy cooking of the North. Tomatoes, salads, melons
and cherries – that's what we eat on holiday – all Provençal
staples.

The Provençals themselves do not think of their cooking
as being like that of the rest of France; the differences
are fuel for their romantic nationalistic dreams of a separate
identity. Acknowledged influences come from the
region's changing foreign allegiances – Italian, Catalan,
Arab. (The county of Nice was part of the Piedmontese
House of Savoy; all Provence was once linked with the
Angevin Sicilian Empire, then with the Pisans, and there
has always been cross-fertilisation with Genoa. At the other

border, Catalonia once governed part of southern France – neighbouring Roussillon.) The French Pieds Noirs and North African immigrants of the 50s brought with them a taste for spices and the now ubiquitous cous-cous. It could never happen in Normandy.

One fifth of all France's market garden produce comes from this most fertile southern region. The figs, apricots, peaches, melons, almonds, courgettes, peppers, aubergines, truffles and tiny purple artichokes, not to mention the olives, grapes and citrus fruit, in the Rungis markets will all have been transported overnight from the southern farms and vineyards.

They also appear, of course, in the local markets, where it would be folly not to shop. Here too are the farmers' wives' cheeses, permeated with the flavour of the herbs that the goats and ewes have munched, and the sachets of lavender and sweet-smelling herbs enclosed in traditional bright Provençal fabric – yellow, red and blue.

The countryfolk appreciate nature's lavishness, and celebrate their good fortune in their village fêtes. The harvests of garlic, olives, lime trees whose blossom flavours the popular tisane, and of course the citrus fruits, are all excuses for an almighty communal binge. The best-known perhaps is the Lemon Festival in Menton.

This cornucopia of good things is put to good use. Dishes you will certainly encounter and should certainly try include the following:

Ratatouille: proportions and ingredients for this colourful vegetable stew vary according to what is available – no two ratatouilles are quite the same – but onions, tomatoes, garlic, red and green peppers are the basics, with aubergines and courgettes optional extras.

Salade Niçoise: again a variable feast, designed to please the eye as much as the palate, usually including amongst the salad leaves black olives, tuna fish, tomatoes, green beans and hard-boiled eggs.

Brandade Even with modern transport there is little fresh fish used in the interior; brandade is the traditional way of pounding preserved salt cod with olive oil, milk, garlic and lemon. Don't be put off by the stiff desiccated corpses you will see in the markets – the end result, a light garlicky cream, is utterly delicious.

Bouillabaisse is a thick stew composed of whatever the fishermen caught last night and could not sell in the market. A good one will include chunks of recognisable prime white fish, as well as shellfish and the bony Mediterranean rascasse. In the market you will see little

piles of motley weird and wonderful fish labelled simply
'bouillabaisse'.

Soupe de Poison, or *Bourride* can be a blended version of
the above, ideally with a shellfish stock base, and often
with tomatoes, served with croutons on which to spread
the powerful *Rouille* – a pungent blend of bread, oil, garlic
and chillies. Along with grated Gruyère cheese the rouille
melts in the heat of the soup and forms a delicious scum.

Sardines are scattered with herbs and grilled over fennel
twigs. If you see them 'en escabêche' they will have been
marinaded with chillies.

Pissaladière is a wonderful onion and tomato quiche,
sometimes made with bread dough.

Aïoli is a garlic mayonnaise, made with many cloves of
garlic and rich olive oil, which can give its name to a whole
dish, *Aïoli Garni*. The aïoli is the centrepiece, into which to
dip the surrounding variety of freshly boiled vegetables and
sometimes fish and hard-boiled eggs. Wonderful.

Tians are layers of mixed vegetable and rice, named after
the clay dish in which they are baked.

Salade Mesclun is one Provençal dish that has achieved
fashionable approval and is copied in many a trendy
international menu. Good ones combine green leaves of
rocket, oak leaf lettuce, watercress, chicory, dandelion,
all scattered with fresh herbs.

The proliferation of vegetables leads to imaginative
presentation. 'Farcis' is a favourite method. Peppers,
tomatoes, aubergines and courgettes are stuffed with rice,
fish, more herbs. Deep-frying in batter is popular too for
courgettes, both flowers and vegetables, and aubergine
slices. Whole heads of garlic are roasted underneath
joints of meat, disintegrating into a meltingly sweet and
mild cream.

Olives are pounded into a *Tapenade* – a strong aromatic
paste used spread on bread as an effective appetiser.
Anchoïade is a similar emulsion based on salted anchovies.
Duck with olives is a classic Provençal combination.

Tomatoes appear in many guises. Ripened naturally in the
warm southern sun, they taste altogether different from
the anaemic hothouse specimens we have to be satisfied
with. A simple dressing of olive oil and lemon juice, a
scattering of chopped basil, and you have the best hors
d'oeuvre in the world, plus the sweet juices left behind
to be mopped up with a slice of baguette. Stewed tomatoes
are a good partner to the young rabbit that is another
extremely popular item on local menus, simply baked with
a topping of breadcrumbs, garlic and parsley, moistened

with good olive oil, they are the perfect accompaniment to a roast leg of lamb or venison.

Simplicity and freshness are the obvious keynotes. The ultimate workman's sandwich, well adapted to be carried to the beach for picnics, is the *Pan Bagnat* – hunks of bread soaked in olive oil to preserve the freshness, sandwiching whatever salad could be picked that morning.

Truly a Cuisine de Soleil. The thought of it makes me ache to head south.

DRINKING WINE IN THE SOUTH OF FRANCE

The four original Appellation Contrôlée wines of Provence were:

Palette – hard and resiny wines from the pine forests near Aix-en-Provence

Bandol – spicy, dark, soft reds and whites and rosés from the terraced vineyards above Toulon

Cassis – mostly fresh-tasting dry whites, some rosés (not to be confused with the blackcurrant liqueur)

Bellet – the Nice wine, red, rosé and white.

Look for these by all means but you may consider them overpriced. All come from limited areas, which have been unable to increase supply to meet the growing demand.

The range of wines available in the South of France today, however, is vast, and overall the quality has improved significantly during the past decade. You will seldom encounter a really memorable wine but all are drinkable and most are very enjoyable.

The rosés are the wines most closely associated with the Côte d'Azur. In the past, many of these had a slightly medicinal flavour which was not to British tastes. This has changed – they are now mildly fruity, short-lasting on the tongue but, properly chilled, ideal drinking especially in a hot climate.

There are numerous Appellation Contrôlée wines in addition to many designated 'VDQS', as well as *vin de pays*. At the lower end of the scale, you may drink some *vin de table*, most of which is not expensive and quite tolerable, although much of it goes into the EEC's distillation programme rather than into a bottle.

Most Provence wines are non-vintage and so quite inexpensive. You can buy acceptable wines in a supermarket for 15 to 40f; 45 to 70f in a restaurant. I have referred only to supermarkets because wine stores don't make much profit out of the low-priced local wines and prefer to stock Burgundies and Bordeaux, Vouvrays and Muscadets.

With so many wines now being offered, it is not too helpful to make suggestions, as they will seldom be among the wines from which you can choose. The following are all worth watching for, however, and all can be personally recommended as being invariably good quality and not expensive.

Côtes de Provence
Domaine de la Bernarde
Château de Pampelonne
Château St-Maurs
Domaine de Feraud
Domaine de Rimauresque
Château de Crémat
Château Réal Martin
Château l'Afrique
Domaine de Rasque de Laval
Commanderie de Peyrassol
Côtes du Roussillon-Villages
Cazes Frères
Château de Jau
Vin de Pays du Var
St Jean de Villecroze (Don't be put off by the *vin de pays* designation. This is an exceptionally good selection of rich, fruity reds from Syrah and Cabernet Sauvignon grapes)
Côtes du Lubéron
Vieille Ferme
Val Joanis
Château de Canorge
Mas du Peyroulet
Coteaux du Languedoc
Picpoul de Pinet (Outstanding value – an excellent dry tasty white at carafe prices)
Coteaux Varoix
Domaine Martin-Pierrat
Château la Condamine Bertrand
(Recent improvements have made these very popular. Reds are warm and velvety, rosés and whites firm and fruity)
Coteaux d'Aix-de-Provence
Terres Blanches
Château Terry Lacombe
Château de Calissane
Domaine de Paradis
Château de Beaulieu
Domaine de Trevallon
Les Domaines de Fonscolombe
Bandol
Domaine de Pibaron
Domaine Tempier
Domaine Lafran-Veyrolles
Mas de la Rouvière

Palette
Château Simone
Cassis
Clos Ste-Madeleine

One of the most pleasurable experiences when visiting the South of France is to go to a vineyard, see the grapes being grown, be shown how they are processed, and then taste the various wines produced. Not all estates welcome visitors but the following is a selection of vineyards where you can enjoy a *dégustation*.

All of the wines you taste are available for purchase – by the bottle, by the case or *en vrac* (in bulk) if you have a pomponne, one of the wicker-covered bottles of 10 or 20 litres you will see on sale in hardware stores and markets. You can expect to pay 15 to 50f a bottle, or 8 to 20f per litre *en vrac*.

Many of these vineyards are well off the road so don't be surprised if you follow the signs and find that you are bumping over a dusty track with nothing but vines in sight.

Château Sainte-Roseline, Les Arcs-sur-Argens, 94.73.30.44.
On the Route des Vins, where you will see vineyard after vineyard. Well-known for its reds and whites.

Domaine Saint-Jean, Villecroze, 94.70.74.30.
The rich fruity reds and the delicate rosés are of outstanding quality. The white is good. All are organically grown.

Domaine de Thuerry, Villecroze, 94.70.63.02.
AOC Côtes de Provence, red, white and rosé.

Castel Roubine, Lorgues, 94.73.71.55.
Another area with numerous vineyards. AOC Cru Classé Côtes de Provence red, white and rosé.

Mâitres-Vignerons de Saint-Tropez, Carrefour de la Foux, Saint-Tropez, 94.56.32.04.

Domaine de Pibarnon, La Cadière d'Azur, 94.90.12.73.
AOC Bandol, red, white and rosé.

Syndicat des Vins Côtes de Provence, Les Arcs-sur-Argens, 94.73.31.01.
This is a wine-producer's co-operative, with over 400 wines on show. The wines may not quite meet the standards of most of the private vineyards but the choice is wide and the tasting a pleasure. There is also a good restaurant.

Most of these are open every day, some are closed on Sundays. Some close on holidays and many close for lunch. Phone if in doubt.

PERCHED VILLAGES

The perched villages of the Var and the Alpes-Maritimes
– over a hundred of them – are a particular feature of this
area, a fascinating and almost unique phenomenon.
These picturesque mediaeval communities are either
perched like eagles' nests on the very peaks of mountains,
seemingly inaccessible rocks and towering hilltops, or cling
to the sheer faces of cliffs or dangle precariously on rocky
ledges.

The reason for such unlikely locations is obvious – for
defence against attackers. There was an unending stream
of these throughout the centuries, but the principal threat
was always the Saracens, those fierce, violent Moslem
warriors who crossed the Mediterranean from Syria,
Palestine, Morocco, Tunis and Algiers and ravaged the
southern coast of Europe, killing, raping, plundering and
destroying. They were the scourge of the French and
Italian coasts and the consequences of their raids can be
seen everywhere there today.

The peoples who were terrorised in this way were mainly
farmers who were obliged to forsake their homesteads
on the plains and seek places offering natural protection.
These were on heights where they then built fortifications
to make their position even more secure.

As such relocation continued, the villages developed a
secret system, a network, wherein several communities
were in visual contact with one another. This mutual
preservation developed, so that the first look-out to spot
invaders could warn the look-outs in other villages in the
network. It is especially intriguing today to be able to go
to a village – for instance, Fayence, Seillans, Montauroux
or Bargemon – and from its highest point spot those four,
five or even more villages in the same web of vigilance. The
terrifying hordes of murderous invaders surging up from
the coast are not hard to visualise.

One result of such defensive organisations has been to
preserve the buildings, the atmosphere, the way of life
and the records of mediaeval living, so that you can virtually
see them as they were 500 or more years ago. You will
tread the same cobblestones that have run with blood
countless times, you will walk through tiny alleys which have
echoed with the screams of the dying, and you will climb
stone staircases which have been piled with bodies.

The castle was usually built on the highest point of a

perched village, but sometimes it was a fortified church. Massive ramparts often circle the hill-top, though other villages are so constructed on the rocky peaks that walls are not necessary and the outer ring of houses is in itself a fortification. Few of these castles have provided complete protection. Most have changed hands many times, but impressive ruins remain.

Most perched villages have two other points in common – they are usually at least a thousand feet high and have around a thousand inhabitants. Today, of course, nearly all of them are accessible by car, although the road may be narrow, winding and tedious. In many cases too, the accessibility is limited and you will probably have to park near the village entrance and climb the rest of the way. Some have become regular stops on the tourist route, while some are deserted and frighteningly silent.

There are other similarities, and after visiting two or three you may find several characteristics in common – and then you discover that the next village is quite different and has its own special identity.

Not all the hundred or so perched villages have been included in this book. Some have had their character changed so much that they have lost their attraction. Some have grown so big (Vence, for example) that they can no longer qualify as a village. Others are no longer isolated because major roads have been built close to them. The communities selected for inclusion here are thus the 'Pick of the Perched Villages' and you will not be disappointed with any of them. They are identified throughout the text as [pv] .

A visit to at least a few of the perched villages is an essential part of any visit to the South of France. The views are always magnificent, history is all around, and you can delight in a blend of past horrors and glories. They are a way of travelling back in time which is unequalled today. See as many as you can, but be warned that they are time-consuming. They will take longer to reach than the distances suggest and the roads are usually narrow and slow.

SPECTACULAR EXCURSIONS

The Gorges du Loup

The River Loup rushes down a terrifying limestone gorge, pours over cliffs to create impressive waterfalls, and carves out deep basins with its swirling waters.

Its wild beauty should on no account be missed, but I wonder how many holiday-makers on the coastal strip have even heard of it. The soaring peaks and desolate rock-strewn plains, approached through olive groves and deep pine forests, are the ultimate contrast to the fleshpots just half an hour below.

The gorges can be toured in a leisurely day, with Grasse, Vence or Cagnes-sur-Mer all suitable starting points. The D 6, the D 3 and the D 2210 make an effective loop, wherever you choose to set off from, and feasible stops on the way include Le Bar-sur-le-Loup (see p. 59) and Tourette-sur-Loup (see p. 208). Courmes, with its population of 40, is only three kilometres off the road, while Gourdon (see p. 109) is definitely worth visiting, though reaching it is a more difficult matter. An incredible zigzagging road wriggles dizzily up through the bare crags to where Gourdon sits perched, scraping the sky.

Few regions of such natural beauty are as accessible as the Gorges du Loup, and you will find the day's tour unforgettable.

MAP 4B **GRAND CANYON DU VERDON** (Alpes-de-Haute-Provence).
25 km SW of Castellane; 40 km NW of Draguignan

This is one of the most spectacular sights in Europe – and one of the least-known. A shame because, as a natural wonder of the world, in the canyon League it is second only to the Grand Canyon of Colorado.

The Verdon River has, over the millennia, slashed through a limestone plateau to form a mighty canyon, 20 kilometres long and 700 kilometres deep. Tourist roads have been built along the cliff tops on both sides, affording dizzying views down into the canyon depths and providing parking areas from which to marvel at the spectacle.

To see the Gorges in their entirety really requires that you drive both the northern and the southern roads. Nailbiters might prefer to drive the northern road in the westerly

direction and the southern road in the eastern direction –
this way the car is always away from the vertical drop side
of the road. Some of the narrow road sections are hair-
raising, in places narrow, in others without railings.

The Canyon can be approached from the east via
Moustiers-Sainte-Marie (the D 952 or the D 957) or via
Aups (the D 619); or from the west via Draguignan and
Comps-sur-Artuby (the D 71 or the D 955); or via
Castellane (the D 952).

Many of the approach areas are natural 'blasted heaths'.
Other areas, unfortunately, have been scorched by severe
forest fires in recent years.

The Corniche Sublime from Aiguines is one of the more
sedate roads, wide and with good parking areas. If you drive
from Castellane, stop at the Point Sublime and you can then
take the route des Crêtes which has more than a dozen
good viewing-points ('Belvédères'). The road from Comps
takes you to 'Les Balcons de la Mescla' with truly
staggering views.

The whole circuit is about 120 kilometres but allow plenty
of time for the hairpin bends and the slow narrow roads.
Fill the tank before undertaking the drive, as there are few
stations.

Should you not want to tackle the whole trip, drive from
Aiguines along the Corniche Sublime and back – finding a
careful place to turn round. You'll still see some incredible
scenery. Climbers run up and down the sheer rock faces
like Spiderman; you'll even see girls making the climb with
babies on their back. Presumably the latter grow up
vertigo-free.

Walkers can park at the Point Sublime and take the footpath
down. You can take a 2½-hour hike through the Samson
Couloir, a half-mile long tunnel, or you can keep going for
nine hours and follow the route des Crêtes to the Chalet
de la Maline.

Another exciting day is to take the Sentier Martel – named
after E. A. Martel, the famous French speleologist who
pioneered the route along the river bed from Rougon to
Mayreste, two very small villages. This walk takes two days,
can only be taken with a group and a guide, and even then
only when the water level is low. The latter is controlled
by the EDF (Electricité de France), the electricity board, who
balance the level according to power demand. This is a
really spectacular trek, not hazardous but calling for a
moderate amount of stamina.

For the less ambitious, there are shorter hikes that can be
made, which do not require a guide or a party. A relatively

easy climb is down from the Falaise des Cavaliers de l'Estellié and up to the Chalet de la Maline, taking about two hours.

Some sections of the roaring torrent along the river bed of the canyon are used for 'whitewater' rafting; seek professional advice in Moustiers before attempting any such venture.

MAP 4A   **LAC DE SAINTE-CROIX** (Var). 6 km S of Moustiers-Ste-Marie; 59 km NW of Draguignan

---

The foaming waters of the Verdon lose their spume as they filter into the Lac de Sainte-Croix, and become a crystal-clear deep green, and the cliffs of the Grand Canyon viewed from below are almost as awesome as when seen from above. The river enters the lake under the Pont de Galetas, where pedalos and canoes can be hired.

The lake is artificial, but it looks real enough. And it will give you an opportunity almost unique in the South of France – you can enjoy a whole kilometre of white beach all to yourself. The area is surprisingly little known, although this will soon change. A German consortium is about to turn the region into a leisure centre and it seems inevitable that the leisure supplied will be a noisier, busier version. But there are still two or three years to enjoy the peace and the silence. The white beaches still sparkle in the sun and the only sound is from the water-birds. Power-boats are banned.

The lake is about 10 kilometres long and about a kilometre wide; its jagged coastline ensures that most of its distant shores are out of sight. This adds to the remote and deserted effect, making it ideal for a quiet picnic. The only villages near the lake are Aiguines, Bauduen and Moustiers. (See the pages on all of these as they are worth visiting.) Trigance with its splendid battlemented mediaeval castle, now a hotel, is a half-hour drive east. Most roads run only about a third of the way round the lake shores.

The Corniches

There are four major roads which run east to west right through the Côte d'Azur. This section will help you decide which one to use to reach your destination most easily, while keeping in mind access to sights and views on the way.

On the A 8 autoroute you have to pay (for instance, it costs about 25f from Nice to Monaco), and in the peak of summer, lines at the tollbooths can be exasperating – but it is usually the fastest and certainly the safest east–west artery.

The three Corniches – upper, middle and lower (Grande, Moyenne and Basse) are part of the history of the Riviera. The term implies a fringe road, one that runs along a corniche or ledge.

The Grand Corniche was built for one purpose only – war. Napoleon ordered it constructed in 1806 – mostly along the route of Ancient Rome's Via Aurelia – with the sole intent of transporting men, guns and munitions into Italy and beyond.

Fortunately, its use for that purpose was limited and today it is a route devoted to peaceful pursuits, mostly holiday traffic. It is unlike many great highways in that it avoids all towns. It starts from Nice and climbs up into the hills, and has been described as 'one of the most beautiful roads in Europe'. The most picturesque stretch is between Nice and Èze. High above St-André, with its 17th-century château, can be seen the curious village of Falicon and further distant is Peille. There is a fascinating view of Cap Ferrat and, at the Col d'Èze, everyone stops to admire one of the grandest panoramas of the entire coast.

Two kilometres past Èze, the Capitaine is reached – the highest point of the Grande Corniche at 542 metres. Then the road descends. Past La Turbie, there are splendid vistas of Monaco and Cap Martin, and the Italian coast as far as Bordighera is visible. Past Roquebrune, the great road ends its romantic run as it joins the Moyenne Corniche and then the Basse Corniche and follows the coast into Menton.

The Basse Corniche, the lowest of the three, tries to skirt the coast all the way but it is a task made difficult by the towering rock-faces which rise clear out of the water. It was begun in 1863, after the annexation of Nice, and reached Monaco fifteen years later. It has some spectacular views; the aspects of the bay of Villefranche are eminently photographable, and now another and quite different view of Èze is presented, for you look up at it and marvel at how the Grande Corniche can look down on any village so high!

The narrowest of the three Corniches – for it is only one lane in each direction for most of its way – the Basse Corniche is nevertheless often the fastest route between Nice and Monaco. It passes right through Beaulieu and Cap d'Ail but is otherwise unrestricted, and there are viewing areas at intervals.

The middle of the three is the Moyenne Corniche, begun in 1910 to relieve the congestion on the Basse Corniche and completed eighteen years later. As it climbs out of Nice towards Mount Boron, there are unparalleled views of the town of Nice. Like its two companion roads, it too shows Èze to great advantage – another quite different aspect and this time from close up as it goes past the road winding up into the labyrinth of tiny streets reaching up to the château.

The slow part of the Moyenne Corniche in summer is the entrance to Monaco from the west, for the parking area by the Exotic Gardens is a constant turmoil of tour buses coming, turning and going. It is well controlled by police but causes delays.

And so, in the approach to Cap Martin, all three Corniches join and one coast road takes you into Menton and then to the Italian border. The A 8 autoroute remains aloof from any such amalgamation and continues on its solitary way, keeping the same distance from the coast, much of it out of sight of the sea.

OLIVE OIL

It has been said that no other tree has exerted more influence on Western culture than the olive. Its principal area of influence has, of course, been the Mediterranean, where it has been incorporated into the cuisines of southern France, Italy, Spain, Greece and the Arab countries.

In the ancient world, olive oil was burned in earthenware lamps for lighting. It was used as an unguent to soften the skin, and the Greeks and Romans believed that it bestowed health and longevity on the body, when used in this way. Modern medicine says they were probably right, for olive oil is high in salicylic acid, the active ingredient of aspirin.

It was used to wash with, and as a lubricant to facilitate the movement of the gigantic blocks of stone which went into the construction of the Pyramids.

Olive oil was used, then as today, for cooking and flavouring, and for the preservation of other foods, such as sardines, tuna and anchovies. Today 90 per cent of olives go into the production of olive oil, and 98 per cent of the olive acreage in the world is in the Mediterranean region, where Provence is one of the biggest producers.

Green olives are the unripe version, black olives have ripened on the tree. Both are pressed without crushing the stones. The pulp is filtered through fibre mats, then put into a press. The unrefined liquid that flows from this first pressing is called 'Vierge'. 'Fine', 'Superfine' and 'Vierge Extra' are the next grades, which come from further pressings. 'Pure' is sometimes seen on supermarket shelves but this is only a mixture of first and second pressings.

'Vierge Extra' is the one to buy. The additional pressings after the first one have removed substances which impart a harsh flavour.

Is there that much difference between the top grade 'Vierge Extra' and a mediocre grade? Yes, there really is, and it is noticeable whether the oil is used for cooking or in salad dressing. The small additional cost is more than justified.

Country markets sell 'Vierge Extra', many of the larger olive groves have their own sales outlets, and some shops, such as Alziari's on place Garibaldi in Nice, are famous. Alziari's sell to visitors from the USA, who wouldn't dream of going back without a couple of cans. The oil is stored in huge barrels and tapped into a can as you order.

Olives are unlike most vegetables in that they have to be processed before you can eat them. A pickling process is used and has remained much the same since Roman times. The olives are soaked in a lye solution and then thoroughly washed. The residue left after this operation is, incidentally, so powerful that it was used as a weed-killer and insecticide in earlier times, so it has to be performed very carefully!

The Château at Cagnes-sur-Mer has a museum depicting the history of the olive and its significant part in the life of Mediterranean communities. The massive stone wheels and huge wooden mills are a marvel of ancient ingenuity. You will learn many astonishing facts about the olive, which in Biblical days was considered to be even more vital than bread. For instance, there are 60 varieties of olive tree and one will grow from the same bole for a thousand years.

Artisan shops in many villages sell olive-wood carvings. It is hard, dense, close-grained and beautifully whorled when polished. It is so strong that in earlier days it was used for spear shafts and dagger handles. Some of the ancient, laborious techniques for carving the wood are still used today.

BLACK DIAMONDS OF PROVENCE

Imagine a food that is almost impossible to cultivate, looks dirty, is dug out of the ground by pigs or dogs (which are able to find it only because it is covered with swarms of insects) has very little taste, has doubtful food value, and is extremely difficult to digest. Such is the truffle, weight for weight more valuable than gold.

A relative of the mushroom in the sense that both are fungi, the truffle is – despite what might seem an overwhelming list of negative factors – the gastronomic ultimate.

The Emperor Caligula ate truffles in huge quantities, believing, as did Mme de Pompadour, that they have aphrodisiac properties. Nuns and monks in mediaeval France were advised not to eat them if they wanted to respect their vows of chastity. In those times, too, it was believed that the truffle grew only where a bolt of lightning had struck the ground.

The truffle is also thought to have mildly hallucinogenic qualities, and in sufficient amounts it provokes dreams. Balzac stated that they augmented his imagination and made him more creative.

Périgord is said to be the region where the best truffles grow. These are black. In Alba, just south of Turin, the (appropriately) white truffle is lauded. But here we are concerned with the Provence truffle, which is found growing around the roots of the Provence white oak. The Var is ideal, a hot summer with occasional rain being the perfect climatic environment for producing truffles. The shortage of rain during the past three years has, however, seen a decline in production there from 2,500 kilos to only 800 kilos. Prices in Paris have risen to around 8,000 francs a kilo, and will go higher unless there is a reversal in the weather trend, and even then it may take a couple of seasons to restore the water table.

Make a point of being in one of the truffle villages on a Thursday during the season, and watch the secretive discussions taking place. Learn what the Provence white oak looks like, pick out one or two and try your luck digging. The odds are against you, but the rewards are sky high. If you see men with guns, dogs or sows approaching it's best to disappear.

Certain villages in the Var – notably Aups – have truffle markets. These bring to mind dealings in the furtive back streets of Cairo or Damascus, the suspicious demeanour of the sellers mirrored in the anxiety of the buyers. You will seldom glimpse the merchandise, although grubby paper packets are produced and corners torn away for a surreptitious sampling.

Grim negotiations are conducted which would do justice to the sale of the plans for a new hydrogen bomb. Then the parties adjourn to the bar, where pastis is consumed and the contents of the paper packets are weighed on pocket-sized scales, held in one hand just as in Roman times. Notes rustle as they pass from pocket to pocket, and the buyers shuffle away, to conduct another level of negotiation, this time with a restaurant owner on the coast.

Needless to say, such clandestine gatherings do not receive (or seek) publicity so there will be no posters on the oak trees, but in the Var, truffle market day is Thursday from November to April.

Truffle hunters operate by night. They will tell you that this is because the odour of truffles can be detected more easily in the cool, still, night air, but the true reason is that a good truffle hunter is like a gold miner in the Yukon – he doesn't want anyone to track him and learn the location of his mine.

German scientists have determined that the truffle produces a pheromone – a musky chemical version of an odour. This is the same pheromone that is exuded from the male pig's saliva and prompts mating behaviour in the sow. This is why sows only are used by the hunters. This too contributes to the universal belief in the aphrodisiac powers of the truffle, for the sows have to be forcibly restrained once the treasure has been located. The equivalent of a thousand francs could otherwise disappear in one satisfying gulp.

The truffle is found two to twenty inches below the surface, an unpleasant knobbly mass, as small as a walnut or as big as a fist. It is even less prepossessing than the mushroom, even after the clinging moist earth has been removed from it.

So what does this ambrosia really taste like? It must be truly a food of the gods, a fitting accompaniment to the nectar of Paradise. Old socks and stale boiled cabbage have been suggested, but the reality is that this enigmatic fungus has little intrinsic taste. Its remarkable virtue is that just the tiniest shreds transform other ingredients. Scrambled eggs, omelettes, salads and sauces became indescribably perfumed.

You will see the truffle on restaurant menus occasionally in Vaucluse and the Var. Try to eat at La Roche Aiguille in Ampus. Madame will be highly offended if you leave one sliver of truffle on your plate and she will stand over you until you eat it.

Taste the truffle in two or three different dishes. Savour it, see if you can take the taste apart mentally and then attempt to describe it.

A classic dish which uses truffles as an essential part of its preparation is Poulet Demi-Deuil – Chicken in Half-Mourning – the name referring to the black truffles in contrast to the white chicken breast.

Caligula, Balzac, Rudyard Kipling, Colette, Dumas, Talleyrand, Baudelaire, Louis XVI and Brillat-Savarin all went into raptures over the truffle. Is it truly 'buried treasure'? Does it really make you feel livelier, happier, more alert?

RUSSIANS ON THE RIVIERA

Visitors to the Riviera are always surprised at the number of Russian churches and cathedrals, and at the many streets and buildings which bear Russian names. The Byzantine towers with their typically bulbous, onion-like shapes are a marked contrast to the sedate churches one expects to find in a Catholic region, and the presence of so many Russians in the past is also puzzling.

A great many wealthy and aristocratic Russians were in fact avoiding the bitter Russian winters by spending them on the balmy Riviera as far back as the 1850s. Grand dukes and duchesses and even emperors and empresses were regular visitors, and with the opening of the Leningrad-to-Nice railway in 1864, these numbers increased tremendously.

Even the occasion when a Russian grand duke shot and killed the French police inspector who was guarding him did not disturb the relationship. Men of cultural distinction such as Leo Tolstoy and Anton Chekhov came here to write, but it was Serge Diaghilev who made the greatest impact.

In 1911, Diaghilev went to Monte Carlo to present the ballet *Scheherazade* – but his efforts extended far beyond the staging of a spectacle. It was Diaghilev's idea to wed to the dance form the contributions of other artists such as painters, composers, poets. Stravinsky, Chagall, Cocteau and Picasso were among those he persuaded to participate and he brought to the Riviera performers such as Nijinsky, Chaliapin and Pavlova. It was from this array of talent that the Ballets Russes de Monte Carlo came to be formed. Its fame was such that it is credited with establishing ballet in the USA through its tours there.

Many Russians came to the Côte d'Azur simply to enjoy the climate. As an example, in 1868 the entire 68 hectares (about 150 acres) of Cap Martin belonged to one person – a Russian countess who did not even live there but in Nice! The Grand Duke Michael built an 18-hole golf course at Valescure near St-Raphaël so that he could indulge in the sport of which he was passionately fond. It was the same Grand Duke Michael who ran his private train from St Petersburg to Cannes one year, keeping the speed down to 24 miles an hour so that he could enjoy the scenery – and thereby disrupting the railway networks of Russia, Belgium, Germany and France.

The Grand Duchess Helen of Russia loved Cap d'Antibes. She stayed there year after year in a villa near the beach of La Garoupe. Every morning, she would bathe in the nude – guarded by a line of Cossacks who kept their backs to her.

The heights above Cannes, known today as La Californie, were a popular area for the Russian nobility to spend their winters. From the magnificent villas, Italy and the Alps are clearly visible. One Russian prince rented a villa there with 787 servants, 48 of them gardeners who worked all night, every night, to change the floral lay-out for the next day.

A few blocks west of the train station in Nice is the boulevard Tzarewitch. This was another area favoured by Russians who purchased many houses here. It is on this street that today you can see the magnificent cathedral that Nicolas II built in memory of his uncle, the Grand Duke Nicolas Alexandrowitch who died in Nice in 1865. It is now known as the Russian Orthodox Cathedral and was constructed as a duplicate of the Yaroslav Church in Moscow. The exterior is gorgeously 16-century byzantine with greenish-gold domes. It is richly decorated inside with some superb icons.

The building on avenue Baumettes which today houses the Musée des Beaux Arts is less obviously Russian but it was built in 1876 as a permanent home by the Princess Kotschoubey of Ukraine who called it Château Ste-Hélène.

In the village of Tourettes-du-Var stands the château – an unlikely-looking French château to be sure, because it is a smaller replica of the school for army cadets in St Petersburg. Born in Tourettes, Colonel Fabre, a French Army engineer, spent many years in Russia building bridges, dams, monuments and roads. When he finally came back to his home village in 1824, he built himself a retirement home – a duplicate of his last project in Russia.

In 1885, the Russian fleet sailed into Villefranche and anchored in the harbour. The King of Sardinia ruled the town at that time and he granted the Russians the use of local premises to stock their coal supplies.

This was the period when the Russian royal family in considerable numbers were spending their winters on the Riviera. One of the Tsar's entourage was a young marine biologist from the University of Kiev, Alexis de Korotneff. He delighted in the rich underwater life of the Mediterranean and set up a research station in one of the buildings left abandoned when the Russian fleet departed.

This subsequently became the Villefranche Oceanographic Research and Study Centre, which recently had a big exhibition to celebrate its centenary.

The name of Marie Bashkirtsheff is undeniably Russian. She was brought to the South of France as a thirteen-year-old and, being very bright and sensitive, she spent her teenage years writing a diary about all the people she encountered, both Russian and French. Her accounts are lively and perceptive and considered by many to convey the most informative and amusing picture of life at the turn of the century.

A more recent Russian to ally his name with the Riviera was Marc Chagall. Born in Russia, Chagall was schooled in Paris, returned to Russia and lived through the Revolution, then came to the Côte d'Azur in 1926. Arrested by the Germans during their occupation in 1940, he was released and spent several years in the USA and then Paris, returning in 1949 to settle in Vence. The Maeght Foundation has organised several exhibitions of his work and the Musée International Message Biblique Marc Chagall in Nice is an enduring memory of his creativity.

WATER SPORTS

These are available at a great many locations along the Côte d'Azur. Rates vary but the following table gives an approximate idea of the charges you may expect for the various activities offered:

Water skiing – 120f per trip
Water skiing lesson – 150f per trip
Ski bus – 250f (for 5 people)
Beach boat – 200f per half hour
Jet Yamaha – 250f per half hour
Fishing boat – 800f per day (plus fuel)
Parachute tow – 200f per trip

SPECIAL RECOMMENDATIONS

The following establishments (marked by an arrow ➤) have been singled out for excellence in one, or preferably all, the criteria of good food, comfortable lodging, good value, welcome, outstanding site. In future editions, backed by readers' experiences, I am sure there will be more.

Antibes. *Mas Djoliba* (HR)M. Reliable and comfortable.

Auribeau-sur-Siagne. *Auberge Nossi Bé* HR(M). Comfortable hotel, outstanding restaurant.

Le Bar-sur-le-Loup. *La Jarrerie* (R)M. Lovely surroundings, superb food.

Beaulieu-sur-Mer. *Le Métropole* (HR)L. Perfect luxury.

Bormes-les-Mimosa. *L'Escoundudo* (R)M. Good food in delightful surroundings.

Cannes. Hôtel Azur (H)S. Convenient and good value.
Gaston-Gastounette (R)M. The locals' favourite.
La Poêle d'Or (R)M. Excellent food and convenient location.
Au Bec Fin (R)S. Good simple cooking, well presented.

La Colle-sur-Loup. *Hostellerie de l'Abbaye* (HR)M – L. Small atmospheric hotel with excellent cooking.

Fayence. *Le Poêlon* (R)M. Excellent cooking in attractive setting.
La Strega (R)S. Modest good value.

Golfe-Juan. *L'Angélus du Port* (R)S. Unbeatable value.

Lantosque. *Hostellerie de l'Ancienne Gendarmerie* (HR)M. Charming small hotel with excellent food.

Levens. *Hôtel Vigneraie* (HR)S. Family-run small hotel with excellent food.
Les Santons (R)M. Outstanding local cooking.

Menton. *L'Oursin* (R)M. Wide range of excellent seafood.

Monaco. *Saint Benoît* (R)M – L. Best cooking in Monte Carlo at an affordable price.

Montauroux. *La Marjolaine* (HR)M. Lovely setting, good food.

Nice. *Hôtel Windsor* (HR)M. Charming inexpensive city-centre hotel.
Primotel Suisse (HR)M. Good value, pleasing situation.

Pégomas. *Hôtel le Bosquet* (H)S. Family-run hotel in peaceful setting.

Peillon. *Auberge de la Madone* (HR)M. Long-established charming hotel in lovely surroundings.

Valbonne. *Le Cadran Solaire* (R)M. Best fish restaurant. Lots of atmosphere.

Vallauris. *Le Manuscrit* (R)M. Good cooking in intriguing decor.

Vence. *Le Château des Arômes* (R)L. Outstanding cooking in outstanding setting.
La Farigoule (R)M. Good-value country fare.

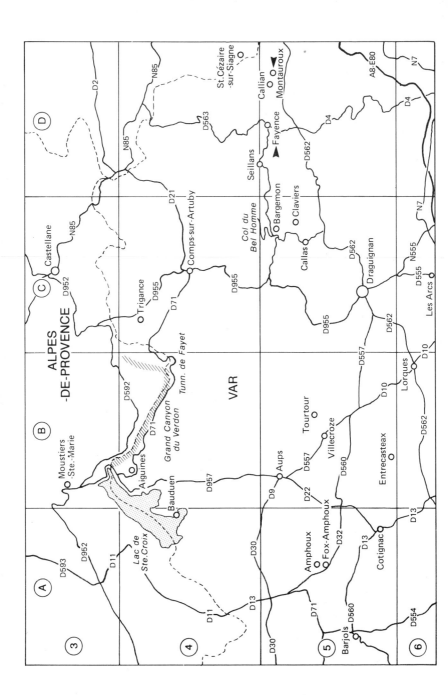

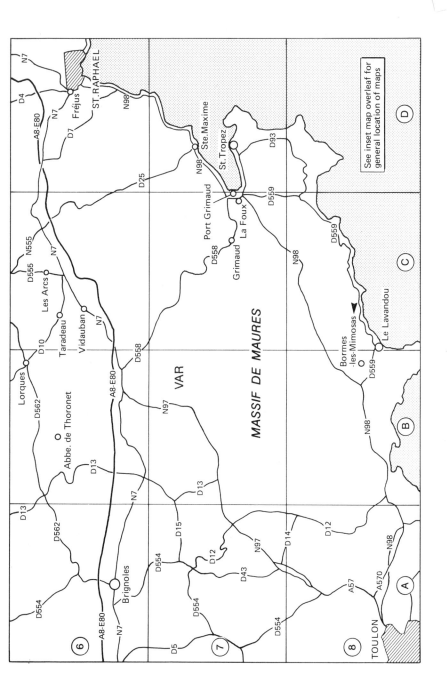

43

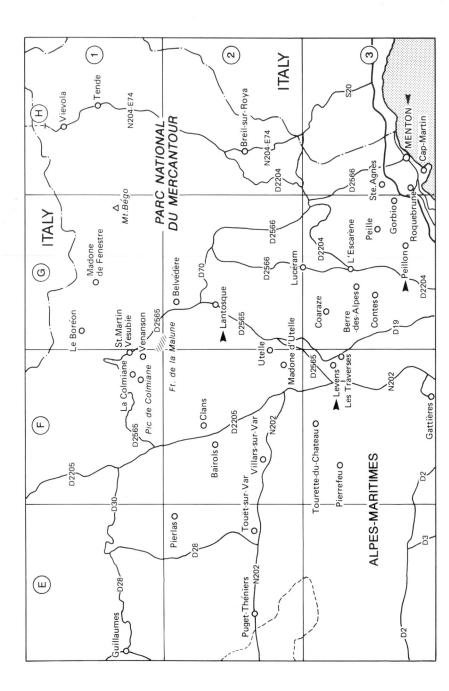

44

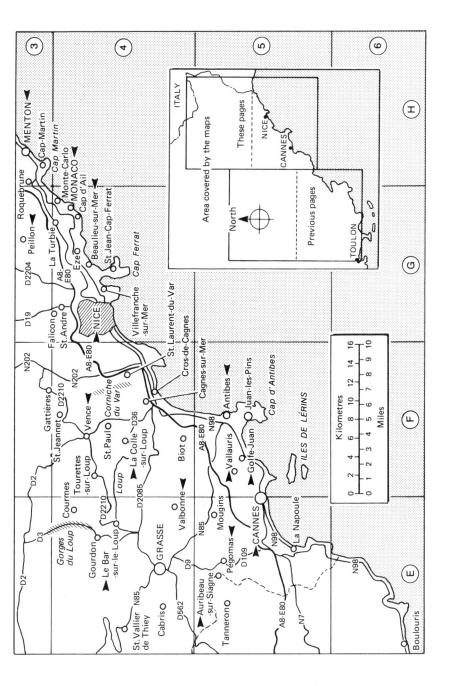

THE SOUTH
OF FRANCE

MAP 4B   **AIGUINES** 83630 (Var). 14 km S of Moustiers-Ste-Marie

Situated where the rushing waters from the Gorges du Verdon pour into the Lac de Sainte-Croix, Aiguines is a tiny village of only 200 inhabitants. Its name comes from the Provençal word *eiguino* meaning spindle and is a reference to the traditional industry of the village, that of turning the local box-tree wood into goblets, cups, beakers, jars and other vessels such as mortars for grinding herbs. As late as the 19th century, the whole village still worked at this trade and their products were distributed throughout Provence.

This unusual historical background has been preserved with the recent establishment of the Musée des Tourneurs sur Bois (Museum of Wood Turners) in the workshop of one of the original artisans of this trade, Albert Rouvier. It is open July and August only, every day.

In the Hôtel des Consuls (a sort of town hall), built in the 18th century, there is a display of Provençal art. The Château d'Aiguines is an attractive square-towered building with pointed roofs on either side. It is now privately owned.

The Festival of St Peter is held on the first weekend in August and is colourful enough, though Aiguines is not a particularly festival-minded village.

The position of Aiguines, with the Lac de Sainte-Croix on one side and the Gorges du Verdon on the other, makes it very handy for visits to both. There are a couple of places that can be recommended for staying:

Hôtel du Grand Canyon
(HR)M *94.76.91.31 Cl. 15/11–1/4; Wed. in Oct. and Nov.   All credit cards*

Situated on the D 71, the Corniche Sublime, and near the Falaise des Cavaliers, this long-established restaurant has fifteen rooms, priced at 240–270f.

The restaurant has a terrace for dining, which looks down a sheer drop into the gorge. The food is good hearty country fare – the dish I can never turn down is the fat, tasty trout, caught that day. Menus from 90 to 180f.

Altitude 823
(HR)S *94.70.21.09   Closed 8/11–20/3   No credit cards*

If you want a really inexpensive place for the night, this is it. The eleven rooms are basic but adequate and priced at 90 to 120f.

The cooking is simple but the portions are large. Menus range from 90 to 150f.

MAP 5F   **ANTIBES** 06600 (Alpes-Maritimes) 11 km E of Cannes;
22 km W of Nice

Ⓜ *Daily*

First, to dispel any confusion . . . Antibes, Cap d'Antibes (p. 89) and
Juan-les-Pins (p. 116) all merge into one another. Each has a
completely different kind of appeal and offers very different
pleasures. If time is really limited it is possible to squeeze all three
into a one-hour drive or half-day walk. You can judge your balance
of interests from the following:

   Antibes is certainly deserving of much more than a fleeting glance.
Its colourful old port area is the interesting bit; its market caters for
locals and its marina is the busiest on the Côte d'Azur.

   Cap d'Antibes: This is where the seriously rich live. There is not
much for the visitor to do except drive, goggling, past their
fabulous villas with electric fences, ferocious dogs and guards,
admiring the sumptuous grounds. The Cap is a peninsula with
beautiful pine forests and an air of opulent seclusion.

   Juan-les-Pins is brasher, the place for beaches, water-sports,
night-clubs, discos, nude shows, bars and cafés. It also has a bigger
concentration of hotels than the other two. Some are very expensive
but there are also lots of reasonable places if you choose carefully.

Patricia Fenn writes: I can think of few greater contrasts than the
one experienced by passing through the gateway from the marina
to Antibe's Vieille Ville. You leave behind one image of the Riviera –
glossy yachts, glossier owners, cosmopolitan chatter, dazzling
brightness, all that is new and fashionable – to find another, where
time has stood still.

   The old iron framework of the market is not at all smart – dark and
drab and usually in need of a coat of paint – but the dimness
immediately relieves the eyes from the glare outside. The colour
comes from the produce piled high on the market stalls. Fresh
from the mountains, so near in distance, so far in character, come
the goat's cheeses and herbs; fresh from the sea come the
glistening fish. Melons, figs, peaches and apricots, asparagus,
peppers, tomatoes all put in an appearance in their due season. How
can anyone resist buying a bargain armful of carnations or roses cut
in Grasse that morning? Young, brown-legged crew members,
who have sailed the seven seas, buy from little old ladies dressed in
black who have probably never travelled further from their farms than
to this lovely heterogeneous market-place in Antibes.

   By midday it's nearly over and the steep cobbled market square
begins to look a bit shabby. It's time to wander through the narrow
dark streets of the old town in search of lunch.

   To be honest, most of the restaurants in the Place are geared for
the tourists; eat here for the atmosphere not the cooking. It's
cheap and very cheerful at any one of the many establishments who
fill the square with tables and chairs, and watch the multilingual
world go by. If you order a plate of moules and the simplest dishes
on the menu you'll get value for money. In high summer, when

the rushed waiters seem to have been recruited especially for their impatience, this is not to be recommended. But where is?

Just inside the walls to the right of the main gate, is another string of restaurants somewhat more geared to the locals. The favourite of Graham Greene, who lived nearby in a very nondescript block of flats, is the Vieux Murs, which is for serious eaters – good but expensive.

Much as I love the atmosphere within the old town, I would never decry that of the marina. A stroll along the jetties is always an eye-opener. The range and number of boats tied up here must be one of the largest in the world. For those of us without helicopter pads it is fascinating to surmise who has. The flags are from many a far-flung land, though with always an interestingly high proportion

Antibes: the foreshore and ramparts

of British red and blue ensigns. Their crew members, often desperately bored, sometimes welcome a chat, and many a riveting lifestyle saga have I gleaned this way. When owners are on board the one-upmanship, not only of bigger boat but of more champagne, more guests, more gladdies, is always good for a laugh.

The rest of Antibes I leave to Peter to describe – I have always found it confusingly traffic-ridden and prefer to spend my limited time by the water.

Behind the old port – on the other side of the massive walls – are narrow streets, driveable but difficult, and packed with shops, boutiques, cafés and restaurants. You are walking into Antibes from here. The rue de la République is a pedestrian street. You will pass the rue Fourmillière, which is bedecked with flowers and very photogenic. The rue James Close is another pedestrians-only narrow street with all kinds of shops, including a new English bookshop. The place Nationale is a popular meeting-place – a busy square with cafés and entertainers, and even concerts in summer.

The Château Grimaldi occupies a commanding position on the ramparts and houses the Picasso Museum as well as other contemporary works. After the Second World War, Picasso was living in a small apartment in Juan-les-Pins, with little space to work, so the director of the Château Grimaldi offered him a studio there. When Picasso moved to Vallauris (see page 219), he left all his works to the Château, now what is known as the Picasso Museum.

It is open 10 a.m.–12 and 2–6 p.m. in winter, 10 a.m.–12 and 3–7 p.m. in summer. It is closed Tuesdays, holidays and the whole month of November. Ask for the guided tour in English. There are about 200 of Picasso's own works – drawings, gouaches, oils, lithographs and ceramics as well as work by Léger, Calder, Mathieu, Modigliani and Max Ernst. There are also eight paintings by de Staël, painted in Antibes during 1954 and 1955 and among his last work. Paintings *of* Picasso by Bill Brandt and Man Ray are here too. A bonus is the spectacular views of the Mediterranean as you look out of the tall narrow windows.

The Archaeological Museum is also on the ramparts and displays 3,000 years of Antibes history. Open 10 a.m.–12 and 2–6 p.m. in winter, 10 a.m.–12 and 2–7 p.m. in summer.

The impressive Fort Carré overlooks the stadium. Building commenced in 1515 and the architect Vauban added the powerful walls more than a hundred years later. These successfully defended the city against attacks throughout the 17th and 18th centuries.

Napoleon was imprisoned here in 1794. This was at the beginning of his military career and was the result of his association with Robespierre. Napoleon was fortunate – he spent only a short time in Fort Carré, while Robespierre went to the guillotine. When Sacha Guitry made his film of the life of Napoleon, he filmed some of it here in the authentic setting. Today there is little inside the walls and it is open to the public only in July and August.

➤ Mas Djoliba

(HR)M   *93.34.02.48   29 ave de Provence   Hotel closed 4–23/1; rest. closed
Nov.–Easter   All credit cards*

The best-known and probably the most reliable hotel in Antibes.
It's a villa set in a 7-acre garden, quiet, with swimming pool, located
between the centre of town and the beach, and within walking
distance of the old town. There are only thirteen, very attractive
rooms (six with baths) so it's usually full. Prices are 290–450f or
320–540f for demi-pension (obligatory in high season).

Meals are served in the vine-arbour during summer. Menus at 80
and 120f.

Hôtel Modern

(H)S   *r. Fourmillière   93.34.03.05   No credit cards*

If you're really on a budget, you need to know about this one.
Who says the Côte d'Azur is unaffordable? There are twenty-four
rooms at 120–280f. Only ten have showers, none have baths. No
TV, no restaurant and no credit cards – but what can you expect from
a central hotel at this price!

Cameo

(HR)S   *pl. Nationale   93.34.24.17*

Many visitors to Antibes have recommended the Cameo, near the
old port. There are only eight, very pleasant rooms, four with bath,
four with shower. Good value at 200–270f; 280–305f for demi-
pension, obligatory in summer.

Auberge de Provence

(HR)M   *61 pl. National   93.34.13.24   Hotel closed 15/4–15/5; 15/11–15/12; rest.
closed Tues. lunch and Mon.   All credit cards*

An old favourite – and very rightly so. Problem is there are only
five rooms so it needs booking well ahead. Prices are reasonable at
250–350f and all rooms have bath. This is really a restaurant with
rooms; the food is highly recommended and you should eat here;
in the shaded garden, even if you don't stay. Seafood specialities
include lobster and crayfish.

Restaurant du Bastion

(R)M   *1 av. Gen. Maizières   93.34.13.88   Cl. Sun. eve and Mon.; Jan. & Feb.*

Bastion by name and bastion by nature – the massive stone
construction on the old ramparts is truly a bastion. Paul and Marlyse
Hammou serve very good food and give very good value. They run a
very smooth and efficient operation and appreciate the importance
of their customers – which, unfortunately, is not the case with all the
restaurateurs on the coast.

The food is traditional Provençal with the accent on fish – as it
should be for a restaurant only steps from the Mediterranean. Menus
at 110 and 170f.

La Marguerite
(R)M   *11 r. Sadi Carnot   93.34.08.27*

Between the old port and the railway station. Gérard Tranchant and Daniel Seguin have been popular here for many years and show no signs of relaxing their standards. Prices are a little higher than in some of the surrounding restaurants but the quality is never in question. Menus at 155, 240 and 320f offer classic Provençal cooking.

La Clafoutis
(R)M   *17 r. Thuret   93.34.66.70*

This is not everyone's idea of a relaxing atmosphere for eating because the startling black-and-white décor can be a little nerve-jangling – unless of course you're only interested in the food, which is why Le Clafoutis is always busy.

For 110f you can have a terrine or rascasse and assorted shellfish followed by civet of rabbit, cheese and dessert. Gérard Montaron seems to have hit an unorthodox formula (for the Riviera) but so far it's a winner.

Le Gouvenail
(R)M   *22 blvd Maréchal Leclerc   93.61.36.95   Open all year; closed Mon. All credit cards*

An elegant but not expensive restaurant with a genial ambiance and just across the street from the Mediterranean.

There are menus at 105, 135 and 180f plus an extensive range of à la carte offerings. The 135f menu is excellent value – fish soup might be followed by supreme de Loup or Saint-Pierre in lobster butter, and finally strawberry bavaroise. Service is good, altogether very satisfying.

La Marmite
(R)M   *r. James Close   93.34.56.79   Cl. Nov. and Mon.   All credit cards*

A local favourite. A tiny, very cozy place on this always busy pedestrians-only street in the old town.

The 96f menu might offer melon, then either peppersteak or halibut in Normandy sauce, and then Iles Flottantes for dessert. The 135f menu is extremely enjoyable if you're a little hungrier. The avocado with shrimp sauce is a good starter, then grilled mussels, while the main course could be fillet of rascasse or (unusual for France) mutton chops! For dessert you could choose one of the delicious pâtisseries or Pears Guillaume.

La Datcha des Arts
(R)M   *93.34.37.39*

If you feel like a complete change of pace – how about some Russian food? On a narrow pedestrians-only street in the old town near the old market.

Ignore the 85 and 140f menus, they are routine French. Have the borscht (beet soup) at 52f or the pirochki (small pies) at 32f. The blinis (Russian pancakes) range from 32 to 75f depending on the filling you choose. Caviare or smoked salmon are at higher prices. Apple Strudel or Sacher Torte at 27f complete an excellent and different meal.

Walking from the port to the old town, you might want to know about the Galerie du Port. It's glitteringly modern and strikes something of a jarring note among the old buildings surrounding it, but it has a strong British feel as it contains so many establishments which cater to the yachts in the harbour, many of which are British.

The Blue Lady and The Rockline Caffee are busy and serve all kinds of drinks including many foreign beers. Both have a strong British clientele. Inside the Galerie is Ashley's, which sells British and American foods, including otherwise difficult-to-get items like baked beans, corned beef, Cadbury's chocolate and chocolate chip cookies. Next door is Mr James Video, which rents English-language videos (3,000 in stock *and* he delivers).

MAP 6C   **LES ARCS-SUR-ARGENS** 83460 (Var). 10 km S of Draguignan; 27 km W of Fréjus

---

This picturesque mediaeval village is really in two parts. The commercial portion is down by the N 7, with a busy railway station covered by what is claimed to be the biggest wistaria in Provence. Don't drive on thinking this is all, though – the 13th-century castle remnants stand high on the upper portion of the village, which is the part to visit. It was once the most powerful fortress in all Provence.

But the principal reason for visiting Les Arcs is that it is right in the wine country. Vineyards stretch away from the road in both directions and many are open for tasting. Some of the best Provence wines come from this area. Neighbouring Vidauban and Taradeau are also wine centres.

The Abbey of Le Thoronet, further to the west, is well worth a visit. Founded in 1146 by the Cistercians, it has been simply but very convincingly organised to give a clear picture of what life was really like in the abbey and the tableaux and descriptions present a comprehensive view of the period. Open every day except holidays. And free.

Logis du Guetter
(HR)S   *94.73.30.82   Cl. Fri. o.o.s.; 15/11–15/12   All credit cards*

Built into part of the château, the Logis is very popular with tourists and locals. The ten large rooms, all with bath, cost 200f. A large room for two costs 420f, plus 41f for breakfast. Demi-pension is 320f and full pension 450f.

The food is prepared from local produce and is served on the

Le Thoronet: the twelfth-century Abbey

terrace in summer, but remember that last orders are taken at
9 o'clock. Menus at 125–355f.

There has been some criticism of M. Callegari, whose authority in
the kitchen and in reception shows signs of relaxing. It is hoped
that this is being remedied, as the Logis is a very enjoyable place to
stay or to eat.

A busy, bustling market town which is notable for two things. First, it is an ideal centre for the exploration of the Haut Var. At least two dozen of the towns and villages mentioned in this book are within a half-hour drive, and so are the Lac de Sainte-Croix and the Grand Canyon du Verdon. Secondly, Aups is the truffle capital of the South of France. Now, this may not excite you wildly but there is more involved here than the mere eating of a food that is more expensive, weight for weight, than gold. (See 'Black Diamonds of Provence', p. 35). Aups is where the trophies from the truffle hunts are brought for sale every Thursday during the truffle season, which is from November to April.

There is not a lot to see in the town, although the unusually large square is frequently the scene of some activity – antique sales, bric-à-brac fairs, carnivals – and I have seen fire-eaters and acrobats there. From the square, the streets wind up and around, and there are plenty of shops and markets where picnic supplies and local products, especially honey, may be bought.

The name comes from the Provençal word *Aup* meaning Alp. Its history was first Ligurian then Roman, and an important military hospital was built here to handle the wounded of the legions. Traces of this still remain in the Quartier des Infirmières. In the 16th century, most of the village population was massacred by the Huguenots, and in the 19th century it was a centre of Republican resistance. One of the villagers, Martin Bidoué, had to be executed twice to ensure his death and his name was revived in 1940 when historical heroes were needed again.

On 12 May every year, there is a procession carrying the relics of St Pancrace, a local man martyred for refusing to bear false witness. The procession goes through the village but avoids the main street where an unbeliever struck St Pancrace. Afterwards everyone goes to the church of St Pancrace for the ceremony of blessing and distributing loaves of bread. Further celebrations include games, contests and a *farandole* (a long line of weaving swaying dancers). And from 15 July to 15 August there is the Annual Festival and Fair of Artisan Products and Agriculture – a sort of County Fair.

Auberge de la Tour
(HR)S   *r. de l'Eglise*   *94.70.00.30*
La Provençale
(HR)S   *pl. Martin Bidoué*   *94.70.00.24*
Grand Hôtel
(HR)S   *pl. Gendarme-Duchatel*   *94.70.00.89*

Aups's casual and unassuming atmosphere extends to its hotels and restaurants. These three establishments combine both functions. Their rooms are adequate and inexpensive, ranging in price from 175 to 195f. And they serve large portions of a wide range of meat, fish and game dishes, well cooked and at very reasonable prices – 90–130f. The last time I ate at Aups, a huge wild boar (*sanglier*), shot by a village *chasseur*, was being dragged out of a tiny van at a restaurant's alley entrance.

MAP 5E   **AURIBEAU-SUR-SIAGNE** PV 06810 (Alpes-Maritimes). 15 km NW of Cannes; 8 km W of Grasse

---

How can a perched village be only 83 metres in altitude? You may well ask. Auribeau looks more perched than many villages ten times its height because it is on the top of what is surely the only rock for miles, high above the Siagne River.

The old village is very picturesque, with narrow winding streets, which, however, like the road approach, are easily manageable. This is a mini-version of many of the more hair-raising perched villages in the Alpes-Maritimes and the Var.

The rue du Portail and the rue Basse lead into a maze of streets full of old houses. Although some people consider that the restoration has been just a little overdone, it is still very pretty and it is worth wandering through its streets and alleys, and visiting its 13th-century church.

From the village, you look out over the hills of Tanneron, which in February and March are covered with golden mimosa. The air always seems especially clear and bright and this must have contributed to the Roman decision to establish a base here rather than in the unhealthy reaches of the Siagne River below.

All the year round local residents come to Auribeau (especially at weekends) to eat, for there are two exceptionally good restaurants here; both of them also have rooms.

On 14 July the village celebrates the Fête des Pompiers (firemen), and on 15 August there's the Fête de Notre-Dame.

➤ **Auberge Nossi Bé**
(HR)M   *pl. du Portail   93.42.20.20   H closed 10/1–28/2; R closed Tues. p.m. and Wed. o.o.s.; Tues. and Wed. lunch in summer A, V, CB*

A charming and welcome auberge in the old style, right on the main street, but Auribeau, with its 1,100 population is not on the route to anywhere so all is quiet. The six rooms are priced at 230f, plus 30f for breakfast; demi-pension is 400f for two persons.

The Nossi Bé's fame lies in its restaurant, and after many years of success with the neighbourhood clientele, this has now spread to tourists. The décor in the dining-room is delightful but in summer you will want to eat on the terrace across the street, from where there are fine views over the wide valley and to the distant hills.

Michel Retoré and his wife Anne-Marie continue to maintain high standards of cooking and service. Menus start at 220f (weekday lunch 150f), with dishes like a gratinée of sweetbreads, fillet of bass with artichokes, and green apple tart with almonds. The latter has been on the menu for years, and they wouldn't dare take it off.

Auribeau-sur-Siagne: La Vignette Haute

Auberge de la Vignette Haute
(HR)M   *93.42.20.01   Open all year   All credit cards*

A romantic sprawling Provençal villa with a tower, stone walls and an impressive view across the valley from its dominating position at the entrance to the village. There are seven rooms, all with bath. They are a little pricey at 600–1,000f, but they are very well-equipped, large and comfortable. Some have a jacuzzi and all but one have a terrace. Breakfast is 70f. Plenty of parking.

Again, it is as a restaurant that la Vignette Haute is best known. Changes in direction have not affected its popularity, and menus are priced at 220, 280, 290 and 300f, including wine. Typical main dishes currently are fillet of beef with three sauces, and mignons of veal with wild mushrooms.

MAP 4E   **LE BAR-SUR-LE-LOUP** PV 06620 (Alpes-Maritimes). 10 km NE of
Grasse

A tiny, fortified village perched on a hill-top, with sweeping views
down over the valley of the river Loup. The church is known for
the 15th-century painting on the wall behind the altar, depicting an
unusually vivid Danse Macabre.

The story is that the local Count persisted in giving a ball during
Lent, despite clerical warnings that this was unwise. The warnings
were justified – several guests were struck down by apoplexy during
the ball and the painting shows Death aiming his arrows at one after
another of the revellers, who are then dragged down to Hell.

After this, you will be glad to get out into the sunshine and stroll
around the Place, which contains a statue of the Marquis de Grasse in
a very unusual pose. The Marquis is a local hero who commanded
the fledgling American navy during the War of Independence.
Surrounding streets have names such as Yorktown in
commemoration.

La Jarrerie
(R)M   *rte de Vence Le-Bar-sur-le-Loup   93.42.51.30   Cl. Tues. 1/1–31/3*
EC, CB

A beautiful old stone building, restored from a monastery and
with a large terrace in a flowered garden, La Jarrerie is an
unexpected place to enjoy a superb lunch or dinner.

In the evening, the large dining-room is candlelit and in cooler
months the huge fireplace blazes with logs. After a warm welcome
and an apéritif, the traditional cuisine is well-prepared from fresh
produce. Agneau sauté au vinaigre et au miel, pigeon rôti avec
galettes de polenta, sardines farcies and escalopes de bar (bass) au
citron vert are among the specialities.

Menus are 80f (not on Sundays), 110, 150 and 200f. The wine list
is well-chosen and reasonably priced. Service is smiling and
helpful.

MAP 5C   **BARGEMON** PV 83620 (Var). 20 km W of Grasse

Ⓜ *Thur.*

Many residents claim it to be the prettiest village in the Var and a lot
of visitors agree. It is certainly very picturesque and has all the features
of a mediaeval past – the ruined castle, the formidable ramparts and
the fountains tinkling in shady squares. The numerous second
homes are mostly owned by British.

In the place de la Mairie is the 12th-century fortified gateway
(popularly but erroneously known as 'the Roman Gate') and near it the
14th-century church with its square bell-tower added two centuries
later. It contains a fine triptych by Puget, a Var artist.

Dominating the village is the Chapelle de Notre-Dame-de-

Le Bar-sur-le-Loup: La Jarrerie

Montaigu, built in 1609. It contains a tiny carved oakwood statue of the Virgin Mary which can only be seen once a year, on the occasion of the Easter Monday pilgrimage. The chapel is open 10 a.m.–6 p.m.

Bargemon has Bronze Age origins but there are no remains to be seen. The Romans fortified it and it was later an important member of the group of 'watchtower' villages – all in visual contact with one another so that warning of attacking barbarians could be exchanged. The other villages in this group are Callian, Fayence, Montauroux, Seillans and Tourrettes.

Figs and olives grow in profusion around the village, whose micro-climate makes it one of the warmest spots in Provence.

Bargemon has a culinary speciality all its own and known in Provençal as *bardoto*. It is like a black pudding and is made from the entrails and blood of a ewe or goat.

There are several feast days in Bargemon, all quite jolly: *February*: Fair, the first Wednesday after Candlemas; Olive Festival, numerous activities including a big Aioli in which the whole village participates. *April:* Easter Monday Fair. *June:* Country Fair and lunch at the Chapelle de St Michel in the now deserted village of Favas, 3 kilometres west of Bargemon on the D 19. *July:* Artisans' Fair. *August*: Feast of St Étienne. *September:* Votive Feast at Chapelle de St Michel-de-Favas. *October:* Village Fair.

The Col du Bel-Homme on the D 25 (about 6 kilometres from Bargemon) has some fine panoramic views and there is a viewing platform at Blac Meyanne, just a little further along the same road with even more spectacular views from an altitude of over 1,000 metres.

Auberge Pierrot
(R)S – M   *94.76.62.19   Cl. Sun. p.m.; Mon.; Feb.   All credit cards*

Formerly known as La Taverne, now with its name changed to that of the new patron M. Pierrot. It has good Provençal cooking and hearty portions. There's a terrace for summer eating. Menus are at 65, 80 and 160f.

MAP 4G   **BEAULIEU-SUR-MER** 06310 (Alpes-Maritimes). 10 km W of Monaco; 6 km E of Nice

---

Ⓜ *Daily*

Calm, quiet, sedate – Beaulieu seems a little out of place on the merry madcap Riviera. Perhaps it's because of the high percentage of retired people, English, Dutch, American, German, Scandinavian. Certainly there is no indication of its venerable past – Neolithic, then pre-Christian, then Greek. Beaulieu is early 20th century – with English teashops and *The Times* on sale at the railway station on intermittent Sunday mornings.

It sits on an evergreen shelf by the sea, pampered by an indulgent climate – another place that carries the label 'Little Africa'. Living up to its name, it is gorgeous with lush and extravagant vegetation, cactus, bougainvillaea, palms, lemons, oranges, prickly pears growing in great profusion; parks and gardens, private and public, are filled with exotic plants and flowers . . . and Beaulieu is said to be the only place in France that cultivates bananas. Inhabited as it is by elegant people and endowed with every attraction that the most exaggerating estate agent could invent, it is no wonder that so many people retire here.

It's a small town, with only 4,000 inhabitants, and there isn't much to see in it, but around it there are many delights.

The Villa Kerylos is the first thing to see. It was built at the turn of the century under the direction of a wealthy German, Theodore Reinach, who was obsessed with ancient Greece. The Villa is an authentic re-creation of a luxurious Greek home, complete down to the last detail. Reinach lived here for twenty years, eating, drinking, acting, living exactly like a citizen of ancient Greece. The bronzes and ivories, the urns and vases, the mosaics and marbles in the Villa beat most museums. Even in Greece there is nothing quite like it. If you are there in the summer, there are frequent concerts – a piano is one of the few concessions to modernity. (Open afternoons only except Monday, all the year round except November. Ask for the tour in English.)

The casino, which is nearby, is very prim but also has concerts and musical performances in the summer. La Rotonde in the Congress Centre, has auction sales, lotto and a Miss Beaulieu contest in May.

In July, be sure to see the folklore festival. It's always very well done and is followed by a ball and fireworks. In August, there is something going on every day – regatta, Battle of the Flowers, Venetian fête, jazz concert, aquatic show, pétanque contest . . . the list is unending.

The Port de Plaisance is the other place to visit. It's only five minutes' walk from anywhere in Beaulieu. It offers an amusing contrast to the busy yacht harbours of Antibes or St-Tropez, for the pleasure port here is as sedate as the town and its inhabitants. Although there are nearly a thousand moorings for boats up to 110 feet long, there is none of the bustle associated with other ports – and never vessels that would let Beaulieu down with peeling paint and general scruffiness.

It is a very relaxing place for a stroll in the sun and a good place to know about if you want a casual meal. At one side of the main entrance, is a row of restaurants, plus the occasional boutique (Valentino, Hermés, Madam). If you feel like a picnic, there is a very good delicatessen, La Traiteur des Gourmets. Their taboulé is excellent and the bouche à la reine, at 18f, is irresistible.

Follow the road on past the port, to Africa Beach or Beaulieu Beach, where you can eat and drink your purchases.

If, on the other hand, you want to have lunch and watch the boats, there is no lack of choice, though the view is better value than the cooking, with many of the restaurants tending to the exotic rather than the traditional.

Despite Beaulieu's small size, it has the extraordinary feature of possessing two deluxe hotels and both in the four-star category. Both date from the fashionable era when only the rich travelled and the standards demanded of the top hotels were very high indeed.

The sedate elegance that has typified Beaulieu for a century remains just as much in evidence today and it is kept alive by these two hotels – La Réserve and the Métropole (see below). You may want to have a look at both of them – they are almost next to each other and both on the sea-front.

La Réserve owes its origin to James Gordon Bennett, the proprietor of the *New York Herald* and best known as the man who sent Henry Stanley to Africa to find Dr Livingstone. Bennett was a larger-than-life character who was probably the first American to have an impact on the social life of the Côte d'Azur. He gave a tip of 20,000f to the sleeping-car conductor on the 'Blue Train', the Calais-Mediterranean express. The amusing corollary to this story is that the attendant was called Ciro and he opened a restaurant with the money.

On another occasion, when Bennett was in Monte Carlo, he found his favourite table in his favourite restaurant occupied. This infuriated him because this restaurant was the only one where he could get his favourite meal – mutton chops. His solution was prompt and simple – he bought the restaurant.

Little wonder then that such a man founded La Réserve in 1880. The name came from the seawater 'reserve', stocked with fish and shellfish, that one kept alive until the chef requires them. 'The King of Restaurants and the Restaurant of Kings' was the adulatory praise bestowed by a journalist of the period.

There are changes in the offing here; one hopes that this Sleeping Beauty of a hotel may be coming to life again.

Métropole
(HR)L *blvd Mar Leclerc   93.01.00.08   Cl. 31/10–20/12*

The fate of many of the great hotels of the Belle Époque on the Riviera has often been a sad one. Either they have been allowed to decline and decay, or have had their site bought up by covetous developers and been pulled down to make way for modern apartments, or they have survived but are now so very grand, so very expensive that neither their image nor their value appeals any longer. Owned by the same family since it was built in 1891, the Métropole has avoided all these dire straits and emerged a century afterwards as exactly the kind of luxury hotel I should love someone to pay for me to stay in.

For a start it has somehow managed to avoid stuffiness. Its manager and staff are kind and welcoming – rare virtues indeed in this haughty neck of the woods. The exterior of the lovely Italianate villa has been preserved, but the interior is now bright and cheerful (in the best possible taste) and not in the least intimidating. The fifty-three bedrooms are furnished in pastel chintzes, the bathrooms are extremely amenable without being excessively marbled. Its site is superb, with a vast terrace and swimming pool overlooking that ridiculously blue sea. It has a beautiful garden, and a private beach.

Demi-pension is obligatory, but with a chef like M. Badrutt, who cares? The restaurant is one of the most famous in the South of France. Demi-pension costs from 740f per person per day, which I think, for this standard, in this position, is good value. Full board is 1,700–2,000f per person in July, August and September, and 1,000–1,100f from January to April.

Beaulieu-sur-Mer: Hôtel Métropole

Le Bâteau Ivre
(R)M   *93.01.27.24   All credit cards*

Simple but well-prepared seafood dishes. Recommended are the Scampi Provençale at 130f and the grilled loup de mer (bass) at 200f. If you want a real feast, order the seafood paella at 280f for two people.

Le Fidji
(R)M *93.01.41.41   All credit cards*

> Chef Marc Hamel offers service from midday to midnight and
> there is an exotic touch to the cooking. Stuffed crab creole is a
> delicious start to a meal and if you wish to stay with spicy flavours,
> there is a range of very good curries. This is also one of the few
> restaurants to serve *mérou*, the grouper fish, a large warm-water
> native, firm and full-fleshed. If you prefer meat, you must have the
> 'Three Meats with Three Sauces' (beef, veal and lamb). The décor is
> also of the islands with a striking Gauguin fresco.
> Menus start at 93f (120f on Sunday).

MAP 2G   **BELVÉDÈRE** [PV] 06450 (Alpes-Maritimes). 3 km N of Lantosque;
20 km N of Nice

> Like many another village in this area, Belvédère has had a turbulent
> history since Roman times. Today it is a farming community and
> life is simple. There is not much to attract tourists except that
> simplicity, and the picturesque festivals which have been kept
> alive to a much greater extent here than in most perched villages.
> The Fête du Brous, held in early October, is the most important of
> these. It celebrates the return of the shepherds from the
> mountains in anticipation of winter. Brous is an unusually tangy
> cheese made from milk curds – the milk coming from the
> mountain sheep – garlic, pepper and brandy. Thick pieces of bread,
> heavily buttered, are spread with brous, and the whole village
> participates.
> Most festivals are, of course, religion-based and one of these is
> the Carnival just before Lent. This is held on Ash Wednesday
> morning, when another food, the Italian polenta (a cornmeal mush
> fried in thick pancakes) is eaten.
> Try to visit Belvédère on the occasion of either of these festivals
> or on the first Sunday in February, when the Feast of St Blaise is
> marked by the farandole, danced in the streets, or the Feast of St
> Pierre, which is held on the first Sunday after 15 August.
> The accessibility from the coast of most perched villages means
> that few tourists look for accommodation in them. Belvédère is
> no different but if you should want some simple solitude . . .

La Valliera
(HR)S *93.03.41.46   Cl. Wed.; Oct.*

> Rooms are modest but quite adequate, and there are fifteen of
> them, more than the usual village inn. Full pension is 160f, demi-
> pension is 140f, and there are menus at 65 and 80f – satisfying
> local fare.

MAP 3G   **BERRE-DES-ALPES** [PV] 06390 (Alpes-Maritimes). 24 km N of Nice

As you approach along the D 215, the village looks like a cone of
houses rising to the peak of the mountain. Although it was a
heavily fortified city, there are no city walls – the outer ring of houses
makes up the ramparts.

Here we are 680 metres high so the views are spectacular, the
surrounding slopes covered in chestnut trees. Berre-des-Alpes is
famous for its de Berre chestnuts, prized all over France, and the
village shops sell confectionery made from them.

The church, built in 1368, is right on top of the village and its tower
seems to reach up to the sky. Inside are a 15th-century statue of
the Virgin and a 17th-century statue of St Sebastian, carved from
hardwood. Both are in excellent condition and are superb
examples of the art of wood-carving.

The ruins of the 10th-century château are in the centre of the
village. Berre was in visual communication with two other villages
– Contes and l'Escarène – and they could warn one another when
barbarians were sighted. On a clear day, Corsica is clearly visible.

There are several local festivals. The ones which would interest a
visitor most are: *March:* Festival of Mimosa. *August* (second week):
Festival of the Patron of Saint Laurent. *October:* Festival of the
Chestnuts (at the time of the chestnut harvest)

Hôtel des Alpes
(HR)S   *93.91.80.05   Cl. Mon. o.o.s.; 2/11–2/12*

Rural simplicity, as you would expect in a village of 600
inhabitants, but quite satisfactory for a short stay.

The Puons family have nine rooms, five with bath, at 180–200f, or
pension at 230f. The rooms are basic – little but a bed and
furniture, and the food is simple and straightforward, with menus at
70–130f. In summer, eat out on the terrace, with its superb views.

Hôtel Beauséjour
(HR)S   *pl. Bellevue   93.91.80.08   EC, CB*

A casual but pleasant hotel with a few more amenities than the
Hôtel des Alpes. There are six rooms with bath and three without,
priced at 130–150f. A good meal in the restaurant costs less than
100f.

MAP 4F   **BIOT** 06410 (Alpes-Maritimes). 8 km N of Antibes;
10 km S of Cagnes-sur-Mer

A popular tourist spot, but happily not too spoiled. There are lots of
artisans making and selling glass, ceramics, olive-wood carvings and
sundials, but at the same time this is a village where you can see

that people actually live normal lives too, so the whole effect is casual and carefree.

The French from elsewhere call it B-O but the locals say Bee-ott, flaunting traditional French pronunciation in favour of the Provençal way. Traces of the Italian language linger still in the patois spoken by the natives, along with a sprinkling of old Provençal.

Biot was decimated by the plague in the middle of the 14th century, and some years later the town was largely destroyed by bandits. They then inhabited the ruins, which became a refuge for outlaws and cut-throats of all kinds for at least a century, when the last bandits departed and left Biot deserted.

In 1460, the Bishop of Grasse sent in fifty families from Genoa to re-build and re-populate. Here, in Biot, they resumed the glass and ceramic industries they had followed in Italy and, with the militant order of the Knights Templars to establish law and security, Biot prospered.

To see Biot today, you must park in one of the muncipal lots marked 'Parking – Obligatoire' and make the fairly steep climb up into the pedestrianised main street. Stroll around the narrow lanes, see the local history museum in the place de la Chapelle. It's small but has some superb examples of pottery made from the local clay. Open 2.30–6 p.m. except Monday, 15 June to 15 October and Thursday, Saturday and Sunday the rest of the year. Entry 5f.

In 1956 a glassworks opened up, reviving the ancient art of glassblowing, and since then Biot has become a centre of this industry. There are now seven or eight workshops, just outside the village, south on the D 4. It's best to park where the signs read 'Commercial Centre – Biot 3000' or just behind it, where there is ample additional parking. You can walk to all the glassworks from either; entry is free.

It is fascinating to watch the artisans colouring and shaping glass by the ancient hand and mouth methods. Art and craft are closely blended and there are shelves and more shelves of fantastic designs and colours in the bowls, vases, jars and decorative pieces. Many really elaborate items are just for display, but many others are for sale. Prices aren't cheap but there is a certain extra satisfaction in knowing that you have actually seen the things made. Subject to transport difficulties, this is a good place to buy gifts. The shops contain a variety of other artisan products too, in wood, pottery etc.

Only about one kilometre south of Biot and on the same D 4 road is the Fernand Léger Museum. It's striking from outside, set on a hillside which is covered with cypress and maritime pines, and displaying on the west façade an enormous mosaic – 3,000 square feet containing 50,000 ceramic plates which reflect colour and sunlight at different angles. The whole façade is then mirrored on the surface of the huge pond below.

The east façade is just as impressive, with three large mosaics. The entire effect is spectacular and you rightly wonder if the interior can match up to it. It does.

It is vast and airy and consists of a series of white rooms with wide walls of glass. It is the only picture-gallery in France to house the works of a single contemporary artist. Fernand Léger, who, with

Braque and Picasso, was one of the pioneers of Cubism, lived and worked in Biot. He purchased the land for the museum himself, just a few months before he died. There are almost 500 works – paintings, drawings, mosaics, sculptures, gouaches, bronzes, ceramics, tapestries, from fifty years of the artist's prolific life.

The museum re-opened recently after enlargement. Parking is easy, entry is cheap, and, because it is so spacious, it never seems crowded. It is a good idea for a wet day and is open all year round, but closed on Tuesdays.

There are few hotels here, but plenty in the surrounding villages. Biot does have several restaurants, however.

Auberge des Jarriers
(R)L   *30 passage de la Bourgade   93.65.11.68   Cl. Mon. p.m., Tues.; last half March; first half Dec.   CB*

Brigitte and Christian Métral have made this old factory into one of the most pleasing auberges on the Côte d'Azur. The atmosphere is warm and welcoming, immediately you walk in the door. The main dining-room has recently been renovated with Louis XIII furniture but you may prefer to eat on the terrace, with its beautiful view of the wooded hillside.

Christian Métral learned his trade from Alain Senderens, the great chef at Lucas-Carton in Paris. Here at Biot, he combines classic cooking with the regional specialities in season. His dishes are elegant without being unnecessarily ornate. Pigeon in thyme and honey is a speciality and so are small fillets of pork, grilled, with a coulis of fresh tomatoes.

The menu at 260f may be a little higher than others in the area, but excellent value. It is called the Provençal Market Menu; you might start with fricassée of lobster in orange butter, or roast fillets of rouget (red mullet) seved with cucumber, black olives and beignets of courgettes, then cheese, then a superb mango tart, served hot with a sage-flavoured ice-cream.

André Toscano is responsible for the wine cellar and his pedigree is impeccable – previously at La Bonne Auberge in Antibes.

Le Plat d'Étain
(R)M   *20 r. St-Sébastien   93.65.09.37   Cl. Mon.*

Right on the main street of the old village, this has been a favourite for years, and continues to hold its reputation. It's small and cosy, fully in keeping with the outside appearance of the tiny windows.

The 89f menu is a winner for a low-budget meal – a salad of crudités, then fillet of rascasse (scorpion fish) Provençale, then choice of desserts. For 130f, fish soup is outstanding; it is followed by leg of lamb in garlic cream sauce and then dessert. The Dégustation Menu, at 195f, could be pâté de foie gras de canard, then rougets in a most unusual fruit-flavoured butter, a croustade of snails, then a small bouillabaisse, and finally dessert – if you are able.

Biot: Le Plat d'Étain

Les Terrailleurs
(R)M *11 rte du Chemin Neuf 93.65.01.59 V, EC*

On the D 4, going south from Biot towards the coast, this large
converted farmhouse building has a relaxed yet elegant atmosphere,
with its flagstone floors and ample space between tables.

The 160f menu is a hot favourite. Try strips of baby rabbit with a
salad of fines herbes, goujonettes of mostèle (a delicious and
uncommon Mediterranean fish), with chocolate roll covered with
almond cream to finish.

A new menu at 230f offers a terrine of foie gras, then lobster with
fines herbes. Magret de canard or médaillons of lotte with thyme
butter are the main course, then cheese followed by dessert.

For lobster fanciers, the 290f menu is irresistible. First an array of
smoked salmon, followed by a whole lobster with pasta and truffle
butter, then cheese, then dessert.

La Pierre à Four
(R)M *15 rte de Valbonne 93.65.60.00*

> M. Portelli has a strong following among local diners and this
> attractive little restaurant on the road to Valbonne is equally popular
> with visitors.
>
> The Menu de la Chapelle at 160f is the one that most people go
> for, choosing items like croquillants de coquilles St-Jacques with
> compôtes of tomatoes and sherry vinegar, cuisseau de marcassin
> (leg of young wild boar . . . well, how often do you get the
> chance?), goujonettes of monkfish, and finally a selection of
> pâtisserie.
>
> There is also a 260f menu, a five-course spread featuring as the
> principal course the tournedos rossini with black truffles.

Café Brun
R(S) *Impasse St-Sébastien*

> A bar with all kinds of drinks, including 30 kinds of beer from
> numerous countries. It always seems so full that there won't even
> be standing room: it's packed with banners and bric-à-brac and
> knicknacks, and wall-to-wall people.
>
> Café Brun is really a Dutch pub but it has become a meeting place
> for the British too, and it's open seven days a week till after
> midnight. You will spot the Dutch East Indies influence if you have
> any of their food – like the chicken satay for 35f and Loempia with
> Katjang Sauce (spring rolls with soya-flavoured sauce); spare ribs at
> 38 or 78f a portion are another favourite.

MAP 8B   **BORMES-LES-MIMOSAS** 83230 (Var) 5 km NW of Le Lavandou

---

> Bormes occupied its strategic far-seeing site high above Le Lavandou
> long before the fishing village existed, and its mediaeval origins are
> still evident in the narrow cobbled streets that twist and turn
> through archways at alarmingly steep angles. Most of the ancient
> grey stone houses have been heavily restored and are used for
> summer occupation only, so that in winter it has a deserted and
> somewhat sad air. But come the swallows, and the flowers in the
> many window boxes, tubs and baskets get planted out, the shutters
> come down, and the faint vanilla perfume from the mimosas after
> which the town was named floats down from the mountains.
>
> It's a very popular and agreeable diversion from the glare of the
> coastal strip to drive up to Bormes's cooler air, appreciating on
> the way up the twisting road the spectacular views of the
> Mediterranean below. At least, stop for a drink or try one of the
> several restaurants now serving honest food in the little town.

La Belle Vue
(R)S *94.71.15.15*

> The Belle Vue lives up to its name. With the best site in town, and
> a splendid view down to the coast, it is understandably popular and
> always full in summer. The food is good if not outstanding; menus
> start at 80f.

L'Escoundudo
(R)M *2 ruelle du Moulin 94.71.15.53 Cl. Mon. o.o.s.; 30/10–Easter CB*

> Escoundudo means a 'hidden corner' in Provençal dialect, and
> again this tiny restaurant is well-named. To find it you must climb
> to the top of the town, duck under dark arches and arrive in a
> picturebook mini-square, always ablaze with simple cottage flowers.
> It is an old favourite of ours, which has had its ups and downs,
> from the extremely simple rustic bistro we first discovered, through
> regrettable pretentiousness, in keeping with the prosperity of this
> tourist village, to its present happy compromise, which is excellent
> cooking, strongly Provençal-influenced, combined with a pleasant
> natural rusticity. Two little rooms and a few tables outside make up
> the accommodation, so booking is advisable.
> Max Dandine used to be a builder before he became chef-patron
> here. I particularly enjoy his pastry-based dishes, like the savoury
> *tourtes* – flans with lids on – and feuilletée de lapereau, but his
> hazelnut gâteau is famous, and he's a dab hand with stuffed vegetables,
> stuffed calamari, stuffed you-name-it . . . All his menus are good
> value, from 125 to 200f, and wines are local and inexpensive.
> Arrowed for good food in delightful surroundings, at prices that in
> this area could be called reasonable.

La Cassole
(R)M *Ruelle de Moulin 94.71.14.86 Dinner only from July to Sept. except Sun.
and fêtes. Also closed Sun. p.m.; Tues. p.m. and Wed. from Feb. to Easter*

> Similar to L'Escoundudo in that Mme Montanard serves
> Provençal-style food in a miniature restaurant built into a mediaeval
> house, but lacking the good-value wine that guarantees the former's
> arrow.
> Otherwise, the food, if anything, is even better, and its atmosphere
> of one big happy family utterly beguiling. Try her bouillabaisse, sea
> bass cooked over vine twigs, and chocolate fondant. Go for the 145f
> menu – no need to pay more.

Paradis
(H)S *Mont-des-Roses 94.71.06.85 Cl. 1/10–30/3*

> Paradise indeed to discover a modest hotel tucked away in the
> verdure of Mont-des-Roses, in the trees of the Du Pin quartier, with
> twenty rooms costing a mere 160–320f. Paradise too to be able
> to breakfast and dine in the lovely garden. How long can paradise
> last at these prices?

MAP 2H   **BREIL-SUR-ROYA** [PV] 06540 (Alpes-Maritimes). 54 km NE of Menton

A perched village at 286 metres altitude, one of the centres where visitors stay for trips into the Forest of Turini, the Parc de la Mercantour and other locations of natural beauty.

Breil is old. It was occupied by the Celts, then the Ligurians and then the Romans. The Porte de Gens and the Porte St-Antoine (now in ruins) were the two main entrances to the village. The mediaeval watchtower known as 'La Cruella' is worth the climb.

On the tiny place Rousse, be sure to see the Chapelle St Catherine and the church of St Alba. The latter is said to have the finest organ in the region.

Breil is a centre of olive production and there is a mill still operating. After the harvest, the Fête de l'Olive is held. There is folk dancing all day and a ball in the evening.

The Fête Patronale runs from 15 to 18 August, with much singing and dancing, stalls, exhibits and a picnic lunch furnished by the Town Hall. The Fête of St Bernard is held at the end of August.

The Fête La Stacada (de l'Estocade) is the biggest fête in village tradition (held once every five years). The last one was in 1989. It re-creates an incident from the early 18th century, when the bailiff of the manor insisted on exerting his *droit de seigneur* despite protests from the men of the village that he was behind the enlightened times. The men finally revolted and the bailiff brought troops against them. Several lives were lost and only the timely arrival of the Lord of the Manor prevented considerable bloodshed. Over a hundred men and women re-enact the pageant, which lasts all day starting with drum bands marching through the streets at 6 a.m. Costumes are worn – infantry and cavalry, abbots and priests, judges, brides and bridesmaids, and a great time is had by participants and viewers.

Hôtel Le Roya
(HR)S   *93.04.48.10   Cl. 1–15/2*

This family-run hotel, with a good view of the lake, has a very attractive and tranquil atmosphere and is popular locally. Its twelve rooms cost 200–220f, or full pension is 240f. Menus are at 60 and 100f, or, with wine, at 100 and 120f.

MAP 4E   **CABRIS** [PV] 06530 (Alpes-Maritimes). 5 km W of Grasse;
20 km NW of Cannes

Sometimes described as a perched village – and it is if you approach from the D 562, the main road between Grasse and Draguignan. The easy approach, however, is directly from Grasse and this is a flat road. From the village itself, though, the ground drops away steeply, and from its 500 metres altitude you can see (on a clear day) the glittering blue of the Mediterranean, as far away as Toulon.

The village has been well-maintained and the mediaeval aspect has been restored as far as is practical. Cabris has always been a popular village for painters, writers, poets and sculptors. Colette lived here when she came down from Paris and wanted to live in the hills as a change from St-Tropez. Yvonne Printemps, Pierre Fresnay, Albert Camus and Jean-Paul Sartre have all lived here; Leonard Bernstein was a more recent resident.

The centre of the village is the place Charles Chauve, where there is plenty of parking near the many bars, cafés and restaurants. Be sure to see the tiny chapel of St Sébastien, built in 1761. It is a little jewel of a place and its twenty chairs almost fill it.

Like many another Alpes-Maritimes village, Cabris was a Roman settlement – indeed, the Roman washing troughs are still in use. There are Bronze Age megaliths and burial mounds within easy walking distance, and in the village are the ruins of the 11th-century château (destroyed during the French Revolution).

Cabris's historic past has been allied to a sophisticated present and it has become a very popular place to eat. Many Grasse residents come out here and there is always a large tourist invasion.

Hôtel Horizon
(H)S *93.60.51.69   Cl. Wed. p.m.; mid Oct.–end Mar.   AE, DC, CB*

There are twenty-five simple but comfortable rooms and a plain family atmosphere at 250–360f, plus 35f for breakfast.

The lounge is a little cramped but you will probably prefer to be outside anyway; the patio garden is charming and has superb views down the valley and of the surrounding hills. André Gide, Jean-Paul Sartre and Antoine de Saint-Exupéry have all stayed here in the past.

The restaurant is now closed, but there are several restaurants of renown within easy walking distance.

Le Petit Prince
(R)M *93.60.51.40*

It has sadly slipped from its former position of culinary eminence, due to change of management. The food and cooking are now variable – one time excellent and the next disappointing. But when it is good, it is very good indeed. Specialities include a millefeuille of smoked salmon, duck cooked in lavender honey, and a wonderful mango dessert.

Midweek menus are from 98f, otherwise from 140f.

Auberge de la Chèvre d'Or
(R)M *93.60.54.22   Open all year*

A pleasant little place, right in the heart of the village, with outdoor dining in the summer. There are menus at 85, 110 and 130f which feature main courses such as trout with herbs, sea bream in lemon butter and perch.

Lou Vieil Casteou (Le Vieux Château)

(R)M   *93.60.50.12   Cl. 1–12/12; Feb.; Mon. lunch; Jul.–Aug.; Tues. p.m.; Wed. Sept.–Jun.*

Built into the walls of the ruins of the château, a small indoor restaurant, with a large enclosed patio with vine-covered trellis roof for between seasons, and a big outdoor area.

Menus are 75, 105, 150, 190 and 270f. On the recommended 105f menu try filleted sardines marinated in lemon with tiny red berries (delicious and unusual), followed by stuffed trout with basil sauce, then goat's cheese, followed by fruit flan.

The 150f menu is equally good value, with a choice of four starters, one of which is snails in parsley and garlic, then a main course choice of leg of lamb rosemary or rabbit (excellent), then cheese, then dessert.

There is a good selection of reasonably priced wines and the service is attentive.

Cabris: ruins of the old château, with 'Le Vieux Château' restaurant

MAP 4F   **CAGNES-SUR-MER** 06800 (Alpes-Maritimes). 21 km E of Cannes;
13 km W of Nice

Ⓜ *Daily, except Mon.*

This is really three towns: Cagnes-Ville is a dull commercial place
which contains only one thing of interest and that is the Renoir Museum
(see below); le Cros-de-Cagnes, the old fishing port, is all high-rise
apartments and supermarkets; that leaves Hauts de Cagnes.

Follow the signs for 'Haut de Cagnes' and then park near the old
château. You will have no difficulty finding it – it will have been
visible for miles as you approach. You may be able to park on the
level just below the château itself or you may have to park down
the hill and walk.

The château belonged to the Grimaldi family and dates from the
14th century. It looks truly like a castle, with its battlemented walls
and its lofty tower, while the mediaeval house, the wandering
alleyways and the large square complete the fairy-tale picture.

The site had been a Roman fortress, built to safeguard troops and
supplies moving along the busy route between Rome and Spain.
Tombs bearing Roman names can be seen today and coins are still
being unearthed with an Emperor's face on them.

It passed into the hands of Rainier Grimaldi, sovereign of Monaco,
in 1309, and he was responsible for the construction of many of
the features apparent today. In 1710 d'Artagnan, of Three
Musketeers fame, in his position as Constable, burst into the
chateau and arrested the then owner, the Marquis of Grimaldi, for
counterfeiting coins in the castle cellars.

You must climb the two flights of outside stone stairs and enter
the courtyard shaded by an old pepper tree. This leads into a shabby
but entertaining museum of assorted interests.

First there is the history of olive production, with old wooden
presses and gigantic stone wheels. Then on the first floor there is
the *boudoir* of the Marquise, now dedicated to Suzy Solidor, a
flamboyant cabaret singer, model and celebrated local character
who was an early and self-professed lesbian. She was the friend of
many of the artists who lived in the area, and Dufy, Cocteau and
van Dongen were among the forty-odd artists who painted her
portrait.

Especially fascinating are the many photographs – mostly a
century old – showing the neighbourhood before roads, cars and
people overwhelmed it. For most of the year too, there is a display
of works by modern artists who lived and worked on the Côte
d'Azur – Vasarely, Bonnard, Chagall and others. In July, August and
September, the International Painting Fair attracts work from
many countries.

The château is open every day from 10 to 12 a.m. and 2.30 to
7 p.m. in July, August and September; from 10 to 12 a.m. and
2 to 5 p.m. (except Tuesdays) in winter. Closed from 15 October to
15 November. Small fee.

The Renoir Museum is only about one kilometre from the château.
The painter had this house, 'Les Collettes', built in 1907 on a 5-

acre plot with magnificent views of the Mediterranean. He was just in time to rescue the numerous olive trees on the estate, many of which were a thousand years old. The house contains Renoir's studio, which is exactly as he left it, and there is no other house belonging to an artist which evokes more splendidly the image of the man who lived and worked there. The now rusty wire netting over his studio window was put up on Renoir's instructions so that the glass would not be broken by his children playing ball outside.

Inside Renoir's studio are his brushes, knives and palettes, his cravat and coat, and the wheelchair and sticks which he was obliged to use during his later years when he was crippled with arthritis. Letters, photographs, sculptures and drawings give an extraordinarily complete view of the painter who refused to yield to his infirmity and had brushes tied to his gnarled deformed fingers, and later the sleeves of his coat, so that he could continue to paint by moving his arms.

Les Collettes is open from 2 till 6 p.m. in summer and 2 till 5 p.m. in winter. Closed Tuesdays, holidays and from 15 October to 15 November. Small fee.

Market day in Cagnes is every day except Monday. On the rue des Oliviers, there are artisan markets on Monday mornings, Thursday afternoons and Friday afternoons.

Cagnes is great on festivals. *Easter:* Flower Festival and Beauty Contest for Miss Cagnes. *1 May:* Corn Festival. *4, 5, 6 July:* Feast of St Peter the Fisherman. *July:* Swimming races at Cros-de-Cagnes. *August and September:* Antiques Fair in front of the Château. This is a particularly good one, very often with some real bargains. *September:* Beer and Sauerkraut Festival. *November:* Antiques Fair on the Hippodrome (the Côte d'Azur's only race track).

There are plenty of places to eat around the square and if you should want to stay here in these romantic surroundings, two hotels are worth consideration.

Le Cagnard
(HR)L *93.20.73.21 Cl. Thurs. lunch; 1/11–18/12 All credit cards*

This is a very well-known and sophisticated little hotel, cleverly converted from several 13th-century houses clinging to the edge of the cliff by the castle ramparts. The guest list has seen many famous names including Antoine de Saint-Exupéry and Jean-Paul Sartre. It is probably the most attractive of all the Relais et Châteaux hotels along the coast.

The 10 apartments and 16 bedrooms are all different and many of the rooms are enormous. Ask for one with a view of the sea, although it will be a little more expensive. All are furnished with antiques. Some have private balconies and three have air-conditioning. M. Barel and most of his staff speak English and all are smiling and helpful. Prices are not unreasonable for such romantic luxury – 320–400f for single rooms, 500–900f for double rooms and 1,000–1,300f for the apartments.

Menus are a hefty 370 and 500f, and it is better to choose carefully from the à la carte menu. You get your money's worth from eating on the stunning terrace or the candlelit dining-room. Try the red mullet sandwiched in bacon, or the *charlotte* of lamb flavoured with mint. There is also a rare opportunity here to taste the Bellet wine from Nice.

Les Collettes
(H)M *93.20.80.66 Cl. 16/11−25/12 All credit cards*

Don't expect to be staying in Renoir's house, although this small hotel/motel does have the same name. It is an inexpensive alternative to Le Cagnard − some people stay here and eat at Le Cagnard with the money they've saved.

The thirteen rooms here are priced at 283−296f and are simple but well furnished. There is a pool and parking; some rooms have kitchenettes.

Restaurant des Peintres
(R)M *93.20.83.08 Cl. Wed. All credit cards*

A long-established popular restaurant, equally favoured by locals and tourists. Jacques Lorquet has kept prices down and standards up and booking is essential in season. The menu at 120f has a strong Provençal accent.

Picadero
(R)M *3 blvd de la Plage 93.73.57.81*

Not in Haut de Cagnes but down on the sea-front in Cagnes and just east of the Hippodrome. It has a devoted following of local residents. Vincent Miraglio maintains high standards, and his menu at 170f is one of the great bargains of the Côte d'Azur. Fish is strongly featured, in interesting combinations like squid and sea urchins as well as more traditional dishes. Leave room for crêpes stuffed with almond cream and pine nuts, and enjoy the Provençal wines.

It's not only the food that is so appealing at Picadero. The whole atmosphere is warm and welcoming, thanks in part to Nicole Miraglio. Catch this one while you can still afford it. A bistro that's going places!

MAP 5D   **CALLIAN** Ⓟⓥ 83440 (Var). 24 km W of Grasse

Ⓜ *Fri.*

Here is an excellent example of one of a network of perched villages; along with Bargemon, Fayence, Montauroux and Seillans.

A Roman fortress once stood on the site where the 12th-century castle was built. The castle fell into ruins but has now been restored very skilfully under private ownership. It maintains its feudal character admirably, surrounded by a maze of lanes, alleys and stairways.

Callian is unusual in having a residential area quite separate from the rest of the village, a feature which has been emphasised by much re-building and restoration of houses for use as second homes by Parisians and non-French. Christian Dior is one of the many who came to live here.

You might also want to see 'The Phantom Village' of Vernasque, two kilometres to the west, silent and empty since 1348 when its population was wiped out by the Black Death.

Festivals – *16 May:* Fête de Sainte Maxime, with many parades. *Early August:* Fête de Saint Donat, with four days of processions, bravades, a fancy dress ball, a trout-fishing contest and a giant aioli feast.

Auberge de Puits Jaubert

(H)S (R)M   *rte du Lac de Fondurane   94.76.44.48   Cl. 20/1–14/2; 16–25/6; 20–30/10; Tues.   V, EC*

There are only eight rooms in this pleasant auberge, priced at 130–180f. However, it is the food that is the principal attraction and the locals patronise it well. Trout from the local lakes is always a good bet, but the menu is well chosen with plenty of variety; three courses for 120–185f.

MAP 5E   **CANNES** 06400 (Alpes-Maritimes) 32 km W of Nice; 9 km W of Antibes

---

Ⓜ *Daily*

Cannes has come to symbolise what the (uninformed) world sees as the Riviera. Its image is expensive, film-star-ish, a touch unreal. True enough, but only half true. There's more to Cannes than that dreadful week in May when all the phoniness of the film-world envelops the town in atypical vulgarity. Don't ever dismiss it as being strictly for the birds. There is something for everyone, if they know where to look. Cannes is like a beautiful woman, who likes to be dressed in classy clothes, thirsts to be admired, and is a lot of fun.

She has come a long way since Lord Brougham and his retinue, deterred by tales of cholera in Italy, rested in the little fishing village here in the Golfe de la Napoule. He saw the possibilities of the stunning bay and natural harbour sheltered by green hills. Quite simply it had the best site then, and in many ways it still has. On a summer's day the technicolour water is dotted with white sails and streaked with the foamy wake of powerboats, and the fine sands are vivid with hundreds of multi-coloured parasols – one colour for each bathing establishment; look again at night when the curve of the bay is animated with red and white car lights flickering like fireflies. Best of all, look at it from the sea, from a ferry, sailing boat, or even a pedalo, and grasp its diversity, from picture-book fishing harbour all the way round to sugar-icing casino; only the terminally blasé could fail to fall a little in love.

Beautiful women, alas, can get spoiled and begin to show their age, and Cannes's prime may well be in the past, when her elegance was legendary world-wide. But the good bones are still there and she has stood up relatively well to what the years have thrown at her. The apartment blocks lack the panache of their Edwardian predecessors, the beaches are crowded, the traffic appalling and it's a total no-no in July and August, but there's still no denying that the lady has style.

Perhaps I'm prejudiced. I first saw Cannes as a very unworldly-wise teenager. It seemed like a fairy tale then, and so often youthful fairy tales have a habit of playing false in later years. Not so with Cannes. I may regret some of the changes but on every subsequent visit the spell has never failed to work. I hope it always will.

Basically there are three principal roads around the bay, the further away from the sea the less fashionable. The promenade – the famed Croisette – is really two promenades, divided by gardens that are unfailingly a blaze of well-tended colour; along the wide sea side parade the families, the children on tricycles, the poodles and their owners, the girls in the clothes that just have to be shown off and, during the Film Festival, the starlets in all their desperation to be noticed. Old men on benches lean on sticks between their plump legs well apart and get the benefit of one of the greatest shows on earth.

On the other side of the boulevard line up the shops that contribute to the Cannes image – Chanel, Gucci, Lanvin . . . and the delightfully naughty-weekend hotels that every starlet dreams of staying in, the Majestic, the Martinez, and the epitome of Cannes – the great Carlton; Cannes without the familiar turrets – shaped, they say, like the breasts of the original owner's mistress (there's Cannes for you) – would be unthinkable.

The rue d'Antibes is the next bracelet, running a couple of blocks behind the Croisette, following its curve for most of the way. Now happily mostly pedestrianised, this is a delightful avenue of beguiling shops with affordable (just) merchandise. If you're in the kind of extravagant mood that only a little dress or shirt or suit or hat or shoes, with that undefinable but unmistakable French flair, will satisfy, look no further. Think of Bond Street with a touch of Gallic wit.

The third road back, the rue Meynadier, starting from the wonderful food and flower market, running behind the central gardens, the Alleés de la Liberté, is probably my favourite, because it refutes so effectively the superficial judgement that Cannes is all sophisticated gloss. This is where the Cannais do their marketing. Mercifully pedestrianised too, since it is always thronged, it is lined on both sides with gourmet's delights. Stock up here for a picnic from the superb charcuteries, like Ernest at No. 52; drool at the windows of the best pâtisserie/chocolatier in town on the corner near the market; queue up for fresh pasta, in confusing variety of shapes and colours; trust the butcher to advise you on what cut of meat to choose for which dish; and spend half an hour or so in the lovely old-fashioned fromagier, Ceneri, at No. 20, learning about the 200-odd varieties of cheese from all over France. If the price tags on clothes in the Croisette and the rue d'Antibes are out of range, the rue Meynadier is also the place to look for a cheap and snappy up-to-the-minute little bargain, and there are always fruit stalls brimming over with peaches, strawberries or whatever crop is biggest and best at that moment.

Another contradiction to the idea that Cannes is nothing but stuck-up is my favourite area round the old harbour. Bully for Cannes that it has never allowed the developers to get their hands on this prime spot of potential real-estate development. Port Canto, the smart marina at the Palm Beach end of the Croisette, is for the gin palaces. There are usually one or two impressive millionaire's playthings docked in the old harbour too, looking rather sulky at having to slum it while relishing the attention they cause. But the vast colourful majority here will be sailing boats from all over the world, their owners aware of their luck at having found a berth in such a setting. There are real fishing boats too, and scruffy dinghies and motorboats, all awaiting the curious inspection of the strolling, peering public.

This is where we usually choose to eat, at one of the several fish restaurants that line the quays. Gaston-Gastounette is our favourite, where (sucks-boo to the Cannes-is-outrageously-expensive school of thought) you can still get a good three-courser for 85f, with the harbour view thrown in. Booking is difficult. Unless it's the impossible high season or the dread Film Festival, parade along, check the menus and play musical chairs for a seat. For drinks or ice-creams we like to sit with the locals at one of the cafés or bars around the Allées de la Liberté, unless the mood is for dressing up and pretending we're rich tourists at one of the bars along the Croisette, where the (considerable) cost of a drink includes unlimited celeb-spotting.

Peter presents another view of Cannes, less starry-eyed perhaps than mine in most ways, but kinder about the Film Festival, and more practical. Between us I hope we present a balanced picture, his of the resident, mine of the visitor. He has the hard facts . . .

Head for the Palais des Festivals first of all. It's next to the old port. Park underneath it – no matter where you are going in Cannes. It's spacious, inexpensive, safe and convenient for almost everything.

Check the posters and see what's on in the Palais itself. There's always something – it may be an antiques fair or a musical concert or a ballet or a jazz concert. The last time I was there it was a festival of mediums, mind-readers, Tarot card interpreters and wizards selling all kinds of entrées into the supernatural world. The 60,000-square-metre area inside includes an auditorium holding 2,400 people and one holding 300 people. There's a theatre that seats 1,000 and ten rooms holding 150 each, and it's rare for several of these not to be active.

From nearby you can take a trip to the Îles de Lérins (see p. 114) – an enjoyable and inexpensive way to see the coast and have a day out. Another nautical alternative is a ride on the *Nautilus*, an 80-foot catamaran, a unique vessel, whose transparent floats and powerful searchlights make possible close inspection of the ocean depths. It cruises for 1½ hours from near the Palais des Festivals out to the Îles de Lérins, for 50f per person.

The old part of Cannes is centred around the hill after which it is named – Le Suquet. The old watchtower, built in 1088, gives a panoramic view of the sea, the Esterel, the Îles de Lérins and the town of Cannes itself. The fortified priory, which is also on top of the hill, has been converted into a museum – the Musée de la Castre, with archaeological exhibits, primitive and contemporary art and numerous artefacts from the Orient. Open 10 a.m.–12 and 3–7 p.m. from July to September and 10 a.m.–12 and 2–5 p.m. October to June. The majority of the streets in the old town are more squalid than picturesque but one stroll that is worthwhile is up rue St-Antoine from the port. It then becomes rue de Suquet. Both streets are lined with reasonably priced restaurants, many serving ethnic food. The best are: **Chez Mamichette**, modelled on a Parisian bistro, **Le Relais des Semailles** (highly recommended with menus at 170, 230 and 260f) and **Le Mesclun** (always book, menus at 150f).

The ancient market of Forville sells fish and flowers and is quite picturesque even though the building itself is a bizarre red stone monstrosity. Continuing west along the coast, there are more hotels and restaurants for those who want to be away from the town. There are also some more sandy beaches, some of which are free and most are quieter than those in Cannes.

Fêtes. Cannes is certainly Festival City. In addition to the Film Festival, there are the following throughout the year: *January* – MIDEM (Records and Cassettes); Amateur Film Festival; Mimosa Festival. *February* – International Games Festival. *March* – Vintage Cars. *April* – International Guitar Congress; MIP-TV (TV programmes). *May* – International Film Festival; International Jumping. *June* – Café Theatre Festival. *July and August* – Son et Lumière on the Îles de Lérins; American Festival (4 July); Musical evenings; International Folklore Festival; Fireworks Evenings; Antiques Fair; Feast of the Fishermen (1 August); Clairvoyance and Astrology Festival; Summer Bridge Festival; plus jazz, opera, variety and music festivals. *September* – International Festival of Pleasure Boat Navigation; Royal Regatta; Cycling Grand Prix. *October* – FIPA (International Festival of Audio-Visual Programs). *November* – Musicians' Festival; International Dance Festival. *December* – Cannes Exhibition; Festival of Sacred Art; Antiques Fair; Christmas Illuminations.

The International Film Festival deserves some amplification as it is now considered by many to be the leading film festival in the world. It is also more accessible to the public than most others. It is held in May, two weeks after Easter Sunday, except when there is some other major event conflicting – the last time this happened was in 1956, the Royal Wedding in Monaco.

Official headquarters of the festival is the Carlton Hotel. Anybody who is anybody will be staying there, but as only 132 of the Carlton's 355 rooms have direct views of the Mediterranean, there is great competition for those. To have a room without a view means you're slipping – to stay anywhere other than the Carlton is close to film-world suicide.

The Film Festival is Cannes's biggest event of the year and has been held since 1947, principally in the Palais des Festivals, which was built primarily for the festival.

Films competing are shown not only in the Palais but in almost every concert hall and cinema in town. The Palais sells tickets a week in advance and if you can flash a card of any kind suggesting membership of – or affiliation with – any film academy or school, it will be a big help. If not, try your library card – if they're rushed, it has been known to work.

La Palme d'Or is the most prestigious award of the event and is awarded to the best film. It has been won by such classics as *Open City*, *The Third Man*, *Black Orpheus* and *The Wages of Fear*.

The history of the festival is packed with incident. There was the year Gregory Peck and David Niven were nearly clapped in jail for using walkie-talkies to communicate with each other while boating. This was during the Algerian War and the rebels were using identical methods. Then there was the year when Henry Miller, one of the judges, refused to wear a dinner jacket and was barred from casting his vote.

Another year, the entire Hollywood delegation threatened to withdraw from the festival if Charlie Chaplin was allowed to attend – and there was the year when budding starlet Simone Sylva stripped off to the waist and pressed against a surprised Robert Mitchum to the accompaniment of dozens of flash bulbs.

Casinos

Casino Municipal – on the Croisette; open 5 p.m. every day, 1 November to 5 May.

Palm Beach Casino – on the Croisette; open 5 p.m. every day, 1 June to 31 October.

Casino des Fleurs – on the rue des Belges; open 3 p.m. till 3 a.m. all year round.

Carlton Casino Club – on the 7th floor of the Carlton Hotel, on the Croisette.

The days of the big showy gamblers have gone and you are unlikely to witness anything as dramatic as King Farouk's appearances. Nowadays people go to casinos simply to gamble.

Cannes has more than 300 hotels, but recommending a few is a tougher task here than in most places on the Côte d'Azur. The seasonal variation which affects prices all along the Riviera is even more severe in Cannes because of the festivals and conferences, especially the Film Festival in May. As a result, hotel pricing is at three levels. One hotel, for example, offers exactly the same room at 420, 500 or 600f depending on the time of year. Even in the lower price ranges the variation at one hotel is 270, 350 and 400f. So in checking hotel prices, pay special attention to the dates.

The great hotels of the Riviera are not just hotels. Many are part of the history of the region and are as important to see as other sights. Wander casually into the lobby, saunter around the public rooms and soak up the atmosphere.

The Carlton, built in 1912, is one of thirty hotels built by Henri Ruhl and by far the most glamorous survivor.

When the Allied armies invaded the South of France in 1944, Herbert Matthews, editor-in-chief of the *New York Times* wrote to the Supreme Commander and asked him to be sure to avoid damaging the Carlton Hotel, 'because,' he said, 'it's the best hotel in the world'.

The stories about the Carlton are legendary. Several of them feature King Farouk, a frequent visitor, who would book forty-two rooms when he stayed there. At dinner, he and his entourage would occupy the entire terrace – never less than seventy people. On one occasion when Josef, the maitre d', inadvertently placed a British peer at an adjoining table, Farouk demanded that Josef be beheaded for the insult.

Captain Guy Puckle, a British yachtsman, was a thorn in the side of the Carlton for many years. With a large supply of wigs, false beards, eyebrows and moustaches, he would impersonate famous personalities in dazzlingly rapid succession, choosing his victims from among the Carlton's regular clientele. He might order a cup of coffee on the terrace as George Bernard Shaw; when it arrived, he would be Edward, Prince of Wales. Then when the waiter returned with the bill, it would be waved away by Harpo Marx.

The expression 'value for money' has, in the case of such hotels, little relevance. If a guest should choose to stay at one of them, it will be for the purpose of savouring a rare experience and with the awareness that such luxury and service are in a class of their own and not necessarily related to money. So ... peak price levels are: Carlton – 1,400–3,000f; Martinez – 1,090–2,390f; Majestic – 890–3,060f. Out of season price levels are: Carlton – 600–1,700f; Martinez – 620–1,350f; Majestic – 490–1,720f. But there are other hotels in Cannes that can be recommended:

Hôtel Univers
(HR)M *r. d'Antibes 93.39.59.19*

Very conveniently located just a few minutes from the Palais des Festivals; the rue d'Antibes is a very busy shopping street but being pedestrians only it is quiet at night. Sixty-eight pleasant rooms, priced at 410–650f during Festival times; 260–380f November to March; and 350–490f at other times. There is a bar and a small restaurant.

Hôtel Abrial
(H)M *24 blvd de Lorraine 93.38.78.82 All credit cards*

Fifty-one air-conditioned and sound-roofed rooms, most with balconies. Located near the Voie Rapide and less than 10 minutes' walk from the Croisette. Prices are 465–500f during Festival times; 280–500f November to March; and 380–500f at other times. No restaurant but breakfast is served on the sunny patio. Parking.

Hôtel de Provence
(H)M *3 r. Molière 93.38.44.35 All credit cards*

Less than 150 metres from the Croisette, this is a small (thirty rooms) and reliable hotel. The rooms are comfortable and well-equipped with TV. Prices 220–430f Festival time; 200–350f November to March, and 200–380f at other times. Small garden.

Cannes Palace Hotel
(HR)M–L *11 av. Madrid 93.43.44.45 Cl. 15/11–15/12 All credit cards*

If you like a really modern hotel in every respect with every convenience, this is the best in Cannes at a reasonable price. There are 100 rooms and all are comprehensively equipped. There is a bar, a pool, a sauna, a disco and parking. The area is residential and peaceful. It is towards the east end of the Croisette but only minutes inland. Prices a little higher than some other hotels but the spacious and beautifully furnished rooms and the range of services provided justify 625–1,000f at Festival time; 450–630f November to March; and 490–770f at other times. Breakfast is included.

Hôtel de Paris
(H)M *34 blvd Alsace 93.38.30.89 Cl. 9/11–11/1 All credit cards*

A hotel could not be more traditionally Riviera than the Paris – white-painted façades, shuttered French windows and tall palm trees in an elegant garden.
The fifty rooms have bath or shower, and some have balconies overlooking the garden. The ambience is delightful and there is a large pool. Excellent value for such quality, at 450–880f in Festival times; 250–420f in November and December; and 350–520f at other times. There is parking but no restaurant.

Hôtel Atlas
(HR)M *93.39.45.45 All credit cards*

About two minutes' walk from the Croisette and five minutes from the Palais des Festivals. Fifty-one very well-equipped and comfortable rooms. Parking is provided, there is a swimming pool, and pricing is reasonable for such a combination: 680–790f in Festival times; 390–430f November to March; and 590–690f at other times. Demi-pension is also available at 135 additional per person.

➤ Hôtel Azur
(H)S *15 r. Jean de Riouffe 93.39.52.14*

Couldn't be more conveniently located – right in the heart of Cannes, just a few steps in from the Croisette. Renovated recently and very good value for money – hotels at these prices are rare anywhere on the Côte d'Azur and especially in Cannes. In Festival times, the fourteen rooms are 140–230f; at other times 120–200f.

Hôtel Atlas
(H)S *5 pl. de la Gare 93.39.01.17 Cl. Nov. & Dec.*

Another very tightly priced and reasonable quality hotel. It's near the station but you can't have everything, and the fifty-two rooms are sound-proofed. Prices are 110–350f in Festival times; 85–200f November to March; and 100–280f at other times.

Félix
(R)M–L   *63 La Croisette   93.94.00.61   Cl. Wed.; 15/11–15/12*

Situated right on the Croisette, one of the best-known restaurants in Cannes although it must be said to be more popular with tourists than residents. Usually necessary to book, and the large terrace out by the sidewalk (where you can have a free cabaret of some of the most extrovert passers-by in the world) is preferred most of the year. Food is mainly fish and the à la carte menu runs from 180f up. Good for a drink too.

Au Pompon Rouge
(R)M   *4 r. Émile Négrin   92.98.90.61   Cl. Mon.*

A busy and extremely popular restaurant even on weekdays and out of season. Only about 20 seats so you need to book or be very lucky. The menu at 89f is most people's choice, with mussels or timbale of aubergines; fillet of loup or daube Niçoise or leg of lamb, followed by cheese or dessert. Many other choices exist – the menu is extensive, so is the à la carte.

Lou Souléou
(R)M   *16 blvd Jean Hibert   93.39.85.55   Cl. Tues.; Wed. o.o.s.*

The view out over the Bay of Cannes is calm and soothing. Inside it's busier because this is a long-time popular restaurant. Their Gastronomic Menu at 97f is hard to beat for value with a long list of choices, mostly seafood and occasionally unusual specialities such as mérou grouper fish. The Gourmand Menu costs 160f. The wines are very reasonable and well-chosen.

Gaston-Gastounette   *Very good*
(R)M   *7 quai St-Pierre   93.39.49.44   Cl. Mon. Dec.–March; 3–25/1*
All credit cards

Right on the quay, looking out on to the port, this is a restaurant that nine out of ten local residents list among their favourites. The interior is air-conditioned and there is a terrace for summer dining. The four-course menu at 150f is the one most customers go for, but the bourride at 150f is a meal in itself and an excellent example of how this speciality dish should really be prepared.

Les Santons de Provence
(R)M   *65 r. du Maréchal Joffre   93.39.40.91   Cl. Mon. (except July & Aug.); 1–23/12; 6/2–21/3   V, EC*

A few minutes from the old port, the atmosphere is very Provençal and it is usually full. Leg of lamb with aubergines, and seafood stew with garlic cream are two of their specialities. Menus at 89f and 115f make Les Santons a very reasonable place to eat and enjoy very good food.

La Brouette de Grand-Mère

(R)M   *9 r. d'Oran   93.39.12.10   Cl. Sun.   V*

M. Bruno was formerly with Cannes's renowned Restaurant Félix before opening La Brouette. The fin-de-siècle décor is appealing and the single menu includes an apéritif and all the wine and coffee you can drink. Among main courses are quail in grapes, and chicken tarragon, and the price is a very accommodating 185f.

La Mère Besson

13 r. Frères Pradignac   93.39.59.24   Cl. Sun.; lunch in July and Aug. All credit cards

One of the most reputable places in Cannes and famous for its Provençal dishes. There is a different fish speciality every day, chosen and cooked under the supervision of M. Martin who has taken over from his famous aunt. The aïoli every Friday is a tradition, and the stuffed baby rabbit is a local dish not commonly encountered. An à la carte meal will cost 200–250f. There is a terrace.

Le Bouchon

(R)M   *10 r. Constantine   93.99.21.76   Cl. Mon.   All credit cards*

A local bistro, a long-time favourite and always deservedly busy. Decidedly unfussy but if you want authenticity and satisfaction, don't miss Le Bouchon.

The aïoli is a meal in itself at 65f.

The 75f menu is a little limited but the 105f one is outstanding value, with fish soup or crab in avocado to start; coq-au-vin or escalope of salmon. You get both cheese and dessert – the charlotte with fresh fruit is not to be missed.

➤ La Poêle d'Or

(R)M   *23 r. des États-Unis   93.39.77.65   Cl. Tues. lunch; Mon.; 15/11–15/12 All credit cards*

Cool, calm atmosphere, suiting the contemporary décor. Some people find the pastel shades a bit cold but there is no complaining once the food is served. Bernard and Corinne Leclerc offer some of the best bargains in Cannes; the quality is not surprising, for Bernard learned his trade at Taillevent in Paris and was voted one of the 'Young Restaurateurs of 1990'.

The menu at 135f can be strongly recommended; there is another one at 230f. Typical dishes are navarin of scampi with olives, served with freshly made pasta, and daurade à la marinère.

Very conveniently situated a few steps from the Palais des Festivals, La Poêle d'Or is likely to go from strength to strength.

St-Benoît
(R)M   *9 r. du Batéguier   93.39.04.17*

Just off the busy coastal strip and in a small side-street, the
St-Benoît has been a popular and reliable restaurant on the Cannes
eating scene for some time. The décor is not elaborate so it's clear
that everybody goes there for the food.

On the 120f menu – ravioli with pistou butter, halibut or leg of duck
with orange sauce, and then a choice of desserts. For a little more
– 155f – you can have a really superb spread. Fricassée of snails with
sweet aniseed cream is an unusual starter. Then fillet of rascasse with
basil sauce or sliced Landais duck with Calvados, then salad and
then dessert.

La Croisette
(R)S   *15 r. du Cdt André   93.39.86.06   Cl. Tues.; 15/12−15/1   All credit cards*

Easy to find on a short street just a few steps up from the Croisette
and a good place to know about when you want something simple
and inexpensive. Grilled sardines, lasagne, steak with shallots are
three of the typical items on the list here; light menus at 74f and 82f.

➤ Au Bec Fin
(R)S   *12 r. 24 août   93.38.35.86   Cl. Sat. p.m.; Sun.   All credit cards*

A simple bistro and long-term favourite. Ingredients are always
fresh, the dishes are well cooked and nicely presented. Their daube
is one of the best on the entire Côte d'Azur. Menus at 75f and 95f
are extremely good value.

Le Monaco — *Pron ford !*
(R)S   *15 r. 24 août   93.38.37.76   Cl. Sun.   No credit cards*

An exceptional combination of modest prices, good food and
generous portions in a simple bistro. Menus at 65 and 85f are true
value for money. Be sure to taste their grilled sardines – they are
unbeatable.

The beaches
You don't *have* to pay to use one of Cannes' famed beaches. At the
Palm Beach end of the bay there is a perfectly good, perfectly
clean public beach. The whole point of patronising the parasolled
beauties is to be seen as well as to see. They all have restaurants
(as opposed to cafés), some of them serving food as rich and rare
as that in the hotels to which they are attached. The waiters (as
opposed to beachboys) wear white jackets and black ties and you
would not be welcome if you tried to sit down in damp cozzie and
sandy feet. Many of their customers have no intention of going
anywhere near the sand, in fact; they have chosen to eat here
because of the ambience and good cooking and not because they
need nourishment after an energetic swim and game of volleyball.

The prices for hiring an umbrella, recliner and mattress may shock those who are not used to regarding their beaches as a bit of valuable real estate, but, if you take into account that they will also entitle you to use loos, showers and changing rooms, I consider them good value for a day spent in luxury on one of the most famous beaches in the world.

The restaurants are open for lunch only and usually only from Easter to the end of October. Among the best are:

Carlton. An exception to the black-and-white waiter rule – the *équipe* here are dressed in white Bermuda shorts and Lacoste shirts. This is probably the best-known of all the *plages*, opposite the famous hotel, and lunch will cost you 190f.

Gray d'Albion. Probably the most chic amongst the young Cannois. Classic cold buffet costs a good-value 100f.

Grand. Best for grilled fish and interesting plats du jour; 150f.

La Madrague. Worth the walk to the far end of the Croisette for probably the best cooking at the fairest prices. Superb fish and a young clientele; 130f.

Martinez. Go for a celebration treat. The grandest of the options, with as many flower tubs and hydrangeas as a charity ball. Changing rooms and showers quite unlike the usual beach variety. Lovely food, and a buffet that lasts all afternoon; 250f.

Majestic. The jet-set's favourite, with the best pontoon as well as a relatively good value menu (200f).

Rado Plage. I'd go for this one – look out for the blue-and-white striped umbrellas. Imaginative salads and good fish; 130f.

MAP 4G   **CAP D'AIL** 06320 (Alpes-Maritimes). 3 km W of Monaco; 17 km E of Nice

---

ⓜ *Fri.*

Small, unassuming, a little passé and with no great hotels, or churches, or museums, Cap d'Ail seems left out of the Riviera scene. Some people have liked it, though, and famous names are scattered throughout its past. Edward Molyneux had a villa here and Noël Coward used it to rehearse *Private Lives*; Greta Garbo came here year after year, staying in the Villa Le Roc.

The location of Cap d'Ail, next to Monaco, makes it a possible place to stay if you want to visit the Principality but don't want to pay up. Frequent and inexpensive bus and train services offer easy means of travelling between the two – or, if you're feeling really energetic, it's a thirty-minute walk.

You might think that such a convenient spot would be worth developing, but this has not happened ('political reasons', say the locals, referring to Cap d'Ail's Communist mayor). The fact is that Cap d'Ail remains unspoiled, an ordinary little place overshadowed by its glamorous neighbour.

The name doesn't derive from any garlicky origin as you might suppose but comes either from the Provençal *Cap d'Aigo* meaning 'place of water' or the Italian *Cap d'Abbaglio* referring to bees. The coat of arms of the community – alongside the Saracen Tower, a squat square edifice just above the Basse Corniche – does, in fact, have two bees.

The Jean Cocteau Amphitheatre on the Moyenne Corniche (near the Centre Méditerranéen) presents various performances during summer, and if you like to stroll, there is a footpath from Mala Beach to Marquet Beach (near Monaco). Avoid it though if the sea is rough – freak storm waves have swept away tourists (and even locals). There is also an old Roman trail from Cap d'Ail to La Turbie, paved with the original stones. When these peter out, follow the little blue arrows.

Festivals – *May:* Corn Festival. *July:* Fête Patronale. *October:* Carnival.

Hotel La Cigogne
(HR)M *rte de la Plage Mala   93.78.29.60   Cl. Nov.–Mar.   V, CB*

A family-run hotel and the only hotel in Cap d'Ail which is down near the beach. It is on a quiet road in a residential area just off the Basse Corniche.

All 18 rooms are doubles and have shower or bath and phone. Prices are 350–365f, including breakfast, or 550–570f for demi-pension (for two people, if the minimum stay is three nights). Menus are 120f and 135f.

Hôtel Miramar
(HR)S *126 av. de 3 Septembre   93.78.06.60   Cl. 3–25/1   CB*

Being located on the Basse Corniche, it's a bit noisy. Ask for a loggia facing the sea (cost no extra). The twenty-seven rooms range from 160–250f, depending on bath or shower – very good value.

MAP 5F   **CAP D'ANTIBES** 06402 (Alpes-Maritimes). Immediately south of Antibes

---

Drive south out of Antibes from the old town, staying on the east coast of the peninsula. The road skirts the beaches and two in particular are worthy of note, being long, sandy and free – three unusual characteristics for Riviera beaches. La Salis Beach is just south of old Antibes and La Garoupe Beach is just south again, before the Cap.

Continuing down the coast, there are impressive views of the bays and the many villas, some of which have had famous occupants. Jules Verne wrote *Twenty Thousand Leagues under the Sea* at les Chênes Verts; La Pomme belonged to Maurice Chevalier, and Mistinguette owned a villa nearby; Cole Porter wrote many of his musicals in yet another neighbouring villa.

The old lighthouse of La Garoupe is the highest point of the Cap. From here, there is a panoramic view of Antibes, the coast, the mountains of the Esterel, the islands of Les Lérins and even the Alps. The huge mansion belongs to Stavros Niarchos. Continuing down boulevard Kennedy, you come to the Naval and Napoleonic Museum. If you are interested in either subject, it's worth a stop. Open 10–12 a.m. and 2–7 p.m. June to September; 10–12 a.m. and 2–6 p.m. the rest of the year. Closed Tuesdays and from 1 November to 15 December. Guided tours.

Following the coast still, round the Cap and proceed up the west coast of the peninsula, past the small Port de l'Olivette with its boat anchorage for small private vessels. Then come several tiny coves with minuscule beaches, then the mooring for – a very unusual sight – microlite aircraft on floats. Next, Port Gallice, with nearly a thousand small craft at anchor; then, past several large villas, *voilà* – Juan-les-Pins.

One of the greatest names in the world of hotels is the Cap Eden Roc. It's on the boulevard Kennedy on the drive around the peninsula so you can take a look at it even if the apartment price of 12,000f per night or the double room price of 3,000f per night are out of your league. George Bernard Shaw and Betty Grable have been among its guests and so have the Emperor Haile Selassie, Henry Kissinger, Sophia Loren, Yves St-Laurent and John F. Kennedy. It is also the hotel that Scott Fitzgerald used as the setting for his book *Tender is the Night* although he changed the name to 'Hôtel des Étrangers'. Sadly it now takes conferences but its loyal international clientele still considers it to be one of the grandest hotels on the circuit.

So it's a sight you will want to see – heated salt-water pool, tennis courts, private beach, 24-hour room service, full air-conditioning, marble bathrooms, huge tapestries and 20 acres of grounds and gardens – the ultimate in luxury.

As for actually staying at a hotel . . .

Hôtel Gardiole
(HR)M   *Chemin de la Garoupe   93.61.35.03   Cl. 11/11–1/3   All credit cards*

Reasonably priced at 320–600f (breakfast 45f), or 420–450f for demi-pension. Ten of its twenty-one rooms have baths, the others have showers. Many open out on to a sea view and the setting in a pine forest is delightful. The terrace is perfect for dining on a summer evening.

The restaurant is known as Chez Gilles and is popular with non-residents as well as residents. Menus at 115 and 210f.

Miramar
(HR)M   *Chemin de la Garoupe   93.61.52.58   Cl. 10/11–15/2*

Again, the fourteen rooms are very reasonably priced, at 385–440f. Four have baths and the other ten have showers. Right on La Garoupe Beach, with a popular restaurant. Menus at 120 and 160f.

Restaurant de Bacon
(R)L   *93.61.50.02   Cl. Sun. p.m.; Mon.   All credit cards*

Its reputation for seafood is legendary and so are its prices. The Sordello brothers are said to have the first choice of the fish catch, and many who have enjoyed the bouillabaisse here insist that it is the best on the entire coast. This always upsets the restaurateurs in Marseille, the traditional birthplace of that great dish, who firmly believe that no one can prepare it as they do.

Fish cooked *en papillote* is a feature of the Bacon. It is an established culinary technique for serving fish, wrapped in paper, preserving the tenderness and flavour, but no other restaurant seems to have the knack of doing it as superbly as here.

The shady terrace looks out over the Mediterranean, the interior is air-conditioned and there is valet parking. You won't be surprised to learn that the Bacon is expensive. Weekday lunch menus are 350f and weekend lunches are 450f. If you go in the evening (and be early as the kitchen closes at 10 p.m. even in the summer), you may be better advised to choose one dish à la carte.

MAP 2F   **CLANS** [pv] 06420 (Alpes-Maritimes). 54 km N of Nice

---

Clans is less mediaeval in appearance than many other perched villages and its history is little-documented, but Bronze Age relics have been found and there is no doubt that it has a long and venerable past. Today it is mainly visited for its wealth of artistic treasures, remarkable for such a small place.

The Roman name was Castrum de Clansis and this gave it its present name. Its more recent history dates from the 11th century, when the church on the square was built. Local legends refer frequently to the village being terrorised by dragon-like creatures called *Tarrasques*. In the church at Bairols, a tiny village on the other side of the river valley and teetering on the highest peak, is a sculptured representation of the Tarrasque. It appears to have the body of a dog, the beak of a large bird, wings and a long powerful tail.

Just before entering the village from the south, you will see the chapel of St Antoine, built about 1490. It is simple and unimpressive from the outside – a minuscule front with a roofed entry, a single small bell above and a wooden cross nearby. Don't be dismayed, though – inside are twenty magnificent frescos covering the walls and ceiling, all in excellent condition, painted about 1500 by Andrea de Cella. Most of these depict incidents in the life of the saint. Below them are scenes illustrating human vices; these are very popular with tourists. Pride is shown by a young king, crowned with gold, resplendent in red robes and mounted on a lion. Sloth is seated on a slow grey donkey, Avarice on a monkey, and as for Gluttony . . . well, you may be going to lunch after visiting the chapel.

Also inside the chapel is what looks like a Black Virgin but isn't. The artist used fig juice to thin his paints and this has had a blackening effect over the centuries.

The time to be here is on 26 July for the Pilgrimage of St Anne, or else for the Feast of the Nativity which starts on the last Sunday in August and is followed by three days of wine, singing, music and dancing. One of the customs observed in the past was the donation, to every head of a family, of a litre of wine, and to every villager a loaf of bread.

Auberge St-Jean
(HR)S   *93.09.20.21*

There are only four rooms here so if you haven't booked, your chances aren't too good. The choice is between pension at 200–210f and demi-pension at 170f. The locals eat here and menus are a reasonable 80–120f. Simple food but always good.

MAP 5C   **CLAVIERS** [PV] 83830 (Var). 21 km NE of Draguignan

---

The inhabitants of Claviers are known as *mange-têtes* because they were forced to eat animal heads when besieged. Its position and its fortifications were such that it was considered almost impregnable. While attackers were thus unable to get in, the defenders seldom had an opportunity to get out, so the origin of their nickname is understandable.

Today, little is left of the fortifications and the population has dwindled to 400. There is not much for a tourist to see except a small, unspoiled village, simple and rustic and overshadowed by its more glamorous neighbouring villages of Bargemon and Fayence.

Local fairs are held on 6 June, 26 July and 8 September while the big Fête de Ste Anne (the grandmother of Jesus) is held on 26 July (the same day as the fair) in the chapel of St Anne, just north-east of Claviers.

There is an excellent restaurant here, ideal if you are visiting Claviers or Bargemon or Callas.

Étoiles
(R)M   *94.47.85.85   Cl. Tues.*

Noelle Eddy is English and describes eating at her restaurant as 'a family affair'. A vegetarian herself, she makes sure that her restaurant offers vegetarian dishes but that doesn't mean that there aren't plenty of other dishes on the menu. The chef, M. Aragon, cooks game superbly and this – like everything else here – is fresh. Fish, lobster, homemade pâté de foie gras all feature and there is even steak and kidney pie. Noelle describes her customers as 50 per cent French and 50 per cent foreigners; Danes are prominent among the latter, with over sixty Danish families in and around Claviers. The five-course menu is 130f.

MAP 3G   **COARAZE** [PV] 06390 (Alpes-Maritime). 26 km N of Nice

The approach is by the D 15, a steep winding road. Coaraze, a mere huddle of ancient houses, sits on a rocky ridge, 650 metres high, looking down on the Gorges du Paillon. It has been devastated by earthquakes on several occasions during the past four hundred years, the last time eighty years ago. Today the inhabitants number fewer than five hundred.

Park near the Mairie, then climb up, through arches, twisting and turning past ancient houses, to the cypress-shaded square. From here, the neighbouring villages of Berre-des-Alpes and Contes are visible – another network of look-out villages able to warn the others of an approaching enemy.

The 14th-century church sits at the top of another cobbled staircase. It contains several very unusual wooden statues of saints. The old stone wall leading up to the church has several enamelled sun-dials mounted on it. One is by Ponce de Leon and another by Jean Cocteau. Their decorative modernity fits surprisingly well into the mediaeval background. Similar sun-dials are for sale in the village.

Coaraze has a remarkable number of chapels for such a small village. There is La Chapelle Bleue just above the village and La Chapelle de Sainte-Eurosie on a hilltop near the village. St Eurosie was a local girl, beautiful and clever, who refused to submit to the Moorish chief Jacca and was killed by him in the 7th century. The villagers still pray to her to intercede when the village is threatened – today this is usually when drought looms.

There are several colourful festivals – *8 May:* pilgrimage to the chapel of St Michel in the nearby, deserted village of Rucca Sparviera (a rather spooky and sombre affair). *23–25 June:* Fête de St Jean. *14 July:* Fête Patronale. *12–15 August*: Fête des Olives. *First Sunday in September:* Fête de Ste Catherine. *29 September:* pilgrimage to St Michel (as in May). There is also an annual jumble sale on 1 May.

Auberge du Soleil
(HR)S   *93.79.08.11*

Very popular and usually full in the season despite the pricing of the seven rooms at 270–440f. This is rather more than you expect to pay in a fairly remote village but then the Auberge offers more than the usual country inn. There is a pool and the style is surprisingly upmarket. The alternative of demi-pension at 260–340f is preferred by most guests but there is also a daily menu at 120f and a good list of reliable à la carte favourites.

MAP 4F   **LA COLLE-SUR-LOUP** 06480 (Alpes-Maritimes). 4 km S of Saint-Paul-de-Vence

Ⓜ *Wed., Fri.*

Despite having a bigger population, La Colle is much less famous than its more glamorous neighbour, St-Paul-de-Vence. Today the two almost merge into each other but as La Colle has little to offer the tourist, it is hardly more than a place to drive through on the way up to the Maeght Foundation or the Colombe d'Or. You may be induced to stop at some of the antique shops you see by the roadside. La Colle must have more of them – and with good-quality merchandise – than any comparable area in the South of France.

One of La Colle's few claims to fame is the mill known as Pagnol's Mill. Marcel Pagnol made considerable use of mills in his stories and he not only used this one in his film *La Belle Meunière* but he lived in it for some time.

If you are approaching La Colle from the coast, it will be up the D 6. Staying on the D 6 will take you to the Gorges du Loup, which you should not miss on any account (see p. 28), while turning towards St-Paul on the D 7 will take you past. . . .

➤ **Hostellerie de l'Abbaye**
(HR)M–L   *rte de Grasse   93.32.66.77   All credit cards*

A 12th-century monastery has been converted along with the adjoining 10th-century chapel into this small sophisticated luxury hotel with a wonderful atmosphere.

The fourteen rooms are all different and all have bath and good views. There is a courtyard, a garden with a swimming pool and a large shaded patio for dining in the summer.

It's all very romantic, very Provençal, and the food is imaginative, well-prepared and well-presented. The good-looking girl staff helps too. Prices 350–800f.

MAP 3G   **CONTES** ⓟᵥ 06390 (Alpes-Maritimes). 17 km N of Nice

A population of 4,500 people makes Contes the largest village in the Paillon Valley and certainly larger than most perched villages.

It is approached by the D 15 then the D 715, which winds its tedious way up the valley. As it is only 290 metres in altitude, it is tempting to say of Contes that for a true perched village it is not high enough, besides being too populous, but as you get nearer you change your mind. Contes has much more of a dominating position than at first apparent, and from it can be seen Coaraze, l'Escarène and Berre-des-Alpes – all considerably higher.

Like so many other villages in the region, it was occupied in prehistoric times, and then by the Romans. Legend tells of a plague of caterpillars which ate all the local crops; appeals to the Bishop of Nice found that worthy baffled, but with true bureaucratic evasion, he referred the matter to legal authorities who arranged a formal court trial of the caterpillars. Despite impassioned defence by counsel, the judge found in favour of the prosecution. The caterpillars were ordered out of Contes and banished to Pierrefeu, on the other side of the mountain. On the appointed day, the villagers exorted the caterpillars to leave and, acknowledging legal defeat, they did so in an orderly manner. Legend further states that Contes has never been bothered with caterpillars since, but unfortunately it does not tell us what the people around Pierrefeu thought of the judgement or the sentence.

The château – *Lou Castel* as it is still called in Provençal – is in excellent condition and is unusual in that it does not sit above the village but below it. It is privately owned but will probably be open to the public by the time this appears in print.

There are some local food specialities. *Brissauda* is one of these – hunks of bread, heated in the oven, rubbed with garlic and then dipped in olive oil. The local version of *soupe au pistou* is much lauded and so is *estocaficado* – dried salt cod soaked in water then cooked with tomatoes, onions, garlic, basil, potatoes and olives.

On 3 May, there is a great procession to the chapel of Ste Hélène, at the exit from the village. The occasion celebrates the saint's intervention in time of drought. The bigger church – in the main square – is Ste Marie-Madeleine and has its annual fête in July. In September, the church of St Martin has its annual fête, celebrating Notre-Dame-de-la-Ceinture.

As befits a village of 4,500 people, there are several small hotels and several restaurants.

Le Cellier
(HR)S   *93.79.00.64   Cl. Sat.; Sun. p.m.; 15–24/8; 20/12–4/1   V, EC*

There are only 5 rooms but they are 120–150f or demi-pension is a very good deal at 140–190f.

The menus at 80 to 145f are excellent value for money, as produce from the area is used, the cooking is careful and the quality is attested by the fact that all the locals eat here.

Le Relais de la Vallée (93.79.01.03), which has similar prices and a pizzeria as well as the restaurant, and Christian Soler's **Le Chaudron** (93.79.11.00) have been recommended.

MAP 5A   **COTIGNAC** 83570 (Var). 24 km N of the autoroute exit at Brignoles

---

Camera buffs love Cotignac. The rue de l'Horloge and the place de la Mairie have heard the ˌlick of thousands of shutters. Follow the path up to the ruined castle with its 11th-century twin towers, and you will see why.

Many say that it is the most picturesque village in the Haut Var. It is located at the foot of a steep cliff which is riddled with caves, tunnels and grottoes. A guided tour will take you through these and then into 'La Salle des Merveilles', with some really spectacular stalactites. It is not a tour for the nervous or unsure of foot – the railings are rickety and paths are precarious.

In the village there are several 16th-century houses and the Chapelle St-Joseph, which was built as the result of a miracle: in the 15th century, the saint appeared to a young farmer and told him to move an enormous rock. Suddenly possessed with superhuman strength, the boy did so – and a fountain of fresh water gushed forth. On 19 March every year, ailing pilgrims come from far and near to be restored to health and vigour.

Notre-Dame-des-Grâces, on the hill to the south of Cotignac, was the scene of another miracle. Representations to the Virgin in this Chapel resulted in Anne of Austria giving birth to the Sun King, Louis XIV, after twenty-two years trying to conceive.

The wide Cours Gambetta which runs through the village is the centre of activity. There are numerous shops along it where you can buy local specialities. Cotignac has a reputation for making wine out of – well, you name it . . . They make lemon wine, orange wine, walnut wine and especially quince wine. Quince is *coing* in French and *coudoun* in the Provençal dialect, from the Latin *cotoneum* – hence the name of Cotignac. The local red and rosé wines are popular too.

Les Rûchers du Bessillon is a shop on the rue des Naïfs which sells local products, including many types of honey and René Vacca in the Quartier Nestuby is a good place for olive oil.

Lou Calen
(HR)M   *94.04.60.40   Cl. 1/1 –mid-Mar. Rest. closed Wed. Sept. –June*
All credit cards

One of the long-established favourites in the Var. Located on the main boulevard – cours Gambetta – it has five apartments and eleven rooms, all very pleasant, reasonably priced at 280–490f, and, despite being on a busy road, quiet. There is a swimming pool. Demi-pension is obligatory in season but that is no disadvantage, as the restaurant is at least as renowned as the hotel.

Fish soup, terrine de grives (thrushes) and daube a la Provençale are three regional dishes which are highly recommended. Menus from 100 to 220f. There is a delightful terraced garden for summer dining.

For cheap and informal eating, **La Falaise** is also on the cours Gambetta and the **du Cours** is a restaurant with inexpensive rooms.

MAP 5B   **ENTRECASTEAUX** 83570 (Var). 9 km E of Cotignac

Hardly worth a special visit, but with time to kill after Carcès, le Thoronet, Aups or Villecroze, and in the mood for a little eccentricity, the McGarvie-Munn Museum might be worth a glance.

The local products on sale are probably more interesting than the
Scot McGarvie-Munn's paintings inside the restored château.

This is Entrecasteaux's only claim to fame. There are a couple of
small cafés, but no hotel or restaurant.

MAP 3G   **L'ESCARÈNE** [PV] 06440 (Alpes-Maritimes). 24 km NE of Nice

---

The name comes from *l'échelle* meaning ladder, and the romantic
origin is that the first houses in this hill-top village had no doors.
They were entered directly by ladders, as this made them more easily
defensible. For many decades, L'Escarène was an important relay
station for changing horses on the coaches between Nice and Turin.

Here is the famous bridge spanning the Paillon which was blown
up by the Germans as they retreated before the Allies in 1944. Its
destruction was a calamity for the village as it was then virtually
isolated. A new bridge was not built until 1961 and, with only the
slightest encouragement, any denizen of L'Escarène will tell you of
his grievance in detail.

With about 1,500 population, the village is a little larger than most
perched villages but there is less to interest the tourist than in
some others.

The Annual Fair is held on 29 and 30 November, and there is a
community festival on 1 August.

Hôtel Castellino
(HR)S *93.79.50.11 Cl. Wed. All credit cards*

A popular hotel for many years, the Castellino has nine pleasant
rooms at 170–230f with the alternative of demi-pension at 200–250f.
Food is good, reliable country fare.

MAP 4G   **ÈZE** [PV] 06360 (Alpes-Maritimes). 8 km W of Monaco;
12 km E of Nice

This is one of the essential visits on the Côte d'Azur. Its perch on a
rock, 1,350 feet up, overlooking the sea, is sublime and its location
is convenient – halfway along the coast between Nice and Monte
Carlo. Be sure to approach it by car along the Moyenne Corniche
– unless you really prefer the agonising climb from the Basse
Corniche or the tortuous descent from the Grande Corniche or the
autoroute.

Èze is one of the most touristic villages along the Riviera, yet it
has managed to retain most of its charm. Restoration has been done
carefully and cars are not permitted in the village – you must park
in the municipal lot (free) and climb the last stretch.

Despite being full of shops, Èze has kept out the tawdry and the
banal. The merchandise is good quality and much is even
charming and unusual – don't miss la Voute, with its working models

Èze

of ancient and improbable aeroplanes, music boxes and moving tableaux.

The tiny narrow streets are slow climbing but well worth the effort, with frequent delightful views of old gardens, archways, and beyond them, the intense blue of the Mediterranean. There are few streets where you cannot reach out with both arms and touch the walls. Don't worry about which way to go – all streets lead to the top and all lead back down to the parking.

History weighs heavily on Èze. It has been damaged or ruined countless times – by earthquakes, fire, plague, fever, starvation under siege and the cannon of warships. It has been invaded by Romans, Lombards, Spanish, Genoese, and pirates of all nations. Èze was the last stronghold of the Saracens on the Riviera and they burned it to the ground when they left.

In July 1986, it was deserted once more when fires in the neighbouring forests blanketed it with choking black smoke and forced the evacuation of the entire village. The slopes are still bare of trees when you look down from the ledges on the eastern side, but Èze takes all this in its stride.

The vaunted Exotic Gardens are not that extraordinary, except for the views, but they offer a pleasant ramble in the sun or a good spot for a picnic.

Adjacent to the village – you can drive over and park there or walk down the steps – is the Fragonard Perfumery. This is not an operating perfumery – you must go to Grasse for that. But the free tour takes you through all the stages of perfume manufacture, shows the ingredients, where they come from and how they are made into perfumes and soaps. The vats, the extractors, the tanks . . . everything is there, but not operative. The final stage of the tour is, of course, the sales room where you can buy all the top brands for less than half the price you would pay elsewhere, including duty-free. This is the perfect place to buy something to take home. All the top brands are made here: Nina Ricci, Yves St-Laurent, Rochas, Christian Dior, Guerlain, Estée Lauder, Coty, Chanel. They can't sell them under their trade names but the sales girls will tell you which is which.

There is a wide range of places to eat but not much choice of places to stay. For hotels, you will do better outside the immediate area and drive in for this visit. A hotel you must at least see is:

Château de la Chèvre d'Or
(HR)L   r. de Barri, Èze-village   93.41.12.12   Hotel closed 1/12–28/2. Rest. closed Wed.; Easter 1/3   All credit cards

The village of Èze is a suitable setting for the Château de la Chèvre d'Or, a thousand-year-old castle converted into a small luxury hotel. There are two suites and eleven double rooms ranging in price from 1,000 to 2,500f. All have spectacular sea views and are furnished with museum pieces. Some have terraces.

The pool and terrace are delightful in summer, and a fire burns in the bar on cooler days.

The restaurant is renowned and the rich and famous eat here. The food is light and elegant; the fixed menu is 350f, à la carte 400–700f. Le Grill offers simpler dishes at lower prices – 98f for the fixed menu or 200–300f à la carte.

Not cheap, but it is an experience and this is certainly one of the great hotels on the Côte d'Azur and can fully justify the classification of 'luxurious'.

Château Eza
(H)L (R)M   93.41.12.24   Cl. 1/11–14/4   All credit cards

Seemingly chopped right out of the rock of the old village, several houses were combined to make the château, which was the home of William, Prince of Sweden from 1923 to 1953. Years of work converted it into a luxury hotel and restaurant which opened in 1983.

Èze: La Chèvre d'Or

It is a superb location with sweeping views out to the horizon.

There are eight magnificently equipped rooms at 1,000–2,500f for a single; doubles at 1,200–3,500f, but you may be more likely to go for the lunch at 280f. Dinner menu at 510f. Bruno Cirino is the Chef de Cuisine and among his à la carte specialities are Daurade Royale from the oven at 210f and fillets of rougets de roche with green garlic and courgettes, also at 210f. Wild duck with spiced butter at 240f is another great dish. The rare Bellet wines are on the wine list.

La Troubador

(R)M   r. du Brec   93.41.19.03   Cl. 15/11–24/12; 1–15/2; Wed. & Sun. (except July and Aug.)   All credit cards

> Built into one of the old houses in the hilltop village where M. Vuille offers more modest prices than his celebrated neighbouring establishments.
>
> The Menu Gourmand costs 160f and offers such starters as 8 oysters or smoked salmon; then you could have fillet of St Pierre, pan-fried with spices and artichokes, or saddle of lamb, or roast duck with figs.
>
> Goat's cheese and a selection of desserts would conclude a most enjoyable meal in a very pleasing ambiance.
>
> If you prefer à la carte choices, the grilled loup at 105f or roast turbot in bandol wine at 120f are excellent value. Another favourite is roast pigeon at 120f while beef-lovers have an *embarras de choix* at 90 to 145f.

Richard Borfiga

(R)M–L   pl. Gén. de Gaulle   93.41.05.23   Cl. Mon. o.o.s.   All credit cards

> Richard Borfiga is a former pupil of Jean and Pierre Troisgros so you can be assured of an excellent meal here. Some have murmured that the atmosphere is a little sedate, but conceded that it may be difficult to be less of a shrine to cooking without losing something essential.
>
> Certainly no one ever faults the food. The menu at 180f of flowers of courgettes followed by aiguilettes of duck with sweet lemon sauce and finally Duc de Prasline is superb value.
>
> On the à la carte menu, there are rouget, loup de mer roti, and daurade at 110–180f, or crapaudine de pigeon (the bird is boned and roasted with garlic) at 160f.
>
> There are other set menus at 250, 300 and 350f. The menu at 300f is a particularly delicious one. It is a meal you won't forget.
>
> In case you're not feeling quite that flush, **La Taverne** on the same street as the **Château** is reasonable, and **Au Nid d'Aigle** up near the top of the village is another possibility.
>
> For something in between, the **Cheval Blanc** down on the Corniche and next to the parking area offers good satisfying food at fair prices.

MAP 5D   **FAYENCE** 〔PV〕 83440 (Var). 35 km E of Draguignan; 27 km W of Grasse

---

Ⓜ *Thurs., Sat.*

> Classed as a perched village and we'll consider it one because it is in a commanding position, once you're up there. The approach, however, is misleading. From the D 562, the main road between Draguignan and Grasse, turn north on the D 563 and you're in Fayence in a few minutes and after only the gentlest of climbs.

Of all the villages in the Var, Fayence has become the most popular with foreigners and Parisians as a location for a second home and has a sizeable international community.

Pass under the big arch which goes straight through the Hôtel de Ville, and park in one of the lots on the left. From here, you can walk to most of the sights of the village.

Fayence dates back to the Romans, who were the first to establish a settlement here; it was not on the hill-top as their garrison was strong enough to have no need for a dominating site. Instead it was on the plain below and was called 'Faventra Castres'. Hence the name of the village today. Succeeding occupiers of the site did not possess the military superiority of the Romans, and invasions by Saracens and other barbarian tribes forced the village to be re-located on top of the hill.

It was there that the château was built in the 13th century and occupied by the Bishops of Fréjus. It is today only a ruin but the old watchtower next to it still stands proud and strong. A 270-degree coloured mosaic on the parapet identifies everything visible – a magnificent panorama, with 1,000-metre peaks ringing the horizon. The watchtower is the perfect place to appreciate the mediaeval early warning system. During the days when Saracen invasions were frequent, the network of neighbouring villages in visual communication with each other was at its most sophisticated, with Bargemon, Callian, Seillans and Tourrettes (not to be confused with Tourette-sur-Loup on p. 208) flanking Fayence, all in a line facing the sea.

The huge 13th-century church of Notre-Dame is on the place Thiers and has many fine paintings. Just west of the village is the Chapelle Notre-Dame-des-Cypres, built by monks from Isles des Lérins in the 11th century and in excellent condition. The old town consists of steep sloping streets and meandering stairways.

The best place to stay is probably the **Hôtel des Deux Rocs** in Seillans, five kilometres to the west, but there are lots of places to eat in the village.

➤ Le Poêlon
(R)M   *94.76.21.64   Cl. Sun. p.m.; Mon.; 15/11–15/12   CB*

An 18th-century stone house on a picturesque steep stairway just off the main street by the Hôtel de Ville. The imposing wooden door opens into a vaulted cellar, now the dining-room. M. Dupas strives for a rustic atmosphere and cooks 'peasant' food in the giant poêlons (like a casserole), which give the restaurant its name. Good fish too. Take the 88f menu – no need to spend more.

Restaurant Provençal
(R)M   *pl. Thiers*

Opposite the church on the place Thiers, this is a simple place with plenty of outdoor seating in the summer. The food is good, simply cooked, but with attempts at a few unusual dishes on a surprisingly long menu.

The Farandole du Provençal is popular (a combination of crudités and charcuterie) and the main course includes escalope of veal or stuffed trout; desserts are unexciting. Menus at 65, 90 and 120f.

▶ **La Strega**
(R)S

Don't expect much in the way of décor. It's really a glorified bar, tiny inside and with two small terraces out front on one of the steep streets going up to the Château.

For value for money, it's unbeatable and, despite the simplicity, the food is delicious. You can start with the pâté of quail at 29f, or the stuffed mussels at 36f. For the main course, two choices are casseroled boar with fresh pasta at 58f, or the sautéed rabbit with herbs at 49f. A bottle of the local white wine at 31f will complete a hugely enjoyable meal, although you may want to end with a tarte au pomme at 18f.

MAP 5A   **FOX-AMPHOUX** 83670 (Var). 10 km NE of Barjols

It's so small it's not marked on a lot of maps. Only 300 inhabitants and it's hard to see where they all are. No connection with foxes, the name combines Fous and Anfous, two Provençale villages.

Today, visitors come to Fox-Amphoux because it is such a perfect little mediaeval village, quite unspoiled, completely untouristic – just simple and charming.

Nothing to see or do, just wander around, take photos and enjoy the views. Many come here just to eat at the only place in the village, which is:

Auberge du Fox-Amphoux
(HR)M   *94.80.71.69   Cl. Oct.–Easter*

It is built into the 16th-century presbytery, adjoining the Church of the Templars. Mme Martha Paule will make you welcome (the previous owners, after doing such a superb job of converting the place, sometimes had a high-handed attitude which kept customers from coming back). Local products are used and the cooking is straightforward, with the occasional exotic touch. Menus are 65, 125, 165 and 245f and the view from the outer dining-room is magnificent. Best to order à la carte – 150–220f for a meal.

The ten rooms are small but adequate. The place for utter solitude, and no distractions other than the early morning cockerel. Demi-pension is 255–600f.

The South of France

MAP 6D   FRÉJUS 83600 (Var). 36 km W of Cannes

(M) *Wed., Sat.*

Fréjus's main claim to fame is its Roman ruins, which exceed those
of any other town on the Côte d'Azur, even if they fail to compare
with the old Roman cities in the Rhône valley, such as Orange. If not
actually built by him, it is thought that Julius Caesar established
a market here – the name is said to derive from *Forum Julii*. Fréjus
had about the same population in Roman times as it has today,
and it was in the harbour here – the finest in the Roman world – that
Octavius built the hundred war-galleys that defeated Antony and
Cleopatra at the Battle of Actium.

The amphitheatre is by far the most impressive relic, and is still
used today for rock concerts and bullfights. The aqueduct, which
brought water to Fréjus from the Siagnole River 50 kilometres up in
the mountains, can still be seen near the road to Cannes, its gaunt
arches striding away to the north to disappear in the pine forests.
The Roman theatre is north of the town and is still used for
concerts. The Porte d'Orée is one of the old gates to the town.

The Cathedral incorporates a 5th-century baptistery, and is of very
rugged construction, for use as a fortress. The 12th-century cloisters
are perhaps the most attractive part of the complex; upstairs there
is the Museum of Archaeology with glassware, statues and
mosaics, many of them Roman, found in the vicinity. Open 9.30–12
and 2–6.30 p.m. Closed Tuesdays.

On a different level, there are the Zoological Gardens, covering
sixty acres and containing all kinds of wildlife.

The old town still goes its Provençal way, with a sleepy square, a
couple of bars, and a variety of small food shops suffering from
the competition from the several supermarkets down the hill, which
have sprung up to cater for the many campers in the district. Most
other visitors stay in nearby St-Raphaël, which has a better choice
of hotels, but the hotels and restaurants in Fréjus include:

Les Residences du Colombier
(HR)M   *rte de Bagnols   94.51.45.92   Cl. 1/1–1/3*
All credit cards

A large Provençal-style villa with 60 bungalows scattered
throughout the extensive wooded grounds, priced at 395–420f.
Supplement for demi-pension is 160f per person. There is a heated
swimming pool and tennis on the grounds.

The public rooms, including the restaurant, are in the villa. The
food is simple but satisfying, with menus at 85, 120 and 175f.

Le Vieux Four
(H)S (R)M   *57 r. Grisolle   94.51.56.38   Cl. Sun.; 1–15/11; 1–15/2*
All credit cards

This is really a restaurant with rooms, which is why the restaurant
is medium-priced while the rooms are inexpensive.

104

There is a charming country atmosphere throughout. The eight rooms are 200f, and the menus are 120 and 235f.

Lou Calen
(R)M   *5 r. Désaugiers   94.52.36.87   Cl. Wed.; Feb.; Mar.   All credit cards*

François Gallione is a careful buyer of high-quality local products and this policy shows in the excellent meals, which are cooked with a flair. Sea food features prominently among the dishes offered – mussels, oysters, red mullet, bass – and all at reasonable prices.
Menus are 150f; à la carte offerings are good portions.

Les Potiers
(R)M   *135 r. des Potiers   94.51.33.74   Cl. Sat. o.o.s.; Wed.; 15/11–15/12; 1–11/3   CB*

Very popular and right in the old town. A loyal clientèle keeps it busy all the year round. Mireille Klein runs an efficient air-conditioned establishment and her husband does the cooking – mainly seafood but also ris de veau, tournedos, breast of duck, and other standard favourites.
The menu at 155f is outstanding value for money. Other menus at 160 and 190f at weekends. Wines are 80f and upwards.

MAP 3F   **GATTIÈRES**   ▣ 06510 (Alpes-Maritimes). 24 km N of Nice; 10 km NE of Vence

---

Looking down the Var valley from its 300-metre-high perch, this fortress village was once one of Julius Caesar's relay stations between Aix-en-Provence and Rome. Since then the Parisians and other 'foreigners' who came, saw and loved the mediaeval village have swelled the number of inhabitants to 2,000, making it one of the larger perched villages.
It is the simple lifestyle, in the away-from-it-all setting high above the vineyards and olive groves, that is the main attraction. Apart from a ruined château, a stark Gothic-Roman church, and the annual fête on the last Sunday in August, there is little else, except of course:

Auberge de Gattières
(R)M   *pl. du Pré   Closed 15/1–28/2   V, EC*

Mlle Rohmer does the cooking and runs the place and gets full marks from her regular patrons and visitors for doing so. Casseroled duck and frogs' legs are on the menu at 120f; or there is a more elaborate one at 200f.
The décor is unassuming, country-style and welcoming. The cooking is honest and always satisfying.

MAP 5F **GOLFE-JUAN** 06220 (Alpes-Maritimes). 2 km W of Juan-les-Pins; 6 km E of Cannes

One of the lesser-known resorts on the Riviera, Golfe-Juan is between Antibes and Cannes, strung along a bay, with safe anchorage and a seemingly endless port. It is sheltered by the Cannes hills and has one of the highest number of sunny days of any place in the South of France.

The utter lack of historical buildings, landmarks or monuments is in sharp contrast to the rest of the Riviera, though there is one touch of invisible history. A blue mosaic plaque on the promenade at the entrance to the rue de la Gare identifies the spot where Napoleon first set foot ashore on 1 March 1815 after he had escaped from the island of Elba. He chose this stretch of beach because he knew it from his days in Antibes and could bank on it being deserted and his landing unopposed. With his tiny army of 800 men, which quickly grew to over a thousand, he set off on the march to Paris, which become immortalised as the 'Route Napoleon'. Three months later, he lost the Battle of Waterloo and went again into exile, permanent this time, on St Helena.

The sandy beach is only about 150 metres long and quite narrow. To the west, the coast is rocky and to the east, it's all port. This, added to the fact that Golfe-Juan only goes inland about three streets before it is stopped by the railway line, is the reason that it is less frequented than most of the Côte d'Azur. There is little to do here unless you're on a boat. No night life, no clubs, no entertainment. There are a few bars and the walk along the promenade, where there are some good and inexpensive restaurants, is very pleasant. Parking is not easy.

You can walk around the port and observe the boats. At the east end, there are working shipyards, and there is also anchorage here for larger-than-usual pleasure-boats.

Between the railway and the sea, you will notice numerous luxurious villas. The largest white one belonged to the Duke of Windsor, and the one next to it to Rita Hayworth.

Hôtel du Golfe
(H)M   *93.63.71.22   Cl. Nov.   P.   All credit cards*

This is the only hotel on the promenade. The nineteen rooms are priced at 280–400f. Parking.

Auberge du Relais Imperial
(HR)S   *93.63.70.36*

Not right on the promenade but on a tiny street only steps behind it. This is a charming little auberge, and one of the few that merit the name. It's open all the year round and locals eat here in the restaurant.

The ten rooms are small but quite adequate and priced at 200–260f. Demi-pension is 180–235f; full pension 280–295f. The cuisine is dominantly fish – hearty portions and beautifully cooked. There is a garden for summer dining.

Hôtel Beau Soleil
(HR)S   *93.63.63.63   Cl. 10/10–23/3; Rest. cl. Wed. lunch   P.   All credit cards*

Like all the other hotels around Golfe-Juan, this one is not directly on the coastal strip. It is about 500 metres inland and on the RN 7, a modern four-storey building overlooking the pool, which has wide lounging decks all around it. It is fully air-conditioned and good value at 250–370f for the thirty rooms, or demi-pension at 225–310f; full pension at 265–355f. Parking.

Hôtel de Crijansy
(HR)S   *av. Juliette Adam   93.63.84.44   Cl. 15/10–20/12   P.   V*

Just on the north side of the busy RN 7 but up a quiet little street. It's a small compact building, all rooms with automatic shutters and balconies. The twenty rooms are 250–260f, demi-pension. Parking.

Tetou
(R)L   *93.63.76.16   Cl. 15/10–15/12; 1/3–20/3; Wed. in season   No credit cards*

If you want to go up-market as far as Golfe-Juan goes, then you can really push the boat out here. Not only because Tétou is right on the beach, but the à la carte menu will run you over 400f. The accent is again on fish, with such specialities as bouillabaisse, grilled langoustes and oven-baked sea bass. Wines include the increasingly rare Bellet.

Chez Christiane
(R)M   *On the port   93.63.72.44   Cl. Tues.; evenings o.o.s. (except Fri. and Sat.); 11/11–20/12   All credit cards*

Christiane has been here for seventeen years and it is surprising that she is not better known. Of course, there are apparently unlimited numbers of good seafood restaurants along the coast but it seems unfair that such outstanding ocean fare as you can get here has not yet brought wider attention.

The tiled floors, basket chairs and pale yellow linen give the dining-rooms a welcoming ambience, and there is an adjacent terrace. All look out across at the boats at anchor. Nothing extraordinary but the food is the thing, as any client here will tell you.

The luncheon-only menu at 170f offers a choice of three starters (the fish soup is excellent), then a choice of three main fish courses which may typically be fillet of sea bream, monkfish, or sautéed shellfish. Then cheese, then dessert.

The four-course evening menu costs 190f. There is also a special menu at 190f which starts with half a dozen oysters and then offers Bourride Provençale, cheese and dessert.

Restaurant Bruno
(R)M   *93.63.72.12   Cl. Sun. p.m. and Mon. o.o.s.; 12/11–19/12   V, CB*

Open-fronted and looking right across at the port, this is another underrated restaurant. Their list of fish specialities is lengthy – bouillabaisse, red mullet, langoustes. . . .

Dominique and Casimir Cassia are always busy, and no wonder with such food at such prices. The 110f menu is a best bet. Soupe de poissons or moules farcies to start, then the salmon trout with lobster sauce, followed by cheese and dessert is a real bargain.

Restaurant La Taverne
(R)M   *93.63.72.14*

On the front, you can look out at the boats from either the summer or the winter terrace. Local specialities figure prominently on the 120f menu. Start with the friture mediterranéen with sauce antiboise (tiny fish fried to a crisp golden brown), followed by oven-roasted fish of the day or a very unusual Provençal dish – blanc de rascasse in mustard sauce. If you have a small appetite that day, there is a menu at 80f. If you're really hungry, the menu at 170f will satisfy anyone. Proprietor and chef Claude Monty tries very hard to do this.

Le Bistrot du Port
(R)M   *93.63.70.64   Cl. Sun. lunch; Mon. (except July and Aug.); 30/11–30/1*
CB

You may feel the urge to eat at a more up-market restaurant with a swankier atmosphere. If so, Le Bistrot offers a menu at 210f. All kinds of seafood and shellfish and some good, moderately priced wines. View of the port here too.

➤ L'Angélus du Port
(R)S   *93.63.71.26*

For a good simple meal at a real budget price this is the place. You can eat in the restaurant looking out at the port across the street or on the terrace right on the promenade. Try the rabbit Provençale with fresh pasta for 49f. Where can you beat that on the Riviera?

Chez Gigi
(R)S   *93.63.71.16*

There are two of these on the front, about 50 metres apart. In both cases, the restaurant looks across the road at the port and also has a wide terrace on the promenade. The waiters risk their lives continually dashing across the road to bring you your food!

One of the restaurants is a pizzeria only. The other offers excellent seafood. Lobster Thermidor features as the main dish in a three-course meal which is an incredible 135f.

There is also a menu at 129f which could consist of fish soup then fillet of John Dory or scallops and choice of desserts.

MAP 3G   **GORBIO** [PV] 06500 (Alpes-Maritimes). 8 km NW of Menton

Sitting just above the autoroute, on the D 23 from Menton, Gorbio
is unquestionably a perched village. At an altitude of 360 metres,
it has a proud position on top of a hill, looking down over the slopes
covered with olive groves.

Like so many other perched villages, it has been pillaged and
ravaged for many centuries, yet it retains a cheerful romantic
atmosphere and has not lost its enchantingly mediaeval look.

Being so close to the coast and with valleys on either side, Gorbio
is frequently swept by clouds of mist so watch out for these when
driving up or down.

The busy place de la République, with its massive 300-year-old
elm, is the heart of village life. From the old Roman gate, the
cobbled stairways climb up through narrow arches, weaving in and
out among the ancient houses, and eventually arriving at the 17th-
century church. This is one of no less than nine churches in or near
the village.

You can climb on past the church up to the ruins of the old château
– another of the castles built by the Lascaris family.

The donkeys of Gorbio have the reputation of being the most
intelligent in the world, according to the French historian Georges
Durandy, but he does not disclose how this strange conclusion was
reached.

Fêtes: *June:* Festival of Cherries; Procession of the Slugs. *Third
Thursday of August:* Feast of St Bartholomew. *Late September/early
October:* Vendanges celebrations.

Auberge de Village
(R)M   *8 r. Gambetta   93.35.87.83*

François Squillace is the enthusiastic and friendly owner-chef who
will prepare excellent local dishes for you. He will probably
recommend the stuffed artichokes, beignets of the vegetable in
season, the ravioli maison and the civet de lapin. Whatever he
recommends you will enjoy. Menus at 85, 105, 120, 130 and 150f.

MAP 4E   **GOURDON** [PV] 06620 (Alpes-Maritimes). 14 km NE of Grasse;
17 km W of Vence

Few perched villages are as perched as this one – 760 metres, on the
peak of a rocky cliff, and looking right down the Gorges du Loup. You
can – if you have the stomach – look down vertically 300 metres.

In such a commanding position, Gourdon was an important link
in the chain of fortresses with visual communication. The sentries
on duty could see as far as eighty kilometres – that is to say, the
coast at Nice to the east and the coast at Fréjus to the south.

The château was originally called Gourdon La Sarrasine when it
was built in the 10th century and, as its name indicates, it was

intended for the purpose of watching for Saracen invaders. There was an ironical reversal of circumstances when it was captured by the Saracens, who then fortified it in their own style. It passed through numerous hands over the next centuries – the Counts of Provence, the family of Grasse, the Villeneuve family and the Lombards. The latter restored it in the 13th century and today it stands in extremely good condition and much as it appeared originally.

Visit the Musée du Château, which is in the Henri IV tower. It has an excellent collection of ancient weapons like arquebuses and arbalests, swords and suits of armour. The dungeons are also open for visits. In the château too is the Museum of History and Naive Painting. The latter lives up to its name rather too effectively but there is a self-portrait by Rembrandt, many valuable paintings of the 16th century and a writing desk used by Marie-Antoinette. The terraced gardens have some very photographable views.

'The Road to Paradise' which runs its dangerous path down the Loup Valley does not, as might be thought, identify a pilgrim route, but the approach to the torrent of water pouring over the huge boulders. *Paradou*, the Provençal word, is simply a corruption of *Près de l'eau*.

MAP 4E   **GRASSE** 06130 (Alpes-Maritimes). 17 km N of Cannes

---

Ⓜ *Daily, pl. aux Aires*

It's still the perfume capital of the world and that's why every visitor to the South of France wants to see it.

Be prepared to be disappointed visually – it's a very ordinary undistinguished industrial town. The aromas that are always in the air from the beginning of August to the end of October are a delight, though. That is the harvest season, while for the rest of the year the smells drift from the factories. A wave of jasmine or a cloud of lavender may engulf you at any time and sometimes there is the tang of orange oil in the air.

It all started with Catherine de Medici, who loved to surround herself with bizarre décor, extreme luxury and rare perfumes, which in the 16th century had to be brought from the Orient. Aware that a profusion of fragrant blooms grew in Provençe, she sent one of her courtiers, a Florentine named Tombarelli, to find a way of making perfumes from these wild flowers.

Tombarelli chose Grasse as the natural centre of a region rich in such treasures, and orders of monks were encouraged to work in what they called 'this blessed herb garden'. The monks worked closely with the glove-makers who always perfumed their wares. The first distillery was established in 1595 and by 1740 there were sixty-five of them. When Marie-Antoinette went to the guillotine on 16 October 1793, she first doused herself liberally with perfume from Grasse.

Lavender, jasmine, geraniums, mimosa and hyacinths grow in abundance, and orange, lemon and lime trees are all there, along with mint, and tuberose – that rarest of white flowers.

Tour one of the many factories – Fragonard, Molinard and Galimard are the biggest. Ask for a tour in English – you will learn how 8 million jasmine blossoms must be collected to produce 1 kilo of essence; and how the flowers must be harvested at dawn while the dew is still on them.

Much of it sounds like fascinating folklore, some of it sheer mystical tradition and most of it historical practice blended with modern chemistry.

The sales rooms are the last stage of the tour and you are unlikely to leave without buying something. All the top-name brands – Dior, Lancome, Yves St Laurent, Estée Lauder and others can be bought at heavily discounted prices. The names will be different but the sales girls will let you into the secret.

Other than perfume . . . well, the Centre International de Grasse present dance spectacles in all their forms with a very active schedule. Jazz, ballet, interpretive, modern and classical dance are all offered, most of them by local groups but often by visiting artists of renown.

The Villa Musée Fragonard has a bigger reputation than it deserves and much of this is due to the attractiveness and historical background of the building which houses it. Formerly the Hôtel de Cabris, built in 1773 by Mirabeau's sister, it was turned into a scent factory but in 1921 was restored as a museum. Today it contains paintings, costumes, glassware and household utensils. Open 10–12 a.m. and 2–5.30 p.m. Closed Saturdays and November.

Little has changed in Grasse during the past 250 years and many of the buildings are much older, but they do not have the air of grandeur that you might expect. The lovely multi-arcaded place aux Aires; the 12th-century cathedral, Notre-Dame du Puy – modified in the 16th century – hosts music concerts throughout the year, often with international artists; the Chapelle de Saint-Michel and the old Hôtel de Théas-Thorenc seem muted by the ordinariness of the busy town. The Musée de la Marine, the International Perfume Museum and the Museum of Provençal Art and History are all of specialised interest.

It is no longer the fashionable resort that Pauline Borghese established, and where Queen Victoria spent several winters. Since then it has been the glamour of the perfume business that has kept the name of Grasse alive.

Fêtes: *second week of May:* Rose festival. *First Sunday in August:* Jasmine festival. *Early August:* Battle of the Flowers.

Cabris and Vence are more likely overnight stops, but there are some restaurants and hotels in Grasse that can be recommended:

Hôtel Panorama
(H)M   *2 pl. Cours   93.36.80.80   Open all year   All credit cards*

One of the best hotels in town. The 36 rooms are pleasantly furnished, fully-equipped with mod cons, and all have a view. 260–325f.

Hôtel du Patti
(HR)M *pl. du Patti   93.36.01.00   Open all year   All credit cards*

> Right in the heart of the older part of town, very good value for
> money. Since it was renovated recently it has been very popular and
> often full, even though there are fifty rooms. They are priced at
> 260–320f; demi-pension at 370–450f. The restaurant serves
> unadventurous but good, satisfying food.

Maître Boscq
(R)M *13 r. de la Fontette   93.36.45.76   Cl. Sun. and Mon. o.o.s.   A, CB*

> One of those restaurants where the owner-proprietor has his
> name out front – usually a sign of confidence in the quality of the
> meals he is offering. M. Boscq makes a sincere effort to please and I
> have never heard of anyone going away from his establishment
> disappointed.
> Several dishes of Provençal origin are always on the menu, and
> there are even a few Grassois specialities, such as stuffed
> cabbage. There is a pleasant terrace and prices are agreeably low.
> The 3 course menu is 108f and à la carte will run 160–200f. Maitre
> Boscq's card has the amusing phrase 'Tries hard to speak English'!
> Well, he tries hard in every area – and succeeds.

MAP 7C   **GRIMAUD** 83310 (Var). 10 km W of St-Tropez

Ⓜ *Thurs.*

> Too close to St-Tropez and too accessible to be a perched village in
> the true and traditional sense, Grimaud nonetheless comes fairly
> close. Its ruined mediaeval castle sits above the village, and the view
> is superb.
> The Ligurians were here, then Grimaud became a Greek trading
> port, and afterwards a Roman base. The bay of St-Tropez was a
> favourite place for Saracen landings and so Grimaud became one of
> the locations for the Knights Templars to build defensive
> fortifications.
> The rue des Templiers leads up to the church of St Michel and the
> house which once belonged to the Templars. Built originally in
> the 11th century, it was restored in the 16th century. The narrow
> winding streets snake around the 15th-century houses, with their
> tiny windows and Gothic arcades. The Musée des Arts et Traditions
> Populaires on the place des Écoles has interesting exhibits of the
> region.
> Two kilometres east of Grimaud is the Chapelle de Notre-Dame-
> de-la-Queste to which a pilgrimage is made every 15 August. It
> contains a wooden statue of the Virgin Mary, very unusual in having
> articulated arms and legs. North of the village, the Pont des Fées
> is generally considered to be part of a Roman aqueduct, although
> more recent historians say it is Saracen.

> Fêtes include: *2 February:* Foire de la Chandeleur. *Thursday after*

Ascension: Woollen Fair. *July:* Country Fair. *August:* Folklore Festival. *15 August:* Local fair; pilgrimage to Notre-Dame-de-la-Queste. *16 August:* Harvest Festival. *29 September:* Feast of St Michel. *25 October:* Feast of St Hubert (Port Grimaud).

That great hotel, Le Kilal, alas no longer exists, having been turned into flats. Les Santons restaurant is still there but unfortunately it is no longer good value for money – two victims of the village's up-market advance. If you want to stay in Grimaud, try these:

Hostellerie du Coteau Fleuri
(HR)M   *pl. des Pénitents   94.43.20.17   Hotel closed 1/11–1/4; Rest. closed 15/10–15/5; Wed. except July & Aug.   All credit cards*

A 12th-century chapel converted into a Provençal-style auberge with tiled floors, and flowers everywhere.

The fourteen bedrooms are small but have good furniture with Provençal prints. All have views out over the mountains; 350–500f.

The food is good and surprisingly imaginative. Dinner costs about 200f.

The Hostellerie is on the edge of the village and so less than three kilometres from the sea.

Ferme La Croix
(HR)S   *94.43.21.81   Cl. Sat.; Sun.; 1/12–15/2   CB*

Really a restaurant with three rooms. A genuine Provençal farm where you are part of the family of Mme Olivier and Mme Bertolotto. It has been charmingly converted, and most of the products served in the restaurant were grown in the garden – where there are tables for dining.

Rooms are very simple, at 150–280f, or 220–280f for demi-pension. Menu at 150f but last orders are taken at 8 o'clock.

MAP 1E   **GUILLAUMES** PV 06470 (Alpes-Maritimes). 97 km NW of Nice

---

Ⓜ   *Fri., Sun.*

The approach to Guillaumes is either along the D 29 or up the Gorges de Daluis, but whichever you take, the impressive sight of the ruins of the old château is the same, towering on top of a mountain and visible from far, far away at its 819 metre altitude.

Both approaches are in themselves picturesque, with bizarre limestone rocks thrusting their bulk out from the cliffs at the roadside, while the road cuts through tunnels.

Guillaumes was probably named after the feudal Count Guillermo, and was constructed about the year 1000. It was originally an entirely fortified city, surrounded by towering walls. Sieges and fires damaged it numerous times and little remains today. The worst of these fires was in 1682 and, forty years later, an itinerant artist painted the village in flames, showing the inhabitants fleeing with their children and meagre possessions. At the foot of the village is the Chapel of Notre-Dame-du-Buyei, a popular pilgrimage destination, where that painting may be seen today.

On the village square is the church of St Étienne, built in 1699. It too contains several paintings depicting various episodes in the history of Guillaumes.

The Friday morning market is a particularly busy one, with farmers and merchants crowding in to the village from all the surrounding countryside and selling everything imaginable.

Guillaumes has originated several dishes which are considered typical and are based on local ingredients. These include courgette tarts, and ravioli stuffed with chopped courgettes, with walnut sauce.

Festivals are an important part of life in any village as remote as Guillaumes. *24 June:* pilgrimage to the chapel of Notre-Dame-du-Buyei. *14 July:* Folklore Festival. *15 August:* Feast of the Assumption (the men of the village dress in ancient military uniforms and march through the village to a drum and fife band). *Second Wednesday in September and second Wednesday in October:* Sheep Fair (commemorating the days when vast herds of sheep paused here to rest on their way down from their pastures up in the Alpes-de-Haute-Provence).

Les Chaudrons
(HR)S   *93.05.50.01   Open all year*

This is a simple but perfectly adequate hotel. It has ten rooms, three with bath, priced at 150–190f. There is a small but serviceable restaurant.

MAP 5F   **ÎLES DE LÉRINS** (Sainte-Marguerite and Saint-Honorat) 6400 Cannes

---

The boat ride to Ste-Marguerite from Cannes takes only fifteen minutes and the onward trip to St-Honorat another fifteen minutes. One or the other in a day is really sufficient. Boats leave hourly in summer and about every 1½ hours in winter. Buy tickets at the office opposite the Palais des Festivals and embark adjacent to the office.

Ste-Marguerite is heavily wooded, with pines and oaks, and the trails through them are for pedestrians only – which makes it tranquil and leisurely after busy Cannes. You can cover as much of the island as you wish in one day – it's only three by two kilometres. The highlight of the visit is the Fort, built by Cardinal Richelieu to defend the coast against the Spanish. It wasn't a success in that regard, although the French ultimately recaptured it.

The main reason to see the Fort is to see the cell in which 'The Man in the Iron Mask' was held. Alexandre Dumas based his book on the prisoner brought there by Saint-Mars, Governor of the island in 1687. Was he really the twin brother of Louis XIV? Or was he Count Matteoli, secretary of the Duke of Mantua, who had tricked Louis by agreeing to sell him the fortress of Casale and then reneging on the deal? Speculation continues, but the cell is real

St-Honorat: the old abbey

enough. Grim, cold and stern. Two hundred years later, the same cell was the scene of a remarkable escape. Marshal Bazaine was serving a life sentence for surrendering Metz and its garrison of 150,000 men to the Germans in 1870. After only five months in the cell, he disappeared; how has never been resolved.

You will be glad to get out of the chilly cells and into the bright sunshine. There are scores of places for a picnic between the beaches and the massive walls of the fort. You can watch boats or survey Cannes and its coast or just bask in the sun. Then perhaps there will be time to see the small museum inside the building featuring finds from the sea – from Roman times up to date. It is run by enthusiastic amateurs who deserve support.

St-Honorat is smaller, more primitive with no tourist attractions, like the Fort of Ste-Marguerite. There are not even any bars or cafés and certainly no traffic. The only buildings are an abbey recently rebuilt on the site of the one founded by St-Honorat around AD 400. It was a powerful institution in those days and many of the French Church's most famous saints came from there (as well as many saints of other nationalities including Ireland's St Patrick). From St-Honorat, missions went all over the world. After 500 monks had been massacred in a Saracen attack in the 11th century, a fortress was built on the island's coast. A tunnel connected it with the abbey so that the defences could be manned without exposure. It is a very imposing and formidable construction.

MAP 5F   **JUAN-LES-PINS** 06600 (Alpes-Maritimes). Immediately W of Antibes

A modern creation, in contrast to the resorts like Antibes and St-Tropez which have histories going back to the Greeks and yet earlier. Juan-les-Pins was deserted fifty years ago and even its name is less than a hundred years old.
A casino was built here in 1909 but it was barely becoming known when World War I caused it to be turned into a hospital. In 1925, Frank Jay Gould, son of the American railroad tycoon, bought it and added a restaurant and a hotel – thus sowing the seeds for one of the most popular resorts on the Mediterranean.
All the beaches – sixty of them – charge an admission fee, and all are sandy. Every kind of water sport is available – scuba diving, windsurfing, sailing, water-skiing – as well as every manner of land-based sport.
Today, Juan-les-Pins could well challenge for the title of the busiest spot on the Riviera. It buzzes with bars, nightclubs, restaurants, boutiques, arcades, ice-cream parlours, coffee-shops, tea-rooms, jazz clubs . . . you name it. It's a beehive of activity, from the Casino to the nude shows, and the crowds seem unlimited. But there is nothing shady or tawdry – all is neat and clean and tidy and honest and you can feel quite safe. But you haven't seen 'busy' till you've seen Juan-les-Pins in the height of the season.
The big event is the Jazz Festival, held every year during the last two weeks of August. Jazz is big all over the South of France but the Jazz Festival here is the most important event of its kind on the whole Côte d'Azur. Artists and music represent true professional eminence and not just commercial popularity. One of the main squares in Juan-les-Pins has been named Square Sidney Bechet which gives an indication of the significance of this musical happening. The great New Orleans saxophonist and clarinet player performed here several times. 'Jazz à Juan' is held in the Pinède with its centuries-old pines and views out over the Mediterranean. The festival seems to be losing none of its appeal despite a reported decline in interest in jazz at other places on the Riviera. Many international names appear still, making this a major musical event.
The International Bridge Festival has been held here since 1949. It

attracts 1,200 competitors, of whom one of the most regular attendants is Omar Sharif.

Les Orangers

(HR)M   *65 chemin Fournal Badine   93.61.09.43   Cl. 15/10–1/4; Rest. closed July, Aug.   V*

Just north of the station but still only a few minutes' walk from the beach. Twenty-eight quite adequate rooms, four with bath, the others with shower. Prices range from 400 to 600f. Dinner 95f.

Auberge de l'Estérel

(HR)M   *21 r. Iles   93.61.08.67   Rest. closed Sun. p.m. o.o.s.; Mon.   EC, CB*

This is really a restaurant with rooms, which usually means that you get extra value for money on the rooms. There are fifteen here (thirteen with shower and two with bath), pleasant and priced at 190–310f, and there is a garden. So many people unhesitatingly recommend the Auberge that it must be one of the best bargains on the coast. Specialities such as roast pigeon are often found on the menu. Meals at 150 and 225f – relatively higher than the rooms but good value.

Pré Catalan

(HR)M   *22 av. des Lauriers   93.61.05.11   Cl. 15/10–15/3   All credit cards*

A few minutes' walk inland from the beach and just behind the Casino. Six of the twenty rooms have baths and the others have showers. Prices are demi-pension only, but the food is good and portions are liberal: 756f for rooms with shower, 806f with bath.

Hôtel Courbet

(H)M   *33 av. Amiral Courbet   93.61.15.94   Cl. 1/10–Easter   All credit cards*

This is another one of those hotels about which I have never heard a bad report. The twenty-seven rooms are good-sized and well-furnished. Every one has a bathroom. The hotel is located almost on the beach and right in the heart of Juan-les-Pins. Prices are fair at 350–500f. The Courbet's location means that there are plenty of restaurants within easy walking distance.

On the rue Dautheville which is a narrow pedestrian-only thoroughfare, there are some inexpensive hotels – nothing fancy, small rooms, minimally equipped and noisy because they are on such a busy street, but at 200–250f, they are very reasonable for Juan-les-Pins and worth knowing about when everything else may be full. These are: **Central** (93.61.09.43); **Casino** (93.61.00.84); **Mexicana** (93.61.31.34); and **Pacific** (93.61.05.36).

Juan Beach
(HR)S *5 r. Oratoire   93.61.02.89   Hotel closed 1/11–1/4; Rest. closed p.m.*
o.o.s.   P.

Only 100 metres from the beach and on a fairly quiet street. There are 28 rooms, 18 with showers and nine with baths. There is free parking, a private beach, a pretty garden and a large covered terrace. Demi-pension is 290–440f and full pension (based on two persons) is 320–380f.

The restaurant is for residents only and serves simple but very satisfying meals. Annyck and Gaby Moreau try very hard to give you real value in this conveniently placed hotel with a calm ambience in the middle of busy Juan.

MAP 2G   **LANTOSQUE** [PV] 06450 (Alpes-Maritimes). 45 km N of Nice

---

Ⓜ *Daily*

Built on top of a spur overlooking the Vésubie Valley, Lantosque is reached by the N 202, which runs north from Nice. When occupied by the Romans, it was a truly walled city with only two city gates. The four- and five-storey houses, which today make up the southern wall, look as if they are about to slide down the mountainside at any moment.

They have, in fact, done so on several occasions – in 1494, 1564, 1566 and 1644, when earth tremors sent most of the village hurtling down the ravine and into the Vésubie or the River Riou which joins it here. The village has been battered too by human hands. It was completely destroyed in a battle in 1300 and from the time that it was rebuilt, the armies of Savoy, Provence, Sardinia, Piedmont and others fought over it for centuries, because of its strategic position on the caravan route along the Vésubie valley.

The villagers say that all the catastrophes of nature to which Lantosque has been subjected are the reason why there are so many chapels for the tourist to visit. St Sulpice is 15th-century and surprisingly modest in decoration; St Laurent is 13th-century and has many old paintings. St Columban, St Roch, St Arnoux, Ste Claire and the Chapelle des Pénitents are of less interest, but if you do want to see them, all are accessible using the small square as the starting point and taking the cobbled alleyways and the zigzagging stone stairs through the maze of ancient houses.

Like so many perched villages, Lantosque has a jolly time throughout the year, with festivals to maintain the customs and traditions of its busy past: *26 and 27 April:* Fête de St Georges. *24 and 25 May:* Fête de St Pons. *15 June:* Community Fête. *14 July*: Bastille Day. *26–29 July:* Fête de Ste Anne. *18 and 19 October:* Feast of Chestnuts. *Christmas:* numerous celebrations around this time, especially Midnight Mass.

In a village of only about 800 inhabitants, you would not expect to find a country inn which has the welcome, the comfort, the service and the food of this one – plus a swimming pool.

➤ **Hostellerie de l'Ancienne Gendarmerie**
(HR)M   *93.03.00.65   Cl. Mon. o.o.s.; 5/11–1/1   All credit cards*

Mme Winther-Solveig from Denmark has made this family-run inn into a renowned hotel-restaurant. As a restaurant, it is very popular with the locals, and as a hotel, it is always full. Its location is convenient for visiting the villages in the Vésubie Valley and it is just off the road from Nice to Saint-Martin. The charming white villa, once the old gendarmerie, has nine rooms at 300–365f for a single, 350–710f for a double, or demi-pension at 370–560f. There is a pleasant garden as well as the pool.

The restaurant serves its own smoked salmon (a Danish talent at work here), which, followed by local trout and a fruit tart, makes a perfect meal. Menus at 110, 145 and 170f.

Auberge du Bon Puits
(HR)S   *93.03.17.65   Cl. Tues. o.o.s.; 1/10–15/3*

M. Corniglion believes in offering good value and many guests come back year after year. The ten rooms all have a bath, and are well priced at 180–240f. The restaurant serves straightforward but good country fare at under 100f.

MAP 8C   **LE LAVANDOU** 83980 (Var) 40 km E of Toulon; 32 km W of St-Tropez

---

The town that I know best of all the region. Too well perhaps for dispassionate summary, since impressions are coloured by glorious escapist holidays in a friend's villa overlooking what is for me the best beach on the Mediterranean, La Fossette.

Having heard horror stories of traffic snarls and sticky short tempers in August, I have never wished to visit in high season, and so experience is limited to the two seasons, spring and autumn, which are just about as perfect in Le Lavandou as anywhere in the world I know.

At these times, even as early as Easter and as late as October, the beaches are at their best, with few bodies, clean sands and sparkling water. I bathe then, but have to admit I am regarded as a nutter. Some of the beach restaurants are open at these shoulder seasons, but many do not find it worthwhile when customers are so few.

It would seem that there is an acknowledged date when the tourists go home and in this outpost of the Riviera, near no big towns, no fleshpots nearer than St-Tropez, there is little local trade. One evening, say in mid-September, we find we have to wait for a table at any restaurant in town. On the next we find ourselves peering not at menus outside but at people within, trying not to be the solitary diners. At these times it is better to make for the town centre, where Zété's always have tables occupied, even in winter, rather than the smarter strictly-for-the-tourists new marina bistros, which only thrive for six short weeks.

There are other compensations for going out of season though. In spring the hills behind the town are a carpet of wildflowers, and flowers not-so-wild in our home-counties gardening experience, like freesias, iris, rock roses, butterfly gladioli, lavender, not to mention broom and gorse. Their perfume, backed up by pine and rosemary, is the most potent evocation of spring I can think of.

We drive up the route des Marguerites behind St-Clair through fields of white daisies, winding up the colourful little road that offers increasingly spectacular views of the coast, and load up the car with firewood, before a picnic feast, looking over the mountains towards Cavalière. In the evenings a huge log fire is both cheerful and practical – the chill of the South of France at these times can be distinctly un-southern, and of course darkness falls early.

Not so very long ago Le Lavandou was an unsmart little fishing village. It's still unsmart but not so little. Substantial vestiges of its unsophisticated past mercifully remain. Life still revolves around the lime-shaded Place, overlooking the wide sandy beach. Surrounding cafés put out their tables and chairs there in summer, but in no way would be allowed to intrude on the much more important boules reserve. Out of season, tourist-free, watching the cloth-capped experts directing their silver balls across the dirt patch in the shade of the pollarded trees, it seems little has changed since the first few clever tourists (like us) discovered Le Lavandou.

Scott Fitzgerald discovered it too. He lived here and described the lifestyle in his books; when a film about his life was made recently, the town and its beaches were the authentic setting. Three thousand years ago it was the Greeks who were the tourists. The offshore waters are littered with wrecks of their ships, from which thousands of relics have been salvaged; so many in fact that in 1681 a law was passed, and is still in force, forbidding treasure hunting without a licence.

Every year we find some change, but rarely to the detriment of the town's character or the enjoyment of its visitors. On the contrary – the pedestrianisation of the central streets has been a great success and it is even more enjoyable to stroll between the tubs of flowers, window-shopping unhassled by through traffic. The new marina is also an asset – well designed and lively with a variety of restaurants, cafés and boutiques, not to mention yottie requirements.

Beaches

The main town beach is vast and golden, but there is a wide choice of others around the town, many of them less crowded:

St-Clair, 2½ kilometres east, has a lovely sheltered beach, facing east towards the mountains, extensive sands, well-equipped with watersports, cafés, restaurants and hotels. Ideal for families.

Le Fossette, further east, is a perfect little horse-shoe with clear sheltered water and fine sand, with a well-known and now, alas, quite expensive beach restaurant, Ma Jolie Fossette. You can hire parasols and mattresses from them.

Aiguebelle comes next, very much busier these days than of yore, but still less crowded than most Riviera beaches. At the very least take an evening stroll along its considerable length, when chattering families have packed up for the day and its natural beauty can best be appreciated. Plenty of unassuming hotels and restaurants to choose from.

The next beach around towards the Pointe de la Chappe is that unexpected phenomenon in these parts – a virtually undiscovered bay. It has no name on the map but is known to our family as Bosom Bay for reasons I won't go into here. To find it, keep your eyes open on the coast road for steps leading down through what looks like a private garden. It's a lovely beach of two coves divided by rocks. Anything less spoiled, less Riviera-typical would be hard to conceive.

A little further along the coast road and you will see an unusual number of cars, many with German plates, parked at the roadside. Investigate further and spot a track leading down through trees to one of the best beaches on the coast. When the dread mistral blows and makes other beaches impossible, this one is always calm and sheltered. It has natural shade, clear deep water, fine sands and a useful bar/restaurant. There is only one snag . . . if you wear any clothes you will be booed off the beach.

From here is one of my regular walks, following the cutting of the old railway line, now lavishly decorated with wild flowers, to *Cavalière*, busy at its eastern end, pleasantly shaded and uncrowded to the west. Here are family hotels unusually situated, actually on the beach.

Le Lavandou is a particularly lively town, with a penchant for festivities in season and out. You can usually rely on something interesting happening during a fortnight's holiday, but look out for the following:
March: Flower Parade. *June*: Artisan and Food Fair; Feast of St-Jean; Feast of St Peter the Fisherman (the big one!). *July*: Folklore Festival; Feast of St Clair. *September*: Tuna Fishing Contest.

Central Le Lavandou does not have as many hotels as you might expect. Families choose to stay in those on the nearby beaches, and many visitors rent villas in this area. There are two wildly expensive hotels, Les Roches at Aiguebelle (1,450f) and 83 Hotel at La Fossette (1,050f), but they are often open only for a very short period in the summer and seem so out of touch with local life and identity that I shall forget them. Otherwise:

La Calanque
(HR)M   *62 av. du Gal-de-Gaulle   94.71.01.95   Cl. 15/10–15/3; rest. also closed Wed.   All credit cards*

Built in the 50s before Le Lavandou became popular, and therefore able to command the prime position, overlooking the harbour and out to sea towards the Îles d'Hyères. All the bedrooms (500–600f) have sea views, and a superb terrace surrounds the dining room. Demi-pension is obligatory in season, at 700–1,976f; this should be no hardship, since the food is some of the best in town. Menus from 195f.

Hervé Vinrich
(HR)M   *11 r. Patron-Ravello   94.71.00.44   Cl. Mon. o.o.s.   All credit cards*

Also known as the Auberge Provençale, M. Vinrich's little hotel-restaurant has thirteen comfortable rooms at 220–320f (demi-pension obligatory in high season at 260–310f). The auberge has a delightfully rustic, deliberately provençal atmosphere. Generally the food is of exceptionally high standard, (menus at 145f), but it tends to tail off at busy periods, when the stress shows. Unfortunate because this would make an excellent family holiday base.

La Ramade
(HR)S   *16 r. Patron-Ravello   94.71.20.40   Cl. 10/11–15/1; Tues. and Sat. lunch*
All credit cards

A Logis de France hotel (rooms a reasonable 248–378f) recommended primarily for its unusually good cooking. Now that the rue Patron-Ravello has been pedestrianised, it is possible – and agreeable – to sit outside to eat. Portions are huge, on menus from 98f.

La Tartane
(R)M   *pl. E Reyer   Cl. Mon.*

Right in the heart of Le Lavandou, always welcoming, always good service, always wholesome food, on menus from 98f. Not a gastronome's delight but not dull either, with plenty of fresh seafood.

Chez Denise et Michel
(R)M   *6 r. Patron-Ravello   94.71.12.91   Cl. Mon.   A, V, EC, CB*

Smaller and quieter than Tartane or Ramade, with a very pretty dining room. Food and service are both good, but wines too pricey. Menus at 98f, 120f and 165f..

l'Escale
(R)S   *pl. E Reyer   94.71.00.25   Cl. Mon.*

Cheap and cheerful, friendly, good value. Outside tables. Less sophisticated than most, with only a limited choice of starters and only one main course on the 82f menu. Quality high enough to rely on anything on offer being acceptable, so long as it's what you fancy. Chips with everything. Other menus at 78f and 98f.

La Favouille
(R)S   *r. Patron-Ravello   94.71.34.29   Cl. 30/10–1/3*

Always bustling – some might say noisy – but with plenty of room to sit outside. Excellent value for money and quick service. Menus 78 and 119f.

Le Provenc'Ail
(R)S *4 r. de la Girelle   94.71.13.38*

> Queues outside are usually an indication of good value, and such
> is the case here, with menus from 75f. The atmosphere in the small
> interior can be stuffy in summer, but there is plenty of pavement
> room too.

Chez Zété
(R)S *41 av. Gal-de-Gaulle   94.71.09.11*

> Zété's has always been good value and is one of the old faithfuls
> that no holiday in Le Lavandou could do without. It's usually full and
> often noisy but somehow being squeezed on to the end of a table
> and forced to communicate adds to the breezy charm – the 70 and
> 100f menus always have plenty of good choices – stuffed mussels
> and langue de boeuf are two regular favourites – but it also prides
> itself on its bouillabaisse and paella served à la carte. At the rear
> is a pleasant shady terrace for summer dining.
>
> The main reason for eating in the new port area is for the interest
> generated by the view and the tourists' promenade. The restaurants
> are more sophisticated than those in the town and lively only in high
> season. The three following are probably pick of the bunch at the time
> of going to press, but there are frequent changes:
> **Le Pêcheur** (menus from 85f), **La Mer** (75 and 110f), **Le Bosco** (85,
> 119, 159f). You can't miss any of them – they all overlook the water.

At St-Clair:

Belle Vue
(HR)M   *Chemin du Four des Maures   94.71.01.06   Cl. Oct.–Mar.*
All credit cards

> A prize-winner in the contest for the hotel with the best garden
> and when you'll see them, you'll know why. The building is in
> provençal style, with red tile roofs, and has a magnificent
> panoramic view over the bay of St-Clair and out to the Îles d'Hyères.
>   The Clare family operate a fine efficient hotel that has charm and
> tranquillity. Their nineteen unexceptional rooms are good-sized, priced
> at 300–600f; nothing wrong whatsoever with the lower-priced ones.
> Half pension at 400–600f obligatory in high season.

L'Orangeraie
(H)M   *94.71.04.25   Cl. 7/10–22/3   AE, DC, CB*

> An unattractive concrete modern hotel but in a prime position
> directly on the beach. The twenty rooms are well equipped with
> good bathrooms and cost a modest 210–480f. Some of the larger
> ones have their own kitchenette.

Auberge de La Falaise
(R)M   *94.71.01.35*

On the Lavandou end of St-Clair beach, overlooking the sea. The lovely secluded terrace is a blissful place to eat on a warm summer's night, but the inside dining room is very attractive too. Just one menu at 98f, with plenty of choice of excellent quality cooking. Madame's quenelles are famous. Service can be on the slow side but the surroundings are so pleasant it doesn't seem to matter much. There are some bedrooms too, but these I've never got round to inspecting.

St-Clair: Auberge de la Falaise

Relais du Vieux Sauveur
(R)S   *r. des Crètes   94.05.84.22*

There is a stunning road running over the mountains between Bormes-les-Mimosas and Canadel, known as rue des Crètes. You can reach it by driving up from la Fossette, where the Vieux Sauveur is signposted from the rue de Plombagos. It's probably too remote – say, ten steep kilometres from St-Clair – to risk for dinner, but for lunch it's an excellent and unusual treat, and a welcome relief sometimes from too much sticky beach. If you use the restaurant you can also swim in the pool, and play tennis, so it's quite a feasible option to spend a whole day up here.

There is no fixed menu but plenty of choice of basic grills, fish, pastas, pizzas and good homemade quiches on the menu. There are no fixed closing dates either – all depends on the weather and the number of customers – so a quick phone call before making the trip up the mountain might be a good idea.

MAP 3F **LEVENS** ᴘᵥ 06670 (Alpes-Maritimes). 20 km NW of Nice

---

A very attractive, carefully restored village, standing on top of a mountain, with a beautiful view of the Gorge of the Vésubie from the square, which is of course the focal point of village activity.

It was once the capital city of the Ligurians, then known as the Leventi. Later it became a Roman encampment and the gates of the old Roman fortress can still be seen. Levens was fortified again in the 12th century, when it was under the control of the Abbot of St-Pons, then it was captured by the Count of Provence and its fortifications strengthened even further. Nevertheless, over the next three hundred years, the fortress changed hands many times and when Annibal, Count Grimaldi, was executed for treason in 1621 the locals rebelled, destroyed the fortress and erected on the ruins a huge conical stone, called a *boutau* in Provençal, to commemorate their liberty.

Every year since, the villagers have performed around the stone a *farandole*, that weaving circular dance of a long line of men and women which is characteristically Provençal. You can be part of that line if you can manage to be here in Levens on 2 September. That day is one of the great symbolic occasions in the history of the village, as the leader of the *farandole* waves the flag of the 1621 revolution. The dance is known locally as 'Lou Brandi Gavot' and is a typical peasant dance, the word *brandi* signifying the side-to-side swaying motion of the dancers, representing the swing of a clock pendulum.

Other fêtes; *20 March, 4 June, 12 September:* village fairs. *10 July:* Fête des Traverses (Les Traverses in a nearby village). *8 December:* Votive Fête of the Immaculate Conception. *24 December:* Midnight Mass, attended by all the shepherds.

Hôtel Malaussena
(HR)M *93.79.70.06 Cl. 1/11–8/12 V, EC*

Not many hotels are named after the proprietor but here is one. Right on the place de la République, the Malaussena has fourteen rooms at 200–270f or 240–290f for demi-pension. The meals, at 65–150f, are good country fare.

Hôtel des Grands Prés
(HR)M   *93.79.70.35   Cl. Jan. & Feb.*

There's a lot of competition in Levens so M. Romulus has to keep
his family-run hotel up to scratch, but he finds no difficulty filling all
the eight rooms. These are 160–250f; 220–240f for demi-pension.

➤ Hôtel Vigneraie
(HR)S   *r. St-Blaise   93.79.70.46   Cl. 16/10–22/1   EC, CB*

A family atmosphere here, where M. Bastien offers eighteen
rooms at 100–180f. The food is so good that demi-pension at 180–
200f is outstanding value. Dining on the terrace in summer is
particularly delightful. The 110f menu might offer: hors d'oeuvres,
then home-made terrine, followed by breast of duck with green
peppers, then cheese and fruit tart.

➤ Les Santons
(R)M   *93.79.70.06*

People come from far and wide to eat in the charming old building,
where M. Péllerin makes great efforts with the food and the cooking,
and booking is essential. Ingredients are always fresh and local, the
results invariably excellent.

Prices are highly attractive too – the menu at 90f (weekdays only)
might consist, for example, of: trout in fresh herbs, then rabbit
with pine nuts, served with fresh pasta, salad, goat's cheese, and a
choice of pâtisserie.

MAP 2G   **LUCÉRAM** ⊡ 06440 (Alpes-Maritimes). 27 km NE of Nice

A delightful mediaeval village, about 650 metres high, above the
Paillon valley, divided by an ancient crossroads. The Ligurians
established the town in the distant past and were succeeded by the
Romans; the buildings you see today, however, are largely
15th-century, four or five storeys high, narrow and clustered close
together.

Entry to the old village is on foot only, so park outside and walk
through the 14th-century gateway or the Portal gate below. If you
use the latter, you are immediately in a dark, cool, quietly eerie world
of the Middle Ages, with the customary maze of winding
cobblestone stairways zigzagging in every unpredictable direction.

Most of the village life today is around the Mairie. With its
population of less than a thousand people, Lucéram is a typical
isolated village community and you will probably hear some
Provençal being spoken. The olive press is still in operation and
the locals still bring in their olives to be squeezed. During the months
of October and November – the harvest time for olives – it is the
custom for the villagers to rub their hunks of bread with garlic, then
dip them in the first of the virgin olive oil.

·Lucéram has several culinary specialities. One is *pissara*, rather like ravioli stuffed with chopped vegetable marrow. Another is *panisse*, similar to Italian polenta, made from chick-pea flour which is rolled out and cooked, cut when cold and then browned in a pan.

The Church of Ste Marguerite stands on the highest point of the village – in perched villages more usually the location of a castle, although the ruins of an ancient watch-tower can be seen. Built in 1487, the church dominates the village and can be seen from far off, the coloured tiles of its dome glistening in the sun.

It contains a surprising number of valuable treasures for such a small village and this is even more remarkable when you consider that the Musée Masséna in Nice has a large number of exhibits donated by Lucéram. The spiritual treasures include relics of Ste Rosalie of Palermo, who worked miracles in repelling the Black Plague, and the earthly treasures comprise silver statuettes made in Italy, *pietàs* carved in wood, and a priceless collection of paintings.

As well as having a great deal to see, Lucéram has several colourful festivals. *March:* Carnival (pre-Lenten). *20 July:* Festival of Ste Marguerite. *15 August*: Festival of St Hubert (Blessing of the Hounds). *6 September:* Festival of Ste Rosalie (big procession).

There are two hotels, both with restaurant: **La Welcome** (93.91.57.12), **La Méditerranée** (93.79.51.54), and a restaurant **Le Ranch de Lucéram** (93.60.33.72).

MAP 3H | **MENTON** 06500 (Alpes-Maritimes) 9 km E of Monaco; 30 km E of Nice

---

Menton has its own very special flavour, quite unlike anything else along the coast. Part of the attraction of the Riviera lies in its contrasts and here is one of the most striking. Just nine kilometres from the glitter and gloss of neighbouring Monte Carlo, Menton is resolutely and delightfully old-fashioned. You will find no smart hotels, no big-name boutiques, no fashionable bars, no starlets on the beach, no sky-high prices, no hassle. Its character is a unique blend of English, Italian and French, all of whom have dominated the town in the past.

As so often on the Riviera, it was the English who first popularised it as a health resort. Queen Victoria found the particularly mild climate – the warmest on the Riviera – suited her and she often stayed here, at the Chalet Rosiers.

The winter climate is so agreeable that foreigners from more northern climes, the British prominent among them, have chosen to settle, ensuring that there are more residents than tourists. An increasing number of young business people who work in Monaco and Nice also find it more pleasing and cheaper to live here.

The Lemon Festival in February is one testament to the climate (although in the freak conditions of 1990 the floats, the lemons, and most of the town were under snow for the first time in living memory). The lemon trees, and oranges too, line the wide central gardens that divide the rue de Verdun. It's a pleasant place to stroll in the evenings, watching the children ride their tricycles and the mothers gossiping in the last of the sunshine. There are arches of roses to duck under and the lavish flowerbeds are always well-tended and colourful. This pleasing prospect leads the eye up to the mountains which frame the view so effectively.

The little town has always been popular with artists and writers. Katherine Mansfield lived and wrote here, in Villa Isola Bella near the station. Guy de Maupassant wrote many of his short stories here and Blasco Ibañez wrote the most famous of all bull-fighting novels, *Blood and Sand*, while living in the Villa Fontana Rosa. The villa has exquisite gardens and pools; one of the gardens is dedicated to the writers that Ibañez admired – Dickens, Balzac, Dostoievsky and Cervantes, whose busts adorn the garden. The villa should be open to the public by the time this appears in print.

The seafront promenade has been extended over the years and is now a long and pleasant walk, past several cafés which offer a particularly agreeable way to take refreshment. They place their tables between two canopied swing-hammocks so that you can rest, rock, and sip in extreme comfort, looking out at the new artificial beach which has been contrived along the parade.

I still prefer the old one, east-facing around the corner, past the lighthouse by the port. Its waters are sheltered, warm and shallow, ideal for children. Wade out and look back above the arches-turned-cafés which back the beach, for a picturebook view of the old town, capped with its beautiful church.

Further round the bay is another, more recently developed beach, La Garavan, and then the road climbs steeply until it reaches the Italian customs. Because it was itself more or less Italian (Mentone) until it became a part of France in 1860, Menton has none of the hastily flung-together feel of most border towns. In fact it resists having any label thrust upon it – it goes on being uniquely Menton.

If you don't want to walk so far from the Casino to the old port along the seafront, take the rue République, which cuts off the Bastion corner and leads past a colourful and much-painted old market square, with the Italian flavour much in evidence. It is still full of stalls, some selling junk, some fruit, some of them cafés, and seems to me to typify the Riviera before the tourists arrived. Old trees provide welcome shade and a lichened fountain a cool-sounding tinkle.

Beyond it are the brightly-tiled halls of the daily market, predictably busy, colourful and interesting, with piles of fish, flowers, fruit, veg and meat, much of the produce supplied by farmers from the nearby mountains.

Nearby is the Bastion (a good place to park), a fortress built by Prince Honoré II in 1619 to protect Menton's southern approaches; it has the resolute appearance of a small but very determined citadel which knows it stands little chance against a really strong attacker. It now houses the Cocteau Museum, containing some of Cocteau's works (local resident, renowned painter-poet). Some of his friends' works are also here, including some Picassos. Open 10 a.m.–12.30 and 3–7 p.m. except Mondays, Tuesdays, fêtes, in summer; in winter – 10 a.m.–12, 2–6 p.m. except Mondays, Tuesdays, fêtes.

An excellent way to get a general first impression of the somewhat strung-out town and its main attractions is to take 'Le Petit Train', a little puffer train, painted in primary colours, that starts its journey at the Bastion, winds round the harbour wall and up the steep cobbled narrow streets up to the Old Town out as far as the frontier, and back into the shopping area, along the promenade, past the market and back to the starting place. The 35-minute ride costs a good-value 25f and operates from 10 a.m.–12 and from 2.15–7 p.m. in season.

Having caught a glimpse of the white and gold church of St Michel, you will undoubtedly want to return to the Old Town and investigate further. It stands in a wide square, unexpectedly bright after the dark mediaeval lanes that lead up to it, and has one of the most striking interiors of any church on the Côte d'Azur. It too was built by Honoré II, the first of the Grimaldi family to carry the title of Prince of Monaco, in 1619, when Menton was part of the Principality. Exotically baroque, with a ceiling painted by the finest Italian craftsmen of the time, and blazing crimson columns and drapes, it is quite breathtaking.

Cemeteries are not usually places for holiday-makers, but all rugby enthusiasts will be interested to know that Webb-Ellis is buried in the Cimetière du Vieux Chateau. John Richard Green, celebrated author of *A History of the English People*, is buried here too.

Le Palais de l'Europe is the artistic and cultural centre of Menton and there is always something happening there. The town is dotted with posters to make sure that no attraction is missed. It is an impressive building, originally a casino.

Le Palais Carnoles was also built by that busy Prince Honoré as a residence of the Princes of Monaco. In recognition of this, Princess Grace of Monaco was invited to dedicate it when it was converted into a museum for paintings in 1977. Today it contains a collection of art from the Middle Ages to the present day, including many canvases by Graham Sutherland, another Menton resident. Open 10 a.m.–12.30 and 3–7 p.m. (except Tuesdays and holidays) in summer and 10 a.m.–12 and 2–6 p.m. (except Tuesdays and holidays) in winter. Entry is free.

A registry office in a town hall sounds like a very unlikely place to see works of art, but the Salle des Mariages in the Hôtel de Ville was conceived and decorated by Jean Cocteau. It is open – even for those not contemplating marriage – 8.30 a.m.–12.30 and 1.30–5 p.m. every day, Monday to Friday, except holidays. Fee 5f.

The Musée Municipal de Préhistoire Regionale is a new building on the site of prehistoric remains. Its skull of a Grimaldi man is famous in the archaeological world. Over 30,000 years old, the skull was found in one of a series of caves known as Les Rochers Rouges near the town – which naturally prefers to call its owner 'Menton Man'.

About five kilometres outside Menton is a remarkable sight. The Sanctuary of l'Annonciade is perched on top of a lonely hill, 225 metres high and has something of the dramatic appearance of those isolated monasteries one sees in Greece. The church here was dedicated to the Virgin Mary and built in the 11th century when it became a Capuchin monastery.

If you really want to soak yourself in regional tradition, don't be satisfied with simply marvelling at the view of l'Annonciade. Take the pilgrimage road on foot – it's known as the Chemin de Rosaire and goes to fifteen chapels, all built in the 17th century by Princess Isabelle of Monaco (sister of Louis I) in order to commemorate the fifteen mysteries of the rosary. There are two annual organised pilgrimages – 25 March and 8 September.

Menton is a great Festival town. The following are only the highlights: *February* – Lemon Festival. One of the biggest festivals on the Côte d'Azur with parades, floats and decorations all over town. *29 June* – Feast of St Peter. *July* – Circuses, musical concerts, dance tournaments, judo concerts, ballets, folklore concerts, jazz and visiting musical artists and performers from all over the world. *August* – The Menton Festival of Chamber Music is world-famous; if you can't get a ticket you can still hear the concert from the quayside. Other events include pétanque contests, more circuses, pop concerts, Viennese music concerts, singers, dancers, displays and exhibitions unlimited. *September* – Feast of St Michael. *Christmas* – Midnight Mass is an exceptionally big affair with lavishly decorated crèches.

Gambling is not as big an activity as in Cannes or Monaco but the Casino du Soleil on the promenade du Soleil is a large, imposing, if somewhat run-down, building. Its restaurant, Le Gourmet, has a terrace looking out to sea, and there is a tea room and an ice-cream parlour; the Salon Embassy room has entertainers and an orchestra on Saturday nights at 10 o'clock and Sundays at 4 o'clock. Telephone: 93.57.11.31.

L'Aiglon
(HR)M   *7 av. de la Madone*   93.57.55.55   *CB, AE, DC*

On the leafy avenue approaching Menton from the west and only 50 metres from the sea, surrounded by a pleasant and peaceful garden, l'Aiglon is a dignified 19th-century house, converted into a hotel with considerable character. The rooms are all different but all spacious and well-equipped; their disparity is reflected in the price – from 290 to 605f. The heated swimming pool is a tremendous asset.

La Méditerranée
(HR)M   *5 r. République*   93.28.25.25   *All credit cards*

If you like to be in the centre of town, this is one of the best bets but the Méditerranée's reputation means that its ninety rooms are booked well ahead in the summer. There is a terrace for outdoor dining and a solarium. The rooms, quite sizeable and nicely furnished, are good value at 270–360f.

Auberge des Santons

(HR)M *Colline de l'Annonciade   93.35.94.10   Hotel closed 18/10–17/12; rest. closed 10/10–17/12*

Located on a quiet street just off the avenue de Sospel, going north towards the autoroute but still close to town. The nine rooms in this family-owned and operated hotel are always booked far ahead; 170–325f or demi-pension at 180–280f. The restaurant offers meals at 105f.

Hôtel New York

(HR)M *av. Katherine Mansfield   93.35.78.69   Cl. 1/11–28/12; 6–27/1*

There are fourteen rooms here, in M. Mena's establishment, all air-conditioned and attractive, at 155–310f, or 215–285f for demi-pension. There is secured parking. Menus from 110f.

Hôtel Paris-Rome

(HR)M *79 Porte de France   93.35.73.45   Hotel closed 31/10–12/12; rest. closed 31/10–5/1*

Mme Castellana runs a very pleasant and personalised hotel with a garage, a garden and twenty-two rooms at 230–390f. Demi-pension is preferred by most guests at 300–570f.
    The location on the Porte de France is away from the centre of town but almost on the beach.

Hôtel Le Globe

(HR)S *21 av. de Verdun   93.35.73.03   Cl. Wed.; 25/10–21/12*

One of the best bargains in Menton. M. Pelletier owns and runs a very good low-priced hotel and the twenty-four rooms are usually filled, being priced at 175–285f. Full pension at 235–310f is a very reasonable charge, for the level of comfort and food. Menus in the restaurant run at 80–140f.

Hôtel Chambord

(H)M *6 av. Boyer   93.35.94.19   Open all year   All credit cards*

Just across from the Casino. The forty rooms are large and airy and very well-equipped. Many look out on to the public gardens. Room prices are 350–430f.

Mentonnaise cuisine is quite different from that of Nice, just thirty kilometres away. The Italian influence, the Provençal style and the Niçois flavours have all been blended together, with some touches of originality. There are several Menton specialities such as *Pichade* – a baked tart of onions and tomatoes with garlic, anchovies and parsley; *Socca* – chick-pea-flour cakes, baked in the oven and eaten hot (Nice has a slightly different version of these); *Barba-Juan* – ravioli stuffed with chopped vegetables, rice, cheese and minced beef; *Tarte de Courgettes*; *La Crousta* – bread dipped in olive oil and anchovy sauce and spread with a layer of tomatoes, plus others.

You will sometimes find a local dish on a menu, but Menton's gastronomic scene is not inspired. Here are the best restaurants:

➤ L'Oursin
(R)M   *3 r. Trenca   93.28.33.62   Cl. Wed.   All credit cards*

You will have to go a long way to find better seafood than here at L'Oursin, right on the Promenade du Soleil, with a sea view. The pleasing blue-and-white décor, the nautical motif of fishing nets and oars, and the paintings, are not overdone.

L'Oursin has a wide range of different fish choices every day – with its namesake, the spiny oursin, always prominent. You might be there the day when there are six oysters for 45f and six oursins for 40f. The plat coquillage is a 160f feast of clams, mussels, oysters, shrimp, crab and whatever other shellfish the day's nets have brought in.

Smoked swordfish is an unusual and superb dish, for only 80f. The medaillons of langouste at 160f and the loup de mer with artichokes, also at 160f, are excellent.

Paris-Palace
(R)M   *1 promenade du Soleil   93.35.88.66   All credit cards*

A big brasserie right on the Promenade, with a few tables outside and a view of the sea.

Busy and bustling with an exceptionally extensive menu. It's hard to think of anything you can't get here, from pasta to frog's legs.

Au Bec Fin
(R)M   *11 av. Félix Faure   93.35.94.73   CB, V*

Right in the heart of the shopping area and on the busy avenue Félix Faure, just a block from the promenade du Soleil, Au Bec Fin has been pleasing locals and visitors alike for a long time. Menus are 90f, 140f and 160f; Italian specialities, particularly the osso bucco, are recommended.

Chateaubriand
(R)M   *14 av. Boyer   93.35.80.82   All credit cards*

A small friendly restaurant near the Casino. Menus at 100f, 130f and 160f include mostly tried and true old favourites with a plat-du-jour like grilled rabbit steak.

Calypso
(R)S   *2 av. Boyer   93.35.81.38   All credit cards*

Specialising in seafood, but with a good range of pastas and grilled meats too, the Calypso is opposite the Casino.

À la carte dishes are more appealing with, e.g., gratin de langoustes with tagliatelle at 98f, fillets of daurade Florentine at 60f, and a great bourride Provençale at 85f.

At the eastern end of Menton and on the **Garavan Beach** nearly twenty restaurants, cafés, bars and bistros are lined, sharing a view of the Mediterranean. They offer a selection of different cooking styles, different national food and a range of prices to suit everybody. Stroll past and make a decision on what you see being eaten; reservations are hardly necessary.

Splendid
(R)M *93.35.60.97*

Fish specialities, pizza and ice-cream. Private beach.

Les Sablettes
(R)M *93.35.44.77*

Fish specialities, including fresh lobster and charcoal-grilled meats.

Le Pargola
(R)M *93.35.44.72*

Italian food and a private beach. Meals in the dining room or under the shade of the beach. Pedalos, surfing and ping-pong, so you can work off the pasta.

La Licorne
(R)M *93.57.12.40*

French cuisine.

Papagayo
(R)M *93.35.34.29*

American bar, pizzeria and restaurant with its own beach.

Scheherazade
(R)M *93.28.52.97*

Moroccan specialities.

Le Skipper
(R)M *93.35.99.60*

Local specialities, particularly fish.

Le Phénix
(R)M *93.35.66.83*

Vietnamese and Chinese food. Beach and terrace. Open all year.

La Tortue
(R)M *93.41.60.46*

      Bouillabaisse, oven-grilled fish and fresh langoustes.

Plage du Levant
(R)S *93.35.36.86*

      Crêperie.

Imperial Plage
(R)M *93.28.29.65*

      Private beach with a bar, a restaurant serving fish and charcoal-grilled meats, and an ice-cream parlour.

MAP 4G   **MONACO** 98000 18 km E Nice; 9 km W Menton

(M) *Daily*

'The Glittering Principality' it is called – a sunny paradise of leisure and wealth, beaches and gardens, glamour and entertainment, sports and famous personalities, all in an area smaller than Hyde Park. It is an extraordinary place in almost every sense. It offers an unequalled range of activities and all in a charming sophisticated atmosphere where you will not be cheated or ripped off and where there is virtually no crime or violence.

Famous throughout the world for its Casino, Monte Carlo is one of the four districts comprising the sovereign state of Monaco, the others being La Condamine (the old port quarter), Monaco-Ville (the old town around the Palace) and the newest, Fontvieille, a suburb and marina recovered from the sea. For tourist purposes, Larvotto with its beaches at the eastern end of the principality should be included.

The Rock (where the old town and the Palace are located) was inhabited in the 6th century by a tribe of Ligurians who were called Monoikos from the Roman name for the port, Portus Monoeci, the Port of Hercules. The Roman fleet made much use of the excellent harbour, but after the fall of the Roman Empire, barbarians ravaged the coast for centuries until they were finally defeated by the Count of Provence. The Emperor Barbarossa gave Monaco to Genoa and it was the Emperor who built a castle on the Rock (the site of the present palace) in 1215 to defend it against the Pope's armies.

At the turn of the 13th century the Grimaldi family gained possession of the Rock and turned it into a powerful stronghold. Monaco was acknowledged by Savoy and France as independent in 1489 but in 1524 it became Spanish. It continued to grow and again became French in 1641 and the Grimaldi family was still in power when Charles III had to sell off what are now Menton and Roquebrune to France. This reduced finances to a danger level due to the loss of the lemon and olive groves and, looking for a new source of income, Charles III decided to build a casino along the lines of the very successful one at Baden-Baden.

It was a spectacularly successful idea and laid the cornerstone for Monaco's prosperity. When Prince Rainier III came to the throne in 1949, he was the thirtieth of the Grimaldi family to rule Monaco. His marriage to Grace Kelly in 1956, a 'Prince and Showgirl' romance, was perfectly in keeping with the fairy-tale atmosphere of this unique little principality.

It was Rainier's astuteness that diversified the attractions of Monaco into areas other than gambling, which now accounts for little more than 4 per cent of the principality's income. Business and finance flourish, and Monaco's other-worldliness does not extend to civic facilities, either, which are highly efficient.

The mundane subject of parking has to rank high on the list of priorities on the Côte d'Azur, but Monaco is better provided than anywhere else along the coast. Follow any of the numerous prominent parking signs. The lots are all underground, large, luxurious, spacious and not outrageously expensive.

There is some street parking but not near the Palace, in the old town or near the Oceanographic Museum. Don't be tempted to violate parking rules as you might in France. Monaco's police force is vigilant (and, given the size of the population, large), and omnipresent too; although you will probably be let off with a warning if you have foreign plates, you will be towed away or clamped if you cause an obstruction or park on a pedestrian crossing. On the other hand, your car is safer here than anywhere else in Europe.

As far as driving is concerned, remember that this is *not* France. This is Monaco and the police enforce the laws of the road rigidly. Drive carefully, don't take any chances and take satisfaction from the fact that all the other drivers are doing the same.

The Casino at Monte Carlo surely has a reputation equalling that of any other building in the world. It was built in 1879 by Charles Garnier, architect of the Paris Opera House. The Salons Ordinaires open at noon, entry fee 50f. The Salons Privés open at 3 p.m., entry fee 100f. The American Room has slot-machines, craps, blackjack and American roulette; the adjacent Pink Salon (formerly called the Green Room) is notorious for its ceiling painted by Galleli, depicting beautiful nude women smoking cigars. The European Rooms are bigger and more elaborately decorated. Roulette, chemin-de-fer, baccarat and trente-quarante are the games, and the gambling is more serious.

Charles Deville Wells has been immortalised as The Man Who Broke the Bank at Monte Carlo. In 1891, he parlayed £400 into £40,000 over a period of three days, using no apparent system other than increasing his bets when he was losing. On the roulette wheel, he put even money bets on red and black, winning nearly every time until he finally exceeded the 100,000 franc 'bank' allocated to each table. In those days, it was customary to cover the table with black cloth and close it for the rest of the day. The third and last day that Wells appeared at the Casino, he placed his opening bet on number 5 at odds of 35 to 1. He won. He left his original bet and added his winnings to it. Number 5 won again – and this happened five times in succession. Wells was never seen at Monte Carlo again. He was known to be a con-man and used as many as thirty aliases. He subsequently went to prison for two years for a crime unconnected with gambling. As far as is known, his win at the Casino was an honest one.

Another famous incident in Casino history began the night when the captain of a Russian warship lost a considerable amount of money. Next day, he sent a message to the Casino management demanding that his money be returned to him and warning that the warship's guns were trained on the Casino and he was ready to fire if not reimbursed. His money was returned and many insist that this is the reason why no person in uniform is admitted today.

The glamorous Mata Hari, courtesan and spy, gambled heavily in Monte Carlo. On one occasion, she was at the roulette wheel when a bearded Russian officer put his arm around her waist and kissed her. She promptly drew a small revolver and shot him in the chest. Remarkably, the damage was only slight but she was asked to leave the principality, which she did – in a huge white Hispano-Suiza.

Kaiser Wilhelm was a frequent visitor and came once with an 'infallible' system devised by Professor Heidelberg, a mathematical genius. Sadly, it served the Kaiser no better than sheer chance. In more modern times, the three Americans who arrived in 1956 with loaded dice specially made for them in Los Angeles were caught after the very first toss and one of them served three months in Monaco's tiny jail.

Also inside the Casino building is the *Opera House*, seating 600 and with perfect acoustics. Massenet and Saint-Saëns wrote operas specifically for it and Chaliapin, Caruso, Melba and John McCormack all performed here. Diaghilev made it the headquarters of the Ballets Russes de Monte Carlo, with Nijinsky its star. The magnificent gardens behind the Casino are a pleasant place to stroll, look out over the Mediterranean, count the dozens of brilliantly coloured hang-gliders floating down and count your blessings – or your losses.

The Palace, of course, is a magnet for all tourists, but smaller than one imagines and somewhat disappointing. It was built in the 16th and 17th centuries in a mixture of styles, even using part of the Genoese fortress erected in 1215.

The Changing of the Guard is one of the most photographed sights in Monaco. Every day at 11.55 a.m., the majority of the 25-strong army is on parade for the full-dress ceremony (dark uniforms in winter, white in summer). They march across the courtyard which is ringed with small cannon and neat pyramids of cannonballs.

The State Apartments are open every day from June to September, 9.30 to 6.30, and in October from 10 to 5. There is a small entry fee and the tour takes about 40 minutes. You will be taken through the Italian Gallery, the Louis XV Salon, the Throne Room, the Palatine Chapel and the Tour Sainte-Marie. The main quadrangle is where concerts are held in the summer and it is paved with three million white and coloured pebbles forming immense geometric patterns.

The Cathedral is very near the Palace. It is in Romanesque-Byzantine style and contains the tombs of former princes of Monaco. Next to it is the Museum, showing the history of the Rock. Open daily from June to September, 9.30 to 6.30, and in October from 10 to 5. Open every day except Monday from December to May, 10.30 to 12.30 and 2 to 5.

The Wax Museum is on the rue Basse, one of the most picturesque streets in the old town. It is small and something of a let-down after Madame Tussaud's but it shows episodes in the history of the Grimaldi family from the 13th century to the present day. The rest of the old town makes an agreeable stroll – centuries-old houses with wrought-iron balconies, narrow alleys connected by vaulted passageways and a thoroughly mediaeval flavour.

Over a million people a year visit the Oceanographic Museum. It is generally considered to be the finest in the world with 4,500 fish in 90 tanks and pools. Every ocean on the globe is represented and the tropical fauna is almost as remarkable as the fish.

The renowned Jacques Cousteau was director until 1988 and one of the exhibits in the entry hall is the SP350, the deep-diving submarine which he and his team developed and which appears in many of his films. Aquatic entertainment is provided by dolphins, seals, sea-lions, tortoises and a host of Mediterranean fish, including some very rare species. It is open every day July and August from 9 a.m. to 9 p.m., from April to June, and in September, from 9 a.m. to 7 p.m., and October to March from 9.30 a.m. to 7 p.m. Small entry fee.

Another popular tourist attraction is the Exotic Gardens, located on the Middle Corniche entering Monaco from the west. More than 7,000 species of succulent plants, mostly cactus, from desert regions all over the world, are spread over the near-vertical slopes which are criss-crossed with paths and bridges. Open daily from May to September from 9 to 7, and from October to April from 9 to 6. In the gardens too are the Grottes de l'Observatoire. These grottoes, homes of early cavemen, are one of the most underrated sights in the principality.

Fanciers of flowers make a bee-line for the Princess Grace Rose Garden in Fontvieille. In April, May and June, the display is spectacular. The 10-acre park is around a charming little freshwater pond with ducks and swans and the air is fragrant with the scent of 3,500 rose bushes, representing nearly 200 varieties. Open every day, sunrise to sunset, no charge.

There are no free beaches in Monaco, but the Monte Carlo Beach Hotel and the Beach Plaza Hotel both have beach facilities and water-sports and the Plage du Larvotto is popular. The sand is imported.

The Monaco Grand Prix may well be the world's most exciting motor race. Two dozen of the most powerful cars on wheels roar through the narrow streets of Monte Carlo at over 200 kilometres per hour along a 3,328-kilometre circuit. Over 80,000 spectators watch legendary drivers whose names have become household words streak around the port and past the Casino while 100 doctors, 250 ambulance men and 50 firemen stand by in case of disaster – as in 1967 when Lorenzo Bandini of Italy crashed, burst into flames and died.

The race has been held now since 1929 and is an annual event held in May. For racing fans, it is a must and even those not normally interested find that they are swept into a fever of excitement on petrol fumes, the roar of the crowd and the snarl of huge engines.

You can buy tickets for the trials run on the Thursday at 100–250f. Seats are free on the Friday. Tickets are 350–500f for the Formula 3 on the Saturday; the big day is Sunday when the Formula 1 race costs 150 and 250f for un-numbered seats and 600–1,100f for numbered seats. The higher prices are for the seats around the port. Tickets are available in Monaco at the Automobile Club at 23 boulevard Albert I, in the place d'Armes, an office on the boulevard des Moulins, and at Voyages Kuoni in Nice.

Hotel rooms are in great demand during these four days as the race can be seen from a great many hotel windows. The owners of apartments along the route find themselves visited by friends they had forgotten existed – or else they rent their apartments out, 50,000f being the going rate. Some bars and restaurants show the race on giant-screen television. It seems incredible that the race authorities should be able to make sure that no others can see the race for nothing. You would think that somewhere you could squeeze into a spot where you can watch the cars screech by – sorry, but you can't!

The Monte Carlo Rally is a lesser event because it does not provide as much spectator satisfaction in the principality itself, Monaco being the finishing line. Nevertheless it is held by many to be the toughest of all the championship rallies because the competitors leaving the various cities in Northern Europe have no idea of the weather conditions they will meet when they cross the Alpine area heading south. In 1990 they came through more than a metre of snow and treacherous icy roads. The purpose of the Rally is to prove the quality of the vehicles, and this is why many of the entries come from the major automobile producers. Private individuals who compete just for the fun of it have understandably felt that the Rally is becoming less and less the kind of event for them. Consequently, the Monte Carlo Challenge, a more recent effort, is confined to owners of privately owned vintage cars. Most are models from the years 1935 to 1965. Over 120 cars take part, starting from Edinburgh and Oslo. Plans are on hand to add Moscow and other cities to this list.

The Rally is in January and the Challenge is in February. Even if you are not on the spot when the cars in either event arrive, you will see them displayed around the port.

Monaco is a shopper's heaven – whether you are a serious buyer or a window shopper, and no matter what you're interested in. The place d'Armes is an outdoor market which delights visitors and photographers. At the other end of the scale is the new Métropole Commercial Centre. This is underneath the Métropole Hotel and 130 sumptuously appointed shops, stores and boutiques are spread over three luxurious floors lit with massive chandeliers. There are art galleries, gourmet foods, and three restaurants: Fuji, a top Japanese eatery with menus at 150, 250 and 350f; Giacomo, pricey Italian food; and Café Mozart, a popular meeting-place for young Monegasques, which is actually two-in-one – there is a snack bar-cum-brasserie with a daily menu at 55f, and a restaurant with menus starting at 65f. Six hundred underground parking places mean that you come up directly into the centre by escalator or elevator.

Les Allées Lumières are luxurious shopping galleries in two locations, both at the eastern end of avenue de la Costa. Platti Gourmet is a fine delicatessen with English specialities among its gourmet delights. Mr Brian at 7 avenue Berceau caters to the British and American communities with otherwise hard-to-find foods. The quality is high and so are the prices.

The boulevard des Moulins is one of the major east–west streets and is lined with shops, stores, boutiques, cafés, tearooms and restaurants

The Monte Carlo Sporting Club is out at the eastern end of Monaco on a promontory reclaimed from the sea. This is considered to be *the* summer sporting centre, even if a lot of the sports are indoors. There is Jimmy'z, the top disco on the Côte d'Azur, where all the celebrities can be seen, and the Salle des Étoiles with a roof which opens and where stars such as Julio Iglesias, Liza Minelli, Stevie Wonder, Charles Aznavour and Tina Turner have recently performed. There is a dinner-dance-cabaret every night here in July and August.

Parady'z is an outdoor disco on the shore of a lake, and on the avenue des Spélugues, just east of the Casino, are several popular night-clubs – The Living Room, where you can dance till dawn, the L'X Club, and Le Tiffany's.

Opposite the Casino is the Sporting d'Hiver (the Winter Sporting Club) which is open all year round and contains shops and boutiques (mainly clothes, shoes, jewellery and art), the Roger Vergé Café (see below) and four cinemas, one of which has films with the original English-language sound-track every Monday and Thursday.

You will have gathered that there is non-stop action in Monaco no matter what your interests may be. Here are just some of the regular events:

January 27 – Feast of St Dévote, a 4th-century martyr and patron saint of the Principality. Relics of the saint are carried in procession from the Cathedral to the Church of St Dévoté. The sea is blessed and a boat is burned. *January and February* – Television Festival. *January–March* – Opera season. *Good Friday* – Procession of the Dead Christ. A torchlight procession through the streets of the old town. *April* – Monte Carlo Tennis Open. All the big names are there. Held at the Monte Carlo Country Club, a delightful location looking out over the sea. *May* – Monaco Grand Prix. *June 23* – The Bonfires of St John. These are lit on the place du Palais and again the next day on the place des Moulins. Folk songs and dances. *July* – Mid-Summer Carnival (Sciaratu) with parades, floats and a fancy dress ball. *July and*

August – International Fireworks Festival. Each evening at 9.30, a different country presents a firework display. A winner is chosen from five competing countries. *August* – Feast of St Roman. A ball is held in St Martin Gardens. *September* – Baroque Music Festival. *November 18* – Monegasque National Fête. *December* – International Circus Festival. The world's leading circus event, attended by members of the Royal Family.

Everyone should sample the Monaco experience at least once. The problem is that there are several hotels of great repute and high prices, but hardly any in the 'S' bracket. There are in fact less than 200 rooms available in that category in the whole principality.

Try at least to look at some of the top hotels (stroll into the lobbies, but not in shorts and curlers) because they are in the category of truly great historic institutions, as interesting and instructive as the museums.

Hôtel de Paris

(HR) *pl. du Casino   93.50.80.80   Open every day*
Restaurant Le Louis XV closed Wed. (except dinner in season); Tues.; 19/2–6/3; 26/11–25/12   All credit cards

The most prestigious, facing the Casino. Opened in 1865, Monte Carlo's heyday, when royalty and aristocrats from all over Europe were guests. During the season of 1887 the register included the names of the Emperor of Austria, the Dowager Empress of Russia, the King of Sweden, the King of Serbia and the Queen of Portugal. In the Second World War the Gestapo commandeered it as headquarters. The lobby is as splendidly ornate and imposing as you might imagine; the 255 rooms are constantly being improved to warrant their price of 1,400–2,800f. The mega-rich of course would take a suite or one of the thirty-nine apartments at up to 125,000f. I imagine all this is of the same kind of interest as what other people pay for a Van Gogh, but as *French Entrée* readers are an eclectic bunch. . . .

I don't think I would pay £12,500 a night for a room in the wildest of fantasies, but I could be tempted to blow a modest ransom for a meal cooked by the great Alain Ducasse in Le Louis XV. Three Michelin stars attest to his talent, menus at 540 and 635f attest to the amount of money about in Monte Carlo – the restaurant is nearly always full.

L'Hermitage

(HR)L   *93.50.67.31   Open every day   All credit cards*
Restaurant Belle Époque also open every day

Suspended on the rocks, with the supreme harbour view, l'Hermitage is Monte Carlo's prime example of the Belle Époque palatial style of building. Rated No. 2 after the Hôtel de Paris generally, but No. 1 in my book. The lobby is even grander, with its pillars and chandeliers, the bedrooms are lighter and more cheerful (though just as luxurious), and the swimming pool is

Monte Carlo: Hôtel de Paris – at night

superb. The restaurant does not begin to compete with the Louis XV for cooking, but is incomparable in its grandeur. A living museum piece this, with red plush paramount, rose marble pillars, painted gilded ceiling and mirrors galore. It is all so vast and spread-out that the innocent stranger should have no trouble at all in achieving a harmless boggle. 246 rooms cost 1,000–2,400f and the sixteen apartments a mere 5,000–9,000f.

Métropole Palace
(HR)L   *94.15.15.15   Open all year   All credit cards*

In its original incarnation the Métropole used to be the favourite of naughty King Edward VII, who revelled in the goings-on in Monte and brought his lady-friends along with him to share them.

Whenever his mother drove through the principality she ordered her carriage blinds to be lowered in case the sight of Bertie embarrassed her.

It is now completely reconstructed on the old site, according to the original plans. The owner has recruited craftsmen and artists from all over Europe to paint and gild and copy and carve. The marble alone cost him a small fortune. The Métropole's boast is that it combines the best of the old (tradition, style, luxury) with the best of the new (plumbing – every room has a jacuzzi).

Rooms are all similar and cost from 1,350 to 1,900f, without the sea view. The restaurant is a disappointment, with a much overpriced lunchtime buffet.

Monte Carlo Beach Hotel
(HR)L   *av. du Bord-de-Mer, St Roman 06190 Roquebrune-Cap-Martin*
93.78.21.40   Cl. 7/10–11/4; rest. closed 16/9–7/6

Not so aristocratic, more *jeunesse dorée*. As dorée they might well be, benefiting from the Beach Hotel's superb position on its private beach, with every incentive for tanning on the elegant loggia overlooking the waves. Olympic-sized swimming pool, tennis and golf. Luxuriant surrounding vegetation. Rooms have been magnificently renovated and now cost 1,650–2,100f. Opening times reflect the summer-only justification for this primarily sun-and-sand hotel. The restaurant cashes in on its position with bills around 500f.

The largest hotel (600 rooms) in Monte Carlo is **Loews**. Occupying a prime site overlooking the sea, it is an anachronistic eyesore. American-orientated in every way from plumbing to one-armed bandits, to plastic food, its rooms cost 2,200f – should anyone be interested. Hundreds of conferences are.

Hôtel Balmoral
(HR)M   *93.50.62.37   Rest. closed Sun. p.m., Mon.; Nov.   All credit cards*

A staid, older hotel with a good location and – almost unique among the medium-priced hotels in Monaco – views out over the port. Seventy-seven rooms at 350–450f for a single and 500–700f for a double, all with bath or shower. Many rooms have a balcony. There is a delightful bar and a TV lounge with a view of the port.

No parking, but a large municipal lot is in the hill under the hotel. You can easily walk to the Casino area and the port.

The small restaurant serves breakfast at 45f but only snacks and light meals the rest of the day.

Hôtel Le Siècle
(HR)M   *93.30.25.65*

An older hotel, opposite the station but in a pleasant area. The thirty-five rooms all have bath or shower and the hotel is air-conditioned throughout; many of the rooms on the upper floors have balconies. Prices are 530–715f.

The ground floor restaurant is glassed-in round two sides, and is a popular brasserie. Menus at 90, 110 and 130f.

Hôtel du Louvre
(H)M   *16 blvd des Moulins   93.50.65.25   DC, EC, V*

A small but pleasing hotel, efficiently run by M. Romain Gilbert and located in the heart of the shopping district. Only thirty-four rooms, priced at 450–650f, and all with bath and air-conditioning.

Hôtel Miramar
(H)M   *1 av. Président J.F. Kennedy   93.30.86.48*

A modern, small and very convenient hotel. There are only fourteen rooms but all have bath and air-conditioning. There are sea views especially from the panoramic bar and a terrace. Access to the hotel is also possible from the avenue d'Ostende. Good value at 470–660f.

Résidence des Moulins
(H)M   *27 blvd des Moulins   93.30.60.86*

Only twelve rooms here but they are priced at a moderate (for Monaco) 325–500f. All have bath or shower, some have balconies. Conveniently located right on one of the main shopping streets, which means that parking and restaurants are nearby.

Hôtel Helvetia
(HR)S   *1 bis r. Grimaldi   93.30.21.71*

Modest but adequate and on the busy rue Grimaldi only minutes from the port. There are twenty-eight rooms, eighteen with bath or shower. They are priced at 170–320f which makes it one of the least expensive hotels in the centre. Mme Adèle Giorcelli gives a warm welcome.

Hôtel de France
(H)S   *6 r. de la Turbie   93.30.24.64*

An old-established low-budget hotel. It's just off the corner of the port and towards the railway station – which puts it in a very convenient location and not too noisy.
　There are eighteen rooms with bath or shower at 200–270f and eight rooms without at 125–190f.

One solution to the problem of finding reasonably-priced, good-quality and convenient hotel accommodation around Monaco is to go to Beausoleil, France, which strange as it sounds, means going only across the street! Monaco is less than 300 metres wide and boulevard Leclerc is one of the streets which is Monaco on the south side and France (Beausoleil) on the north. The contrast is remarkable – twenty-storey ultra-modern apartment blocks of glass and concrete on the south side of the street and old, three- and four-storey houses with washing hanging over the wooden shutters on the north side. Being so close to Monaco, however – indeed a physical part of it except on the map – it is ideal for a budget hotel location. From boulevard Leclerc it is only three minutes' walk to the Casino and five minutes' walk to the port. Parking St Charles is only a minute away and the Monaco markets are adjacent, well worth a visit if only to compare the old street market portion with the gleaming modern part.

There are three hotels on Beausoleil's side of boulevard Leclerc, all close together.

Hôtel Cosmopolite
(H)M   *19 blvd Leclerc   93.78.36.00   All credit cards*

An attractive building decorated with elaborate wrought-iron balconies. Rooms at the back are quieter. The twenty-three rooms are simple but pleasant, 130f with shower and 200–300f with bath. The young staff are friendly and helpful.

Hôtel Olympia
(H)S-M   *17 bis bvd Leclerc   93.78.12.70   All credit cards*

This is a pretty five-storey building on a corner. The thirty-two rooms are sizeable and simply but nicely furnished. All have bath or shower and air-conditioning. Most have balconies. There is a lift and a bar. Rooms are 220–260f.

Hôtel Diana
(H)S-M   *17 blvd Leclerc   93.78.47.58   All credit cards*

Adjacent to the Olympia, this is another very agreeable hotel. There are thirty-five rooms, 190f with shower and 250–290f with bath.

Just to encourage those who might be intimidated by Monaco's glossy image, here is an immediate contradiction and incentive to read on: inexpensive hotels may be difficult to find, but inexpensive restaurants are not.

La Crémaillière
(R)S   *31 blvd Princesse Charlotte   93.50.66.24   Cl. Sun.; 15/12–15/1   CB, V*

Half a roast guinea-fowl in a sauce lightly flavoured with chestnuts, a potato pancake, and assorted fresh vegetables, accompanied by a half-bottle of very good Provence Rosé costs 65f. A very pleasant restaurant, with an outdoor terrace used year-round.

Beausoleil: Le Cosmopolite

Roger Vergé Café
(R)M   *Sporting d'Hiver   93.25.86.12   Cl. Sun.   All credit cards*

Don't let the name frighten you away. The prices are surprisingly reasonable if you have seen the astronomical numbers associated with eating at Roger Vergé's legendary Moulin de Mougins.

The café is located underground in the Sporting Club which is its only drawback. If you come in from the sun, you will like the shops and boutiques in this mall. It is bright, spacious and cheerful and ideal for a light lunch. It is open from 9 a.m. till 11.30 p.m.

There is a two-course menu at 100f and a three-course one at 120f. Pasta dishes are a speciality and on the à la carte they are priced from 39 to 48f. Entrecôte steaks are 87 and 92f, and a feature rare in France and very popular with customers wanting a light lunch is the serving of wine by the glass, at 20 to 35f a glass.

➤ Saint Benoît
(R)M-L   *av. de la Costa   93.25.02.34   Cl. Mon.; 28/11–28/12   All credit cards*

If you feel like spending a little more than usual in order to enjoy a really good meal, with a superb view of the port of Monaco – this is it.

Menus are 150f (two courses) and 210f (three courses) and the emphasis is strongly on seafood. On the à la carte menu, fish specialities include coquilles St-Jacques, lotte, pageot, loup de mer and chapon, and are priced at 95 to 225f. Service is swift and polite. Parking underneath the restaurant. Arrowed for the best cooking in Monte Carlo at an affordable price.

Rampoldi's
(R)M   *3 av. des Spélugues   93.30.70.65   Cl. 1–30/11   All credit cards*

An institution in Monte Carlo, and where you may see one of the younger members of the Royal Family. The food is definitely Italian and all à la carte. The minestrone at 45f is superb. A wide choice of pastas, all at 70f and risottos at 80–100f. Fish dishes are excellent, most at 150f; meat dishes are 100–150f.

Always busy, you need to book.

Polpetta
(R)M   *2 r. Paradis   93.50.67.84   Cl. Sat lunch; Tues. o.o.s.; 15/2–10/3; 15–30/10   All credit cards*

The atmosphere may be family-rustic, but this is where Roger Moore eats when he is in Monaco, and where Pavarotti and Frank Sinatra are patrons.

This confirms that Polpetta serves Italian food – some say the best in Monaco – and that it is a place where you will probably see some celebrities in the picture-lined bistro or on the large terrace. The food is authentic and enjoyable and the portions are generous. À la carte only, with pasta dominating – a dozen or so at 40–80f. Italian specialities such as ossobuco with rice, scallopine Marsala, or scampi gratinée cost 60–120f. The Italian wines are all good buys at 65–120f a bottle – try the Santa Cristina, a gorgeous rich full-bodied red.

Polpetta is busy and usually full, even out of season, but the service is prompt and efficient.

D'Avüta
(R)S-M   *1 r. Bellando de Castro   93.30.71.99   Cl. 4/11–22/12; Fri. o.o.s.   All credit cards*

In the heart of the old town, right by the Place des Carmes and so only 50 metres from the Palace.

Pasta is its speciality but there are other Italian dishes too. Menus are 60, 70, 85 and 95f.

Eat on the terrace in summer; this is made easier by the fact that it is larger than the indoor restaurant

Pulcinella
(R)M   *17 r. Portier   93.30.73.61   Cl. Wed.; 10–20/1   All credit cards*

One of the most popular restaurants in Monaco and deservedly so; Italian again.

Starters like Parma ham with melon or carpaccio cost around 70f. A good range of interesting pastas come cheaper.

Brochette de gambas (giant prawns on the spit) make a light but very satisfying main course at 100f.

Desserts are disappointing.

After eating, stroll across the street and veer to the left where you will see the little treasure of a house that Edward, Prince of Wales, built for Lily Langtry.

Sam's Place
(R)S   *1 av. Henri Dunant   93.50.89.33   Open all year   All credit cards*

No frills here. It's always busy, the tables are close together and it's therefore noisy but it's hard to beat for a good reliable satisfying meal at a low price. Main dishes from 45f. Open till midnight.

MAP 5D   **MONTAUROUX** 83440 (Var). 18 km W of Grasse

From the D 562 – the main road between Grasse and Draguignan – take the D 37 north, and Montauroux is only a few minutes' drive. Despite its proximity to a major highway, it is a perched village sitting on a mountain top. The approach is quite easy for a car – but must have been infinitely more difficult for an attacker centuries ago.

Montauroux is another of those villages which were part of a look-out network, in this case linked to Bargemon, Callian, Fayence, Seillans and Tourettes.

The D 37 leads directly into the square, which is always busy. The lanes and houses fanning off have been well-maintained, so that the whole village has a prosperous air, but this has not obtruded on its mediaeval character. On the edge of the square, see the chapel of St Barthélemy with its elaborately painted walls and ceilings.

On 24 August every year, there is a fête with folk-dancing. The high spot of the fête is the burning of an effigy of the Duc d'Épernon, who in 1592 hanged six officers of the garrison and murdered sixty villagers who resisted his tyrannical rule.

Just outside the village is the château on the Domaine de la Colle Noir, which was restored by Christian Dior as a family home.

There are two good hotel-restaurants here:

▶ La Marjolaine
(HR)M   *93.76.43.32   Rest. closed 1/11–15/12; 10/1–15/3   All credit cards*

In a calm and peaceful location, with a pretty garden, a panoramic view and nineteen rooms at 185–300f, La Marjolaine has been *the* place in Montauroux for a long time. Jean-Charles Dazon and Christian Couineau are justly proud of their restaurant, which attracts customers from far away.

Le Relais du Lac
(HR)M   *94.76.43.65   Open all year   All credit cards*

On the CD 562, the name refers to the Lac de St-Cassien, a very popular and still unspoiled place for swimming, sunbathing and picnicking in the summer.

The thirty-seven rooms in the hotel are 100–280f; demi-pension at 150–230f. The rooms are comfortable and quiet, and there is a pool as an alternative to the lake.

MAP 5E   **MOUGINS** 06250 (Alpes-Maritimes). 8 km N of Cannes; 11 km E of Grasse

---

A pretty hill-top village, once full of mediaeval charm but now, alas, steam-rollered into a dismaying uniformity – a victim of its own popularity with tourists.

Some villages have survived such an invasion, viewing the tidal waves of tourists with alarm (the residents) or anticipatory glee (restaurateurs, hoteliers and shopkeepers), then doing their own thing and emerging, scarred but unshaken, from the encounter. Mougins, sadly, has not. It consists today of restaurants offering mediocre food at inflated prices and art galleries displaying overpriced art of inferior quality. The only visitors seem to be foreign tourists so don't expect any 'little places where the locals eat'.

Mougins's boast is that it contains more restaurants per square kilometre than anywhere else on earth – this is easy to believe. All this concentration should have sharpened the competition, but all it seems to have done is stabilise prices in the upper regions and inhibit creative cooking. The natives blame this on Roger Vergé's Moulin de Mougins. One of the top restaurants in Europe and run by an entrepreneur-chef who is now mass-marketed all over the world, the Moulin has established sky-high price levels (600–800f per person).

But you will still want to visit it. You must park and then walk to the village itself. When the parking lots are full, the police will block off the approach roads and wave you off elsewhere. You should see the art gallery, Le Lavoir, which is built around the long rectangular stone tank which was where the villagers used to wash their clothes. There is also a tiny museum in the Mairie and an interesting photography museum near the Saracen Gate with many photos of a century ago.

Outside Mougins is the Musée de l'Automobile – at the Aire des Breguières turn-off from the A 8 autoroute, and clearly marked.

Over 100,000 people come every year to see the spectacular vehicles, which include an 1894 Benz, a 1938 Bugatti Galibier and a 1925 Rolls-Royce Phantom. Over seventy cars are displayed at a time out of a total of more than 240, so that the display changes and there is always a theme. The cinema seats 150 and shows a very entertaining film on the history of the automobile. Check the screening times when you enter.

An unusual exhibit is the garage abandoned on 4 September 1939 – the day general mobilisation was ordered in France. It has been preserved to the last detail and you can still smell the motor oil. The museum is open 10 a.m. to 7 p.m. from 1 May to 30 September, and from 10 to 6 p.m. from 1 October till 30 April.

If you really want to eat in Mougins, the best place is:

Le Feu Follet
(R)M *Mougins Village, pl. de la Mairie   93.90.15.78   Cl. Mon. o.o.s.; Sun. p.m.   A, V, CB*

The best value for money in the area. The food is not remarkable but of reliable standard and portions are generous. The fixed price menu at 145f might offer asparagus terrine with fresh tomato sauce, saddle of lamb en croûte, plus cheese or dessert. Good local wines.

The terrace is usually crowded in summer, being adjacent to the fountain. Must book.

Pat Fenn adds: My view of Mougins is somewhat different from Peter's, he being a resident and I merely a tourist. However, assuming that most readers will be tourists too, here is my angle: I actually *like* Mougins. I see it as a pastiche of an enchanting old French village, set so near the fleshpots that the contrast between fumes and fret and pedestrianised peace is all the more appealing. The whole village is like a stage setting, cleverly masterminded for maximum charm, and I can see nothing wrong with that. Banish the concept of phoniness and stroll through the steep streets, footsteps echoing on the cobbles. Pass the ancient fountain and massive old tree that spreads its deep shade over the village centre, sit at a café and enjoy the sheer prettiness of it all, contrived or not.

The inflated prices at the Moulin are of course a huge commercial joke and I doubt if any local would dream of patronising it. Because its clientele is largely American, I personally would put it bottom of my list of the three-star restaurants I should dearly love to visit, and we have been disappointed with l'Amandier, Vergé's other Mougins restaurant. It should, however, not be forgotten that Roger Vergé is one of the top chefs in France, if Michelin is to be believed, and that there are several establishments in Britain which nowadays more than match his prices.

Whenever we stay in the area we like to visit Mougins once and thoroughly enjoy the experience of finishing our stroll with a meal either at **Le Feu Follet** or at:

Le Bistrot

(R)M   *pl. du Village   93.75.78.36   Cl. Tues. o.o.s.; Wed.; 2/12–20/1   AE, CB*

An ancient (genuinely) stone building in the heart of the village, with two small vaulted dining-rooms and an uncommercial smiling welcome. The menu at 150f has a strong Provençal flavour, and the ingredients are generous and patently fresh. I remember the rascasse cooked with anchovies and olives with particular affection. Good cheeses and desserts follow. Booking essential.

MAP 3B   **MOUSTIERS-SAINTE-MARIE** 04360 (Alpes-de-Haute-Provence).
45 km W of Castellane; 62 km NW of Draguignan

Ⓜ *Fri.*

This is a most unusual village and in a very strange setting. It sits at the foot of a gigantic gorge, 500 feet deep – a mighty crevice cleft by the water which roars down from the Alps, slashing through the soft limestone rock.

Across the top of the gorge and high above the village, an iron chain stretches from peak to peak and from the middle hangs a gilded iron star. 'The Chain of the Star', as it is called, was put up by the Chevalier de Blacas, a knight from Moustiers, who was captured by the Saracens at the Siege of Damietta during the Fifth Crusade. While in captivity he vowed to put a golden chain over his home village if he was ever released. When he did finally return home, he could only afford an iron chain with a gilded star. No one knows how he accomplished the formidable task of stretching a chain across the 750-foot gap – even today with modern technology it would be no mean feat.

Moustiers has been famous since the 17th century for its faience, delicate blue-and-white pottery which is prized all over France. It is said that the secret of the glaze, which makes this pottery quite different from any other, was brought from Faenza by an Italian monk. Apparently the transplantation of the industry was successful, for it flourished immediately and, less than a hundred years later, four hundred mules laden with *faience* pottery were scrambling down from Moustiers to the famous fair at Beaucaire every year.

Moustiers is small. You can walk and climb up and down the two sides of the torrent which hurtles down the gorge and under the bridge over the main street, then you can walk along the main street which crosses over that same bridge . . . and that's about it. There is a museum of faience in the town hall which has been there since the 17th century when the first pots were made. Most of Moustiers's population of 500 are in the numerous shops busy selling the faience porcelain; prices for the highly decorative porcelain are high, but I have never taken a visitor there yet who didn't buy something and it seems that not only foreigners buy there – people from all over France revere faience porcelain, in the way Germans view Dresden.

The Chapelle de Notre-Dame-de-Beauvoir is up in the ravine and quite accessible. It is very picturesque, with its 12th-century Romanesque nave, its Gothic choir and its Lombardy belfry.

Moustiers doesn't have much to offer in the way of any recommended accommodation. Aiguines, Trigance and Aups are all within a short distance and you will enjoy a stay in any of these. If, however, you are here at lunchtime . . .

Les Santons
(R)M   *pl. de l'Église   92.74.66.48   Cl. Mon. p.m. o.o.s.; Tues.; 15/11–1/3*
All credit cards

An extremely ancient boulangerie-turned-rustic-chic-restaurant, with solid cool stone walls. The vine-covered terrace offers a stupendous view of the peaks of Notre-Dame – eat there whenever the sun shines; inside in the stone-flagged dining-room when it rains.

André Albert makes the most of local resources. One of his favourite dishes is farm chicken cooled in the lavender honey for which the region is renowned; trout from the mountain streams and pigeons cooked in sage are good too, while his cheese-board is a lesson on all the best local goat cheeses. Prices are unexpectedly high for such a remote village, but an investment of 195f for the cheapest menu, or the cost of just one à la carte dish, will not be regretted.

MAP 5E   **LA NAPOULE** 06210 (Alpes-Maritimes). 8 km W of Cannes

Ⓜ *Wed.*

The principal reason for going to La Napoule is to visit its château. Originally Saracen, there remained only three towers and a gateway added in the 14th century when Henry Clews, a rich American sculptor, bought it in 1918. He and his wife Marie, who was an architect, restored it over a period of twenty years. They did all the work themselves, with only the occasional help of a mason and his son.

Formal gardens were created and every night Henry and Marie Clews, dressed in mediaeval style, dined in the huge hall, waited on by servants in Provençal costumes and entertained by musicians in the minstrel gallery.

As a sculptor, Henry worked in alabaster, wood, metal and marble for five years until he died, just before World War II. His widow refused to leave the castle even when the Germans occupied it to billet troops there, and to ensure that they did not loot the sculpture, she hid it.

When the war was over, she opened the château as a museum. Clews' work is certainly grim and eccentric; inspired by mediaeval and pre-Columbian art, it depicts grotesque birds, animals and men. The museum is open all year except December and there are guided tours only. Hours are in the process of being changed yet again – may be closed weekends but call 94.49.95.05.

A small pretty harbour is adjacent to the château, separated only by a sandy beach. Be sure to take the walk along the rocky path which runs around the foot of the château walls, by the water's edge.

Le Boucanier

(R)M   *93.49.80.51   Open all year   All credit cards*

A beautiful location – right on the sandy beach next to the château and looking up at its imposing walls. Seafood is the speciality here and stars the magnificent platter of clams, oysters, mussels, winkles, crabs, prawns and other shell-clad cousins at 340f for two people.

On the à la carte menu are langoustines, grilled gambas and loup flambé, at prices from 120 to 210f.

There is one fixed menu at 130f, with a choice of terrine de rascasse or moules marinières as the first course, and the daurade grillé is among the best of the main courses.

Even out of season, the large outdoor dining area, virtually on the beach, is popular.

La Maison de Bruno et Judy

(R)M   *93.49.95.15   Cl. Tues. o.o.s.; 15/11–15/12   All credit cards*

A popular favourite for a long time and directly across the street from the château.

The inside dining-room is pleasant and relaxing and outside there is a patio for the summer months. The menu at 150f offers a really delicious terrine de poissons with mousseline sauce for instance, then the crab is a superb main course, as is the hare. The pâtisserie display is of very high quality.

At 190f, you should have the mussel soup, or, for something different, the crêpes stuffed with lumpfish. The main course of tournedos of salmon with dill is a real problem because the spare ribs with honey thyme are so good too. There is cheese to follow on this menu and then dessert, of which I recommend the nougat glacé.

MAP 4G   **NICE** 06000 (Alpes-Maritimes). 32 km E of Cannes; 18 km W of Monaco

---

Ⓜ   *See text*

One of Europe's most renowned tourist cities and 'Queen City of the Riviera'. It's the fifth largest city in France, with a strong commercial presence in addition to its status as a resort.

You may have read about its politics, the charges of corruption in local government, its mayor who is in hiding in South America and the allegations of Mafia control – not to mention Graham Greene's book *J'Accuse*, exposing the seamier side of the city. As a visitor, these won't bother you at all, so just enjoy its sights, its beaches, its restaurants, its museums and its climate.

The cultural amenities of Nice are extraordinarily varied and extensive – its shopping, which offers a mini-version of Paris, its casino, its water-sports and its famous Carnival, plus an unending stream of summer attractions – which means there are always things to see and do.

First the beaches. They are rocky, covered with pebbles which are hard on the feet and the back unless you are suitably equipped. For sandy beaches, you must go to Cannes or Juan-les-Pins. This does not stop thousands of people converging in the summer months on the Nice beaches, which are kept clean and tidy, while the water is monitored frequently, so you need have no fears.

The approach to Nice is by either the A 8 autoroute or the RN 7. The promenade des Anglais, one of the great boulevards of the world, is one of the first sights you will see; it has several lanes in each direction, runs right along the coastal strip and provides rapid transit for cars, little impeded by signals or stops. It is unrivalled in Europe for its magnificent wide sidewalk, which is on the Mediterranean side – that is to say, between the promenade des Anglais and the beach. It is always busy but seldom crowded. An endless throng of holiday-makers, retired pensioners, dog walkers, parents with children, joggers, skateboarders, roller skaters, and others, is readily absorbed and there are no billboards or stands or booths or any other commercial intrusions.

The port used to be a place to enjoy a stroll, but it's much less fun now, with fewer pleasure boats but more commercial vessels as well as the giant Corsica ferries.

The château is no longer there, although you will see it marked on all the maps. The hill on which it stood is now merely a wooded height converted into a delightful public park. Among the trees are the occasional remains of the ancient citadel, pieces of tumbled masonry and a part-buried arch or the remnants of a doorway. The view from the 185-metre top stretches southwards out to sea, and northwards over the rooftops of the old town. It is not difficult to see how the fortress proved to be impregnable even to Barbarossa, the most ferocious of the Barbary corsairs, when he besieged it in 1543. There is a funicular if you don't feel like the climb.

The old town of Nice is extremely picturesque and quite safe. Much of it really is old yet it blends in with the posh restaurants and the smart shops which have moved in but not taken over. The first thing you need to do is park; there is also lots of street parking, though limited to two hours. Advice gets difficult from here on! Occasionally you will get a ticket for being ten minutes over. Most of the time you can leave it five hours and nothing happens. You will also see cars double-parked – in places marked appropriately, this is legal. The Niçois double-park anywhere, even blocking narrow streets. You may want to do the same and you may get away with it, having foreign licence plates. Another hazard of double-parking is that you frequently get blocked in. The local policy is to ask first at the nearest shops and if that doesn't work, lean on the horn until someone comes to let you out. Parking lots are the best answer and they are not too expensive – 8 to 10f for the first hour and reducing by the hour. Never leave anything of value in the car – break-ins are not uncommon, especially when the car is foreign.

The quai des États-Unis is a continuation of the promenade des Anglais and runs to the cape at the foot of the castle. It was formerly known as the Plage des Ponchettes and used to be lined with many of the best restaurants in Nice. There are still a few there but most have moved inland and the whole strip seems to be awaiting redevelopment. Housed in the old Sardinian naval arsenal is the municipal art gallery, Galeries des Ponchettes, which has periodic shows of painting and sculpture by modern artists.

Just behind the gallery and across the cours Saleya is the Cathedral of Ste Réparte on the place Rosetti. Here is one saint who deserved to have a cathedral dedicated to her. Refusing to denounce Christianity, she had molten lead poured over her and red-hot iron stakes driven into her body; as she survived, she was thrown into a furnace, and, when the flames went out, she was decapitated, whereupon a white dove ascended from the corpse. A painting in the cathedral depicts these tortures. Don't be put off by the somewhat mediocre aspect of the outside because the interior blazes with crude colours. It is far from the sanctuary of peace and contemplative calm that you expect – instead it is laden with extravagant ornamentation and lavish detail.

Not far away from Ste Réparte and near the station is the Cathédrale Russe ('Russians on the Riviera', p. 38, gives the background on this unlikely combination). This, the Russian Orthodox Church, is a typically ornate Byzantine building, with one large central onion-shaped dome, surrounded by four smaller domes. It is, appropriately, on the boulevard Tzarewitch and was built just after the turn of the century but in the old 16th-century Russian style. Its building was ordered by Nicolas II in memory of his uncle, the Tsar Nicolas, who died in Nice in 1865. The structure is a duplicate of the Yaroslav Church in Moscow and inside are some fine icons; the church interior is richly decorated, the gold glittering in the sun.

Rue de France, rue Masséna, rue Paradis and rue Maccarani comprise a shopping area in the old town, which is all pedestrian streets. There are boutiques, shops, cafés and restaurants, and when you get tired you can drop in at the English-American Library behind the Anglican church and read the English newspapers.

The cours Saleya deserves a special mention all of its own. You can park directly underneath it and emerge into a pedestrian precinct or even into the market itself. First, the outdoor markets. You will have seen others but not as large as this one, not as busy and not with more spectacular produce. Camera-bugs go crazy here. The luscious fruit, the succulent vegetables, the chickens, meats, cheeses, herbs and spices are a food-lover's paradise, and the flowers fragrant and dazzling. The fruit and vegetable markets are open every day, mornings only, except Monday. The flower market is open every day except Monday, 1 to 3 p.m. On the shadier, southern side are the fish stalls, several of which are also restaurants.

Through white stone arches, you will catch glimpses of the Baie des Anges. At the foot of the hill bearing the château is a yellow stucco building which once housed Matisse's studio. This is certainly one of the most attractive corners of the old town.

Monday is the day when the markets and most of the shops are closed but this does not mean inactivity by any means, for the antique dealers and second-hand merchants set up their stands in one of the biggest shows on the Riviera.

The cours Saleya is also restaurant-row and many of the best restaurants in Nice are here. The emphasis is on seafood, naturally, but, remembering that the city was Italian until it was re-united with France as recently as 1860, there are many Italian places too.

The rue Droite also contains some interesting antique and bric-à-brac shops, while on the rue Gaëtan, just off the cours Saleya, is Aux Essences de Grasse, selling over a hundred different flower essences, soaps, oils, eaux de toilette and perfumed oils for burning in lamps.

If you walk through the pedestrian area, you reach avenue Jean-Médecin, off the magnificent place Masséna. On the corner is Galeries Lafayette – a five-storey department store which covers the entire block and sells nearly everything. Their gourmet food section in the basement is stocked with delicacies from many nations. Further up the avenue Jean-Médicin are numerous stores and boutiques, then Nice-Étoile, another large shopping complex, containing different stores and shops, including Pier Import, which specialises in Oriental imports; Habitat; and FNAC, with perhaps the biggest selection of records and cassettes on the Riviera.

Henri Auer on rue St-François-de-Paule sells superb chocolates and crystallised fruit, while Nice's most renowned purveyor of cheeses is Paul Chervet, who supplies Jacques Maximin and the West End Hotel as well as the Chèvre d'Or in Èze. He is located at L'Edelweiss, 55 rue de France, and at La Poulette, 12 rue de la Préfecture in old Nice.

Street markets selling old books, maps, documents and papers are held every Sunday morning on boulevard Risso and place Durandy.

Don't miss the Palais Lascaris on rue Droite, a gem of a Genoese palazzo of the 17th century, restored as a national monument. The entrance hall contains the armoury of the Lascaris-Vintimille (Ventimiglia) family and the balustraded marble staircase leads up to the apartments on the second floor, where Flemish tapestries hang beneath ceilings frescoed with scenes from myth and drama. The rooms are tiny but exquisite. The chapel is beautiful and the furnishing and hangings throughout contribute to the feeling of a truly royal residence. Admission free, open 9.30 a.m.–12 and 2.30–6 p.m. every day except Monday.

Just opened is the Museum of Modern and Contemporary Art, a splendid building, purpose-built on the newly named Promenade des Arts. It is intended to provide a showcase for living art and it does this in sumptuous style.

First, the building itself: unusually, it was designed by a local architect, Yves Bayard, who has done a superb job in designing an edifice which is as modern as the works it houses. Outside, long elevated walkways lead through hanging gardens and past pools.

The front of the building is a bold composition of four square marble towers connected by metal and glass wings. Massive curved girders support the grid structure, giving grace and elegance. The museum is not a separate but an integral part of all this and there are also two theatres, one 1,100-seat and one 300-seat. These perform principally serious French drama but there are a few exceptions – the Royal Shakespeare Company, for instance, has performed a play in English for a run of five nights.

Parking is easy and convenient – clearly marked and underneath the complex so that you emerge by steps or a lift directly at the museum.

The work on display dates from the 1960s to the present and there are both temporary and permanent collections with a strong emphasis on Yves Klein, Arman and Martial Raysse, all Nice artists. The American abstract school is represented by Andy Warhol, Robert Rauschenberg, Roy Lichtenstein, Claes Oldenburg, Jim Dine and Gilbert and George.

There are several bizarre 'moving' tableaux – flashing neon lights on canvas, inverted bicycles which emit strange noises when the pedals are turned, spinning dolls – and some pop-art, with crushed automobiles, sculptures of welded turbine-engine blades, coloured plastic columns which are puzzles, and torn Elvis Presley movie posters.

As you ascend from floor to floor by escalator, the views of Nice are magnificent, seen through the connecting wings of clear glass.

Four changes of exhibits a year are planned, in addition to the permanent exhibits. The café is open from 9 a.m. to 1 a.m. and the grill is open from 7 p.m. to midnight. The museum is open every day from 11 a.m. to 6 p.m. except Tuesdays and bank holidays, and on Fridays it is open till 10 p.m.

The Museum of Prehistory known as the Terra-Amata is at 25 boulevard Carnot, just off the north-east corner of the port. The life of hunters of mammoths, bears and elephants of 400,000 years ago is interestingly told. Open in summer 10 a.m. to 12 and 2 to 7 p.m.; in winter 10 a.m. to 12 and 2 to 6 p.m. Closed Mondays.

Two other museums are within short walking distance and both are well worth visiting. There is the Musée Masséna (65 rue de France and 35 promenade des Anglais – it runs right through the block), which gives the history of Nice since the 11th century. There are furniture, vases and candelabra from the First Empire, doors and wood-panelling and paintings from the former residences of the kings of Italy, French and German weapons from the 15th to the 18th centuries, jewellery and porcelain, costumes and coins and medals. . . . Open 1 October to 30 April from 10 a.m. to 12 and 2 to 5 p.m.; 1 May to 30 September from 10 a.m. to 12 and 3 to 6 p.m. Closed Mondays and public holidays and all November.

The Musée des Beaux Arts is at 33 avenue de Baumettes, just behind the promenade des Anglais and is still often referred to by its earlier name of Musée Jules-Chéret, a painter who worked in Nice and died here in 1932. The building, constructed in 1876, was formerly the private residence of Princess Kotschoubey of Ukraine. It shows paintings and sculpture from Italian primitive to French impressionist, arranged so as to demonstrate progress through the various schools – Romantic, Realist, Oriental, Symbolic and Academic.

Jules Chéret, being a local painter, is well represented and so are the van Loos. Carle van Loo was a Dutchman, born in Nice, who became well known here as an artist. Van Dongen, Mossa (also a Niçois), Dufy, Matisse, Bonnard, Braque, Monet, and Sisley are featured too, along with sculpture by Rodin. An amount of work by other artists is less exciting but the variety is remarkable.

One of the more interesting groups of paintings are those by Marie Bashkirtseff, a Russian better known for her memoirs than her painting. Seen from the viewpoint of a thirteen-year-old girl in Nice, these are a major source of information on the life and times, people and places, of the late 19th century, for she was unusually observant and her impressions are sensitive and quite unique. The Beaux Arts is open 10 a.m. to 12 and 3 to 6 p.m. from 1 May to 30 September; and 10 a.m. to 12 and 2 to 5 p.m. from 1 October to 30 April. Closed on Mondays, public holidays and all November.

Just off the promenade des Anglais in the Quartier de Fabron, towards the airport, is the Château Ste-Hélène, built by Raymond Blanc, the founder and director of the Casino at Monte Carlo. Anatole Jakovsky bought the château from the Coty family (of perfume fame) and here, in the Musée International d'Art Naif, he has gathered more than 600 naive paintings, drawings, engravings and sculptures from twenty-seven countries, with more than two hundred artists, mostly European, some North and South American and African. Names mean less in this style than most, but Rousseau, Generalić, Séraphine and Peyronnet are here as well as some of Jakovsky himself. Open 10 a.m.–12 and 2–5 p.m. from 1 October to 30 April; and 10 a.m.–12 and 2–6 p.m. from 1 May to 30 September. Closed Tuesdays and most public holidays. Admission free.

After all this culture, you may be ready for something a little lighter. Parc Phoenix, on the promenade des Anglais and near the airport, is a very recent addition to the attractions offered by Nice. It is a large amusement park containing the biggest plant house in the world, the Island of Remote Times, a Mayan temple, an Astronomic Garden (which shows the history of the planet earth as seen from space), a butterfly park, fishes, birds and flowers. Special events are presented in a steady series – 'Dinosaurs' was a stupendous attraction with moving monsters provided by Hollywood technology. It was followed by 'Japanese Gardens' and then 'Insects'.

There are waterfalls, lakes, bars, restaurants, coffee shops, fast food kiosks and plenty of easy parking. Admission to all attractions

costs 59f for adults and 35f for children. The park is open 10 a.m.–
5 p.m. from 1 October to 31 March (closed Mondays); 10 a.m.–
9.30 p.m. from 20 June till 19 August (open every day); 10 a.m.–
6.30 p.m. from 20 August till 30 September (closed Mondays). Closed
completely from 4 January till 3 February.

Nearer to Nice and just in from the promenade des Anglais is the
Parc des Miniatures intended for the young, though ticket sales
indicate that more adults visit it than children! The history of the
Riviera through 400,000 years is displayed in miniatures at a scale
of 25 to 1. Buildings, characters and automated models, spread over
a wooded area of 35,000 square metres, tell the story of Nice and
its surroundings. There is a restaurant, snack bar, souvenir shop and
free parking. Open all year.

Less than a kilometre north of the château in Nice is the Musée
National Message Biblique Marc Chagall. This is a most unusual
exhibition. Located on the avenue Docteur-Menard, it is a permanent
collection of paintings, sculpture, mosaics, tapestries, stained
glass windows, drawings, ceramics and lithographs. Biblical and
Russian themes dominate the work of Chagall. Open in summer
10 a.m.–7 p.m.; in winter 10 a.m.–12 and 2–5 p.m. Closed Sunday
morning, all day Monday and all November.

Cimiez, now a northern suburb of Nice, was originally a Roman
city, Cemeneleum, with the great Roman road from the Forum in
Rome to Arles passing through it. It grew to have a population of
about 30,000, but was destroyed by the Lombards in the 6th
century. Little is left, but the remnants of a 10,000-seat arena, Les
Arènes, may be seen; and there are the remains of some 3rd-
century baths, and what may be a part of the Temple of Apollo. In
the Archaeological Museum (164 avenue des Arènes), housed in
a villa in the Genoese style of the 18th century, there are many
objects found in the excavation of the site including a statue of
Antonia, the niece of Augustus Caesar. It is open from 10 a.m. to 12
and 2.30 to 6.30 p.m. from May to September; from 10 a.m. to 12
and 2 to 5 p.m. from October to April. Closed Sunday mornings and
all day Monday.

The villa used to house the Matisse Museum on its first floor but
by the time you read this, it will have been re-opened in a new
building adjacent. Check the times as they have not yet been
announced. This will be an important addition to Impressionist
art, as paintings from every period of the painter's life will be
represented. Matisse spent much time in Nice from 1916 and in
1921 he took an apartment here. He died in Cimiez in 1954 at the age
of eighty-five and so it is appropriate that a museum of his works
should be erected where he produced many of his finest works.
Besides paintings, on exhibit are all the books which he illustrated, a
complete collection of his sculpture, and objects which belonged to
him.

Three types of exhibition are planned: Thematic (based on a
significant aspect of Matisse's creativity or his time); Historic
(based around a work by Matisse or of his time), and Contemporary
(featuring painters and sculptors who followed his style). Matisse
is buried in the adjacent cemetery.

Within walking distance is the Franciscan Monastery and Church and Museum. This recalls Franciscan life in Nice from the 13th to the 18th centuries. There are guided tours of the cloisters, sacristy and oratory with displays of sculpture, frescos and books. Open 10 a.m.–12 and 3–6 p.m. every day except Sundays and public holidays.

The block of flats at the top of the boulevard de Cimiez used to be the Hôtel Regina where Queen Victoria stayed every year. Her statue still stands in front. Matisse lived in this hotel too, from 1942 on.

Nice's most famous event is unquestionably the Mardi Gras Carnival, which ranks close behind the Carnivals of Rio and New Orleans. For two weeks before Lent, King Carnival holds sway, with a big fireworks display on Shrove Tuesday and the Battles of the Flowers. These are parades of floats and cavalcades of 'big heads' – grotesque masks caricaturing well-known and topical figures. Brass bands blast away, and all the fiacres of Nice are pressed into service, carrying loads of pretty girls.

The best grandstand seats are expensive and need to be booked well in advance. The place Masséna is a favourite spot with most spectators.

The tradition of a pre-Lenten parade has existed for over five hundred years but the Carnival in its present form dates from 1876, when the first Battle of the Flowers was held on the promenade des Anglais.

If it's gambling you're looking for, the Casino Ruhl on the promenade des Anglais at the place Masséna is the place for you. French and English roulette, 30/40, blackjack and punto-banco every day from 4 p.m. on. There are 190 slot machines open from 10 p.m. till dawn, plus a cabaret, a night club, a discotheque and a bar-restaurant, Le Louisiane. The Casino has re-opened recently after the closure which resulted from a sensational corruption case.

Many other events take place in Nice throughout the year. Principal among them are: *February:* Festival of Modern Music. *April:* Dog Show; Book Fair; Tennis Tournament; Automobile Rally. *May:* Fête de Mai, folk singing and dancing every Sunday in the Parc des Arènes in Cimiez. *29 June:* Festival of the Fishermen; ritual burning of a boat on the Plage des Ponchettes. *July:* Grand Jazz Parade; International Folklore Festival in Albert I Garden. *August:* Wine Festival in Cimiez Park. *October:* Automobile Rally; Nice Philharmonic Orchestra Music Festival.

The Riviera has several hotels which are part of the social fabric and their names glitter prominently in the history of the Côte d'Azur. Only one such hotel is in Nice but in the opinion of many, it is the greatest of them all.

The **Hôtel Négresco** was built in 1912, at a cost of 6 million gold francs. It was the creation of Henri Négresco, a Rumanian violinist in a gypsy orchestra before he decided to go into the hotel business. It was designed by the architect who designed the Moulin Rouge and the Folies Bergère – and for further contrast, the Négresco was erected on the site of a former convent.

It is one of the grandest hotels on the Riviera, due in no small part to the lavish uniforms of the staff; the chandelier in the Salon Royal was specially made for the Tsar, there are Légers and Picassos on the walls and the toilets in the lobby are resplendent with gold fittings. The 150 rooms are in the styles of many different periods.

The hotel is frequently used in films as a landmark identification when the camera moves slowly along the promenade des Anglais. Its restaurant, Le Chantecler, featured prominently in the recent James Bond film *The Living Daylights*.

So many celebrities have stayed here that it is difficult to determine which ones have not. Isadora Duncan deserves special mention, though – she spent the last years of her life here, owing the hotel so much money that she could not afford to leave.

Rooms are 1,300–2,000f per night, and apartments up to 6,000f – but there is no doubt that this is one of the grandest hotels in the world.

Hôtel La Pérouse
(H)L   *11 quai Rauba-Capéu   93.62.34.63   All credit cards*

Many return to La Pérouse year after year, confident of a spacious room, many with a balcony and some with sea views. All sixty-three rooms are well-furnished, air-conditioned and fully equipped.

The hotel is quiet and convenient for walks through the old town, into the market area and around the port.

There is a sauna and a solarium, and in the summer grills and snacks are served by the pool. No restaurant, but there is room service. Rooms are priced at 365–975f, the higher end of the range naturally relating to the rooms with a view.

➤ Hôtel Windsor
(HR)M   *11 r. Dalpozzo   93.88.59.35   Open all year   All credit cards*

It is always difficult to find a good hotel in the heart of a city. Hôtel Windsor is an unreserved recommendation, only steps away from the beach, the promenade des Anglais and the pedestrian shopping streets.

The sixty air-conditioned rooms are charmingly furnished. The public rooms are spacious; there is a pool, which was used as the setting to film François Truffaut's *Day for Night*; and there is a beautiful flower garden. The service is attentive and helpful, and the prices surprisingly reasonable for such quality in such a select and convenient location: 300–550f for a double room.

➤ Primotel Suisse
(HR)M   *15 quai Rauba-Capéu   93.62.33.00   All credit cards*

The Provençal-named location is the small cape which juts out into the sea from the foot of the castle hill. Consequently there are superb views from many of the forty-two rooms, which have period furniture. The whole hotel has a very pleasing ambience and it is perfectly placed for a stroll along the promenade des Anglais or into the old town. The rooms are priced at 300–350f which is very hard to beat in Nice. Demi-pension is 300–400f.

Little Palace Hotel
(H)M   *26 r. Paris   93.88.70.49   V, CB*

One of those hotels that the guests keep to themselves. Otherwise everybody would want to stay here. In the musicians' quarter of Nice, it is only minutes from the beach. There are thirty-four rooms, all with bath and shower, and at an amazing 250–300f. No parking, but the Mozart parking lot is one minute away.

Hôtel Alfa
(H)M   *30 r. Masséna   93.87.88.63   All credit cards*

Recently modernised and all of the thirty-five rooms re-decorated. Situated on the lively shopping street rue Masséna, which is restricted to pedestrians, therefore quiet at night. Cafés, restaurants and bars are in profusion all around and it's only 200 metres to the promenade des Anglais and the beach.

All the rooms have air-conditioning and bath or shower. They are modestly priced at 235–445f. There is a lounge, a bar and a breakfast room. There is a municipal parking lot nearby.

Relais de Rimiez
(H)M   *128 av. de Rimiez   93.81.18.65   Cl. Jan.   All credit cards*

Large, comfortable and quiet air-conditioned rooms. There are twenty-four of them, priced from 180 to 230f. The sweeping terraces have fine views.

There is a drawback – inevitable at these prices. It's located just north of the A 8 autoroute (minutes from the Nice–Ariane Nord interchange).

Hôtel Mercure Opéra
(H)M   *Quai des États-Unis   93.85.74.19   All credit cards*

It looks a little grim from the outside, part of a long grey façade of buildings. Inside, however, it's quite different, with fifty pleasant rooms, all sound-proofed and air-conditioned. Views over the Mediterranean are superb, and the rooms are priced at 350–480f.

There is no parking but the large municipal parking lot in place Masséna is only three minutes' walk.

L'Oasis
(H)S   *23 r. Gounod   93.88.12.29   P.   All credit cards*

There are thirty-eight simply furnished but perfectly adequate rooms in this inexpensive hotel right in the centre of downtown Nice. All are now equipped with private bath or shower and colour TV. There

Nice: Hôtel l'Oasis

is a private car-park. Reliable hotels like this, with rooms at 300–350f, are not easy to find.

Le Gourmet Lorrain

(HR)S   *7 av. Santa Fior   93.84.90.78   Cl. Sun. p.m.; Mon.; 1–10/1; Aug.
All credit cards*

It is hard to know which to recommend first here – the hotel, the restaurant or the cellar. The fifteen rooms are simple but pleasingly furnished and are priced at 130–185f. Demi-pension is obligatory in season, at 150–270f, but the food is so good that you are much better off with that arrangement. Soupe de poisson, roast quail, cheese and chocolate mousse, at 90f is a bargain. Remember, though, that the kitchen closes at 9.30 p.m.

The cellar is one of the largest in France with a bewildering selection at all prices.

What's the catch? you ask. Well, the only disadvantage at all is the location which is just north of the railway station. Although not a fashionable area, it is quite respectable and less than ten minutes from the promenade des Anglais.

Lou Balico
(R)M   *20 av. St-Jean-Baptiste   93.85.93.71   Open every day till midnight*
All credit cards

Located next to the new Museum of Modern and Contemporary Art, this is the ideal place to taste true Niçois cuisine. Several

Nice: Lou Balico

restaurants claim to offer it but you won't find it better or more authentic than here.

The Menu Dégustation at 180f, or the Menu Balico at 140f, are the ones to go for, but if you want to do your own selecting, you can't go wrong with the moules Balico at 45f, followed by the tuna Provençale at 70f, an enormous steak with a delicious sorrel sauce, accompanied by pasta. There is a toothsome array of pastries and desserts and a selection of inexpensive Provence wines.

L'Esquinade
(R)L *5 quai des Deux Emmanuel Cl. Sun. & Mon. p.m.; Jan.   All credit cards*

Considered by many to be one of the finest seafood restaurants in Nice, l'Esquinade has recently been redecorated, and Pascal Roche, formerly with Jacques Maximin of Négresco fame, is now the chef.

Most of the familiar faces in politics, business and showbiz may be seen here. It's not cheap, but the quality is superb. In summer, dine on the terrace overlooking the old port.

You might think twice before spending 420f on a lobster or crayfish, but the more modest 195f menu has plenty of good things to offer. You might choose the stuffed courgette flowers, then the red mullet with ratatouille ravioli and scampi cream, then lamb cutlets sprinkled with herbs, and conclude with Paris-Brest – choux pastry covered in chopped almonds, filled with butter praline cream and served with thick orange sauce. You'll need a walk around the port after that!

Le Farniente
(R)L *27 promenade des Anglais 93.88.29.44 Cl. Sun. o.o.s.   All credit cards*

Major hotels are unlikely locations for good restaurants but the Westminster-Concorde Hotel which houses Le Farniente is the exception.

The new chef, Jean-Pierre Barnard, master of classic cuisine, offers outstanding seafood meals at 180f. There is a large terrace with a view of the sea for summer dining, and the restaurant itself is plush and air-conditioned.

Chez les Pêcheurs
(R)M–L *18 quai des Docks 93.89.59.61 Cl. Tues. p.m. & Wed. o.o.s.; Thurs. lunch and Wed. in season; 1/11–15/12 All credit cards*

Chef Roger Barbate is a Maître-Cuisinier de France and his speciality is seafood. Devotees come from all over the Côte d'Azur to his restaurant on the quayside, with its marine décor. You can watch the action in the busy kitchen if you're not too engrossed in the superb food.

Good starters around 65f are the terrine de poissons or the cuissons de crevettes roses. The two dishes that Roger Barbate is famous for are the bouillabaisse, 340f for two persons, and the

Nice: Chez les Pêcheurs

bourride, 390f for two persons. Both are a meal in themselves. Leave room for good desserts like the marquise of dark chocolate.

Jacques Maximin:
Gastro Restaurant
(R)L   *93.80.70.10   Cl. Mon.; Tues. lunch*
Bistro
(R)M   *93.80.68.00   Open every day*

The great chef from Chantecler Restaurant in the Négresco Hotel in Nice recently opened his own restaurants just behind the Galeries Lafayette, a site which used to house the old Casino Theatre and which Maximin has transformed into a temple to food.

The opening was described as the 'No. 1 Gastronomic Event of the year on the Côte d'Azur'.

Maximin's pedigree is impeccable. He worked with Michel Rostang and Michel Guérard and at Prunier-Traktir in Paris. Originally influenced by Roger Vergé, he quickly developed his own style and he is sure to reach even greater heights – although one may ask, 'After achieving 19½ points out of 20 in Gault-Millau, how much higher is there to go?'

The two establishments you will consider visiting are the **Gastronomic Restaurant**, where a meal costs 500–600f and the **Bistro** which has menus at 150–170f, which change every day. Another establishment, the Boutique, is actually a catering operation.

St Moritz

(R)M *5 r. du Congrès   93.88.54.90   Cl. 15/11–12/12; 11–29/1; Wed. o.o.s. All credit cards*

Small and cosy, not posh but only a block from the promenade des Anglais and always busy because of its very good food and reasonable prices. Fish or onion soup, for instance, cost 45f; and main dishes, from 85 to 185f, include sautéed chicken with wild mushrooms, leg of lamb with garlic and red wine sauce, coquilles St-Jacques à l'Ancienne, and loup de mer in pernod sauce.

La Petite Maison

(R)M *3 r. de l'Opéra   93.85.71.53   Cl. Sun.*

Bistro-style, with lots of character, right in the old town and serving mostly fish. You can choose from all the catch of the day here – sea bass, crayfish . . . and four or five specialities daily. An unusual item on the menu is an assortment of six hors d'oeuvres with two glasses of wine at 150f for two people – ideal when you feel like a midday snack. Nicole Rubi and Bernard Olle are becoming well-known and it seems likely that their fame will continue to spread.

La Baieta

(R)M *28 cours Saleya   93.62.32.94   Cl. Sun.   All credit cards*

Outstanding seafood in a street with so many good seafood restaurants. A wide range of Mediterranean fish is cooked in a variety of ways. You can make a preliminary choice outside, where the sole, red mullet, loup de mer, crab, prawns, oysters, clams, mussels and others lie in serried ranks, glistening fresh.

The 99f menu has three courses, but the best bet here is the assortment of grilled fish. It's 180f but it's a full meal in itself.

La Toque Blanche

(R)M *40 r. de la Buffa   93.88.38.18   Cl. Sun. p.m.; Mon.; 15/7–15/8 A, AE, V, EC, CB*

Since Alain and Denise Sandelion took over here and refurbished the place, it has grown rapidly in stature and popularity. La Toque Blanche is small and the menu is not extensive but everything on it is carefully selected, and the fish dishes are the ones to choose. Menus at 130 and 160f during the week; 160f on Sunday Gastronomic menu at 280f. Note that the kitchen closes at 9.30.

Chez Don Camillo
(R)M *5 r. Ponchettes 93.85.67.95 Cl. Sun. All credit cards*

In spite of the name it's really Italian cooking – a quaint, gracious, almost formal restaurant on a street of tall elegant old buildings at the eastern end of the cours Saleya. The noodles with black truffles are excellent, as are the saltimbocca, the various scallopines and the osso bucco.

Franck Cerutti changes the menu very frequently but whatever is being served is sure to be good. The most recent fixed menu was at 180f and offered baby rabbit stuffed with herbs, then morue (cod) with mixed peppers, haricot beans, anchovies and tomatoes, and then dessert.

The à la carte choices may be preferable, with a fine blend of familiar dishes and many that are different and imaginative.

La Farigoule
(R)M *93.87.11.21 Cl. Sun. EC, CB*

You are sure to walk along the rue de France, the pedestrian-only street which is lined with boutiques and shops. If you are stricken by hunger during such a shopping safari, there is no shortage of places to eat. One of the best is La Farigoule which sits just far back enough from the road to be reasonably quiet.

The food is Niçois and Provençal, served in a modest auberge, with a smile. Menus are 80, 95 and 135f, and there are à la carte choices ranging from 45 to 120f. A popular favourite is the mini-bouillabaisse at 110f.

For local colour in bars and cafés, try the **Caves Ricord** at 2 rue Neuve – they serve pizzas and other snacks, and wine by the glass, in an old-fashioned atmosphere of slow decay. Otherwise, there is a Dutch bar, **Le Klomp** (6 rue Mascoinat), which has a lot of British customers and is always crowded and noisy, and there are even English and Irish pubs.

More decorous surroundings can be found in the bars of the major hotels – although the drinks are inevitably more expensive. The piano bar has been discovered by the Côte d'Azur and these have sprung up, mushroom-like, everywhere. The **Bar Terrasse du Phoenix** at 405 promenade des Anglais, the **Iguane Café** at 5 quai Deux Emmanuel has live salsa music, and **Le Mississippi** at 5 promenade des Anglais are among the most popular places.

La Taverne du Château
(R)S *42 r. Droite 93.62.37.73 No credit cards*

Madame Bonifassi is hospitable and efficient but at lunchtime, the place is hectic. It's a little easier in the evenings. You need to reserve.

On a narrow street (no cars) in the oldest part of Old Nice, this is one of the great 'character' restaurants of the city, where the locals meet for their anis at the long zinc bar. Ropes of garlic, gourds and drying peppers hang from the ceiling.

Now to the food – of which there is an absolutely bewildering selection. There are a dozen kinds of pasta, two dozen meat dishes, a dozen fish dishes and no matter how you put it together, you won't spend over 100f. The beignets of sardines, the gnocchi au pistou, the crispy friture (like whitebait) and the magnificent osso bucco can be recommended. A simple but substantial set menu costs 74f.

You can't fail to enjoy an evening here at La Taverne.

MAP 5E   **PÉGOMAS** 06580 (Alpes-Maritimes). 7 km W of Mougins; 11 km NW of Cannes

---

The area is heavily wooded with pine trees; the name of the village comes from the resin which is extracted from the pine nuts. Pégomas is a nondescript village and there's nothing to see. So why is it in this book?

Many visitors like to stay in a small, casual, unassuming hotel in a quiet, rustic atmosphere and still be able to drive down to the coast when and if they wish. Pégomas is ideal for this purpose, being only eleven kilometres from Cannes. It has several places to stay.

➤ **Hôtel Le Bosquet**
(H)S   *83.42.22.87   Cl. 1/11–1/12*

You know when you're approaching Le Bosquet by the smell. No, not of Provençal garlicky cooking – there is no restaurant here – but of jasmine, roses, lavender and all the other sweetly smelling plants that the original owner, a parfumier from Grasse, chose for his own garden. There's a rich fruity smell too in the autumn when the plums and apricots drop from the trees that line the drive to the house.

Simone Bernardi, the lovely smiling granny who runs this very special hotel with her husband Jean-Pierre, turns the fruit into jams, which feature in the breakfasts served on the terrace to those guests who do not want to cook for themselves in the cuisinettes with which seven of the eighteen rooms are furnished. It's all very much a family concern, with daughter Chantal and her daughter Romain helping out, but it's Simone who is the benign driving force.

The simple two-storey building, set amid the orchards that Jean-Pierre has planted, is blissfully peaceful after the hurly-burly of the coast, a mere hop and a skip away, and the atmosphere of friendly casualness will, I am sure, win many faithful friends. The one problem is getting a booking, since I am not the only one who has loved Le Bosquet.

The value – 230–280f, or 300–370f for a room with mini-kitchen – is extraordinary in this area, and together with the welcome, earns the bosky Bosquet an undoubted arrow.

Les Jasmins
(HR)S   *92.42.22.94   Cl. 1/10–30/3   V, EC*

M. Latour has fourteen rooms here, priced reasonably at 180–270f, while the full pension at 240–320f is a very good deal, with way-above-average cooking. The restaurant also serves an adequate meal at 65f, but in other menus, ranging up to 200f, you will find some surprisingly sophisticated dishes.

MAP 3G   **PEILLE** [PV] 06440 (Alpes-Maritimes). 10 km N of Monaco

Peille prides itself on being the birthplace of Pertinax, Emperor of Rome, in AD 193, even though he only reigned for three months before being assassinated for his democratic reforms. The inhabitants of the village have long had a reputation for being independent – the whole village has been excommunicated several times for refusing to pay taxes imposed by the bishop.

Despite its population today of nearly 2,000, Peille has lost none of its mediaeval character. It sits at 630 metres' altitude on top of a mountain – very much a perched village although it is readily accessible by the D 53 from Monaco.

The ruins of the old Lascaris château sit high above it and ancient houses straggle out and around, while others are scattered down the mountain slopes.

The rue St-Sébastien is lined with historical buildings – the Palais de la Gabelle, the place du Mont Agel with its delightful 14th-century fountain, and the Palais du Juge Mage, the former seat of the Counts of Provence. One of the entrances still has the original date inscribed above it – 1149.

See the old church of Peille, 12th century but with a baptismal font dating back to the 4th century, and the single nave to the 7th century. Above one altar are 16th-century wood panels depicting the Rosary.

Fêtes: *1 January:* Festival de la Pomme Fleurie. *End July:* Fête de Ste Anne-de-la-Grave-de-Peille. *First Sunday in August:* Feast of Wheat and Lavender. *15 August:* Feast of the Assumption. *First Sunday in September:* Feast of the Nativity (known locally as Festin des Baguettes).

Peille is considered to be the ideal starting point for three excursions: to Les Banquettes Pass, 741 metres' altitude, from which one can see Menton and Castillon; to St-Sébastien Pass, 754 metres' altitude, and to Col de la Madone, 927 metres' altitude, a hair-raising drive from Peille to Ste-Agnès.

Hôtel Belvédère
(HR)S   *93.79.90.45   Cl. Mon.; 1–25/12*

Most visitors stay at nearby Peillon, which is better provided with hotels, but there are five rooms in this small and rustic establishment, more a restaurant than a hotel. They are priced at 140–260f.

Menus at 70–150f are well-cooked and nicely presented using local products and M. Beauseigneur rigidly supervises all the activities.

Restaurant Cauvin
(R)M *pl. Carnot 93.79.90.41*

At least a couple of generations of the same family has run the Cauvin, so honour is at stake and you will always find good food.

Help yourself to mountains of hors d'oeuvres, which will include country pâtés, sausages, pickled fish, vegetables and an immense array of salads. Restraint is advisable, as next come home-made ravioli, and then a main course of something like gigot of lamb with mounds of frites and beignets of aubergines or courgettes or whatever else is in the garden. Then there is salad, and a cheese selection, followed by home-made fruit pies.

Clearly you will not go hungry and throughout you can also enjoy the view from the dining-room windows. Menus are 90 and 140f (140f only on Sunday).

MAP 3G   **PEILLON** [PV] 06440 (Alpes-Maritimes). 19 km NE of Nice

---

A strong contender for the title of 'prettiest perched village in Provence'. The name of Peillon is the diminutive of Peille, the neighbouring village from which it was separated in the 13th century. It is said today that not one more house can be built in Peillon – there just isn't space, even for one!

A lot of work has been done to restore the village but it retains its mediaeval charm. For instance, there is only one gate into the village and it is carefully closed every evening with heavy iron bars.

Park by the shaded square and walk up the rest of the way. You will find Peillon to be as mediaeval a village as any you have seen and history oozes out of the ancient stones. The crooked stairways zigzag their way through arches and round abrupt corners, always climbing, always difficult, as they wind up to the 16th-century church (a little disappointing although it was built on the site of a 12th-century edifice).

Just off the square is the 7th-century Chapelle des Pénitents-Blancs. The wooden altarpiece also dates from the 7th century and there are some 16th-century frescos, although more magnificent ones are to be found in other churches in the region.

The Fête Patronale in August is a colourful festival.

➤ **Auberge de la Madone**
(HR)M *93.79.91.17 Cl. Wed.; 29/5–5/6; 15/10–15/12   No credit cards*

Popular for many years, the Auberge is run by Christian Millo and his family who have created a friendly atmosphere here. The seventeen rooms range from 380–580f and those at the higher end of the range have large balconies. There is a terrace for outdoor eating and the view is terrific.

M. Millot likes to make ample use of Provençal herbs. The cooking is good and the products well-chosen. I have specially enjoyed the quails in grapes and on another occasion the tournedos with red peppers. Menus are at 120f and 190f. Demi-pension is 400–540f, and, with such good food, this is a very attractive price.

MAP 2E **PIERLAS** pv 06260 (Alpes-Maritimes). 73 km NW of Nice

---

Perched villages you may have seen, but you haven't seen any like this one. It is completely and thoroughly perched on top of a solitary mountain peak – so solitary that there is hardly any of the population remaining. The few several-storeyed houses that are here are occupied only on weekends so that the effect is usually that of an utterly deserted village.

Adding to the isolation is the twisting, turning, narrow D 428 which is the only approach road to Pierlas. It is a road of hairpin bends and dangerous corners which has led to many a driver giving up in dismay and turning away to find an easier village.

The only entrance to Pierlas is through a small tunnel, which leads out on to a tiny empty square. There is really nothing to see here and nothing to justify the terrifying approach – nothing except the ghostly atmosphere which will raise the hackles on your neck and have you glancing over your shoulder. Was that just a bird? Did that shadow move? Recommended only for those with a taste for the bizarre.

MAP 7C **PORT GRIMAUD** 83310 (Var) 10 km W of St-Tropez; 6 km E of Grimaud

---

'Fake, phoney, retrograde,' said the critics when plans to build a Provençal-style 'fishing village' in the drab approaches to St-Tropez were revealed in 1967. This was an era when Le Corbusier reigned supreme and if a community were going to be devised there was only one way to build it and that was starkly upwards. Architect, yachtsman, François Spoërry thought otherwise and had the courage to see his dream of an assembly of housing, varied in dimensions, colours and especially roof heights, united by its Provençal style, brought to fruition. He saw no reason why fine old materials, beams, roof tiles, wrought iron, planks, salvaged from surrounding countryside should not blend well with new materials. He believed that decorations, like mosaics, lanterns, benches, tiled name-plates, enhanced his buildings and did not detract from them as the unadorned architecture of the time dictated. He took his colours from the Provençal landscape – a natural palette of honey, sand, ochre, rust.

But his houses were not just a pretty face. Inside, the sense of space was brilliantly exploited. All the ugly mechanics of hi-tech deemed necessary for modern living were hidden underground. The outstanding effect is of solidity, longevity, minimum waste of materials – all good peasant precepts.

A sailor himself, his dream village had to be near the water, and every residence must have direct access to it, so that the owner could step directly from his house onto his jetty, onto his boat. He devised a system of curving dredged canals, with fingers of water probing towards each group of dwellings, so that residents could go about their business, to shop or to work, by boat. Cars must be left outside this 'Cité Lucustre' – there is no need for them.

The architectural press continued to ignore this non-event, big financial backers had no faith in its possible success. Spoërry's unwavering confidence in what he was achieving urged him on to find the money himself. All he needed were customers sympathetic to his vision.

The first four-bedroomed houses were ready in 1967 and offered for sale at £8,000. They sold like hot cakes, purchasers backing their own tastes rather than that of the pundits. As the money flowed in, Spoërry was able to build another tranche and another, and competition to buy has never wavered.

The whole site was reclaimed from sand dunes and salt marsh. Old roof tiles were transported from the Drôme, and local craftsmen were brought in to make staircases with treads of acacia, and wrought iron for the balconies which overlook the canals. It is now a sophisticated lagoon village complete with shops, boutiques, banks, restaurants, cafés, a hotel, a post office and even a church. The houses are expensive and no two are alike. It is remarkably well-done and though purists may prefer ancient villages that are genuine, it is certainly worth a browse.

So how do they figure today? A walk around the village, over little hump-backed bridges, along the canal walks, is highly rewarding. The materials have weathered attractively with time. The money is there to maintain them and improve them. The gardens have matured and softened the outlines. After the increasing fret and fumes of the busy coastal road outside, the peacefulness engendered by the car-free zone and the proximity of water comes as a particular joy. A four-bedroomed house would fetch at least £250,000.

The shops and restaurants are a bit disappointing, and I would not recommend eating here, but it is most agreeable to have at least a drink in one of the several cafés overlooking the water, and make an assessment of just how successful was Francois Spoërry's dream.

MAP 3H   **ROQUEBRUNE-CAP-MARTIN** [PV] 06190 (Alpes-Maritimes). 7 km E of Monaco; 5 km W of Menton

---

It's really extraordinary how many different perched villages there are. Many are alike in some respects but you will continually run across yet another which is quite unlike any you have seen before.

Roquebrune is one of these. When seen from afar, it has a

thoroughly ancient and romantic aspect and you wonder what it must be like close at hand. It turns out to be a cheerful little town, neat and trim in its mediaeval splendour. It is a town of stairs and steps. They go straight and they go crooked. Some soar up into dark passageways and are seen no more. Some climb openly up the side of a house and some stand alone, for the place they led to has gone long ago. Some stairs are bleached white by the wind and the sun and the rain, others are green with weeds and others are blackened with time.

Roquebrune seems to have been piled up on itself rather than built, rather as if it were a natural growth of living rock. Its streets twist and turn, dip and rise, seek alleys and doorways, arches and steep cobbled slopes.

As you walk around Roquebrune, you wonder to yourself 'Is anywhere flat?' Yes, there is a place. It is a piazza, a public square called place des Frères. On two sides, the ground falls away down a sheer precipice. There is a café, two hotels, a fountain and a school. Most of the time you will have to park somewhere along the side of the steep approach road and then climb the rest. It's steep but worth the effort.

The old castle (mostly 15th century) stands on top of Roquebrune, its keep the sole surviving example in France of a 10th-century Carolingian stronghold. Wander through its great hall and its many vaulted rooms and up the stairways which ultimately lead to the very summit of the castle. It takes only a minimum amount of imagination to picture which was the guardroom, which was the chamber of justice and which were the ladies' quarters. You will easily identify the dungeons. Visits are unguided so you are free to roam through the castle and speculate at will. It is open 9 a.m. – 12 and 2–7 p.m. in summer, 10 a.m. – 12 and 2–5 p.m. in winter, closed on Fridays.

After centuries of conflict, siege and conquest, the castle, now in ruins, fell into the hands of an Englishman, Sir William Ingram, in 1911. He was a rich tourist who immediately conceived a passion to restore the ruins to their earlier glory and the large signs you will see – 'Ingram Tower' – testify to his efforts. These were enthusiastic but became more and more tasteless and less in keeping with the true style of the times. Fortunately, Ingram was restrained from wreaking too much architectural havoc after vigorous protests from the local community. Happily, he abandoned his 'restoration' and donated the castle to the village.

Today the castle is a vibrantly active part of the life of the community. During July and August, there is something happening almost every day – musical concerts, ballets, pétanque contests, poetry readings, processions, *dégustations*, jumble sales, fancy dress balls, acrobatic competitions – and many of these make use of the castle as a setting.

One organisation which does this quite spectacularly is the Monaco Drama Group who perform Shakespeare in English in the castle grounds annually. It is an unforgettable experience, with the moon illuminating the natural outdoor amphitheatre and the arc of the Mediterranean glittering 'backstage'. Also in early August is

Roquebrune: the old village

the Procession of the Passion, a historical pageant with the participation of 150 local residents as actors.

Roquebrune's most famous visitor was probably Winston Churchill, who loved to paint there, but in the annals of art there is another name that is closely connected with the town – Hans van Meegeren. Driving through the south of France looking for a place to paint, the Dutchman's car broke down in Roquebrune. Staying in a lodging house while it was being repaired, he and his wife saw the Villa Primavera and fell in love with it. His is a fascinating story . . .

Rembrandt has always been the best-known Dutch painter but he produced well over a thousand paintings. Jan Vermeer was less known but as he painted only thirty-six works in his lifetime they were far more valuable. Consider the astonishment of the art world therefore when a thirty-seventh painting was discovered, confirmed as authentic by every expert and sold for $300,000.

When Nazi Germany collapsed in 1945, the fabulous collection of Hermann Goering was found to contain yet another Vermeer. Suspicions were aroused and the whole story then emerged. Hans van Meegeren had painted both these 'other Vermeers' while living in the Villa Primavera in Roquebrune – mainly in order to get revenge on the Dutch art clique which had criticised his early work ('arrogant scum', van Meegeren called them). He received a prison sentence of twelve months but died six weeks after his release.

Hôtel des Deux Frères
(HR)M   *93.28.99.00   Cl. 1/11–7/12*

In the main square – the place des Deux-Frères – you will find the Hôtel des Deux Frères, superbly converted from what was the original village schoolhouse. There are ten rooms, all with bath or shower, priced at 380–490f. The chef spent some time working with Michel Guérard and has built up a strong reputation. Meals about 250f per person, including wine, although the wine list needs improving.

Il Piccolo Mondo
(R)M   *15 r. Grimaldi   93.35.19.93   Cl. Tues.*

On a more or less flat section of cobbled alley – rare here – with tables outside in the summer. The Italian influence is obvious from the name and Tony Minetti is indeed Italian, but he cooked in Jersey for many years. Recommended are the delicious starter of tiny pieces of rabbit, saltimbocca, piccatas and a superb blend of mousse, sorbet and fruits. The menu is 150f, but there is a wide à la carte selection.

La Dame Jeanne
(R)M   *Chemin de Ste Lucie   93.35.10.20   Cl. Sun. p.m.; Mon.; Feb. & Mar.*

Up one of the winding little streets from the square you will find this delightful restaurant, converted from an old house. Claude

Nebbio cooks traditional dishes but adds to them his own original touches. There is a menu at 150f and an à la carte meal will run 200–250f.

Au Grand Inquisiteur
(R)M   *18 r. du Château   93.35.05.37   Cl. Mon.; 1/11–26/12*

Higher up from the square, near to the Château and up a steep stairway where you can't even touch both walls with arms outstretched (unusual in Roquebrune), this is a very popular place with locals and tourists alike. The interior is charming farmhouse style and the service is attentive. Menus at 125 and 205f are excellent value.

MAP 3H   **SAINTE-AGNÈS** PV 06500 (Alpes-Maritimes). 7 km NW of Menton

The highest village on the entire Mediterranean coast, Ste-Agnès, at 750 metres' altitude, is remarkably only four kilometres from the coast and perched just above the autoroute. A very steep and winding road leads up to it – early guide books used to recommend an hour's ride in a bus to go up and then walking back down in half a day! Modern tourists are not made of such stern stuff, I fear.

The question of why Ste-Agnès came to be up there is easily answered – to place it out of easy reach of the marauding Saracens. The question of how it was placed there is much more difficult to answer. Even an unthinking eagle would not build a home at such a height. When you see Ste-Agnès – from a distance, you consider it ridiculous – when you see it from closer up, you can't quite believe it.

Its layout is just as jumbled and incoherent as any perched village – the same winding cobbled passageways, the same erratic stairways and vaulted arches. It all seems amazing that Ste-Agnès still has a population of about 500.

Behind the village, you must climb the track about a hundred metres of hard going to reach the ruins of the Saracen castle. All of the castles on the Riviera were assaulted by Saracens at one time or another but this one was named for a different reason. The Emir Haroun fell in love with a young and beautiful Provençal girl and renounced the Muslim religion to become a Christian. The main street has been named after him.

Small shops sell leather, pottery and woven goods but not very many because Ste-Agnès is not a well-trodden place on the tourist route. It has an air of unconcern about the world, perhaps because it has remained almost unchanged through so many centuries.

On the last Sunday in August, the Fête Patronale is celebrated with a parade. The Fête des Vallées is on June 24.

You are not likely to want to stay overnight, which is just as well, but if you should be here at lunchtime, you don't have to go back down to the coast.

La Vieille Auberge
(R)S   *93.35.92.02*

Extremely popular with the local residents, which means good food, ample use of regional products and heaped portions. The rabbit with herbs is the dish I can never resist but others have enjoyed the pastas which are prepared with an Italian flair.

There is a large terrace for outdoor dining in the summer and prices are very reasonable 60–110f without wine or 80–130f with wine included.

MAP 4D   **SAINT-CÉZAIRE-SUR-SIAGNE** 06780 (Alpes-Maritimes). 21 km SW of Grasse

Once a fortified Roman village but not really a 'perched village' in the truest sense. The main reason for visiting St-Cézaire is to visit the grottoes, about three kilometres out of the village, which is itself quite ordinary.

The cave entry to the grottoes is steep and descends over 150 feet. Cleverly illuminated, the stalactites and stalagmites are vivid red in the chalk. Open 1 March to 31 May and all October, afternoons only.

Just outside the village too are several megaliths and burial mounds. These date from about 2000 BC – the Bronze Age – and many bracelets, rings, necklaces and bangles of bronze have been found.

Roman wells, for the use of the Eighth Legion, are just outside the village too – Les Puits de la Vierge (the Wells of the Virgin), they are called locally. These still contain water and have done so ever since they were ordered to be dug by the Legion's commander, Julius Caesar. The village is named after him.

La Petite Auberge
(HR)S   *93.60.26.60   Cl. 15/12–15/1   V*

There are a great many places to eat and stay within a reasonable range of St-Cézaire so La Petite Auberge has had to keep up its standards in order to compete. M. Philoppoteaux has only six rooms but they are priced at 90–145f; demi-pension is 158f and full pension is a very good deal at 205f. Non-residents eat here too – very satisfying meals at 45, 70, 90, or 145f.

MAP 4G   **SAINT-JEAN-CAP-FERRAT** 06230 (Alpes-Maritimes). 10 km E of Nice

It's a long peninsula, sticking out three kilometres into the Mediterranean. At the tip is Cap Ferrat, while St-Jean is the active area round the port.

The walk down the west coast (no cars allowed) is one of the world's most beautiful promenades (about two kilometres) but you can drive around most of the peninsula and make a mini-circuit. It's all a little disappointing, because St-Jean-Cap-Ferrat is the most prestigious residential area on the whole Côte d'Azur but the seclusion of the luxurious villas behind their electric gates, towering walls and armed guards does not exactly shout 'Welcome, tourists!' and you drive on because there is not much else you can do or see other than the occasional tantalising glimpse of the blue sea.

Famous names have owned many of the villas, including Somerset Maugham, David Niven and Count Agnelli, founder of the Fiat empire. The coastline is almost entirely rocky so there is only the rare minuscule beach – only two or three bodies wide. Parking is not possible, or very difficult in most places.

The neighbourhood of the port is the nearest thing to a thaw in the atmosphere. Nearly a thousand boats bob at anchor – but only very, very gently for it's a tightly enclosed port. There are several shops, restaurants, boutiques and cafés, and it's a popular place for a stroll. If you feel really energetic you can follow the path along the coast out past Paloma Beach (private) and out to Point Saint-Hospice where stands the Chapelle Saint-Hospice, built in the 17th century.

This commemorates the saint who came here with a handful of followers in AD 560 to establish an outpost of the Christian religion. Hospice (or Auspicius) was a man with the gift of prophecy and the power of working miracles. When he predicted the invasion of the cape by the savage Lombards, he sent his converts to seek safety in the hills while he shut himself up in an old deserted tower. The barbarian Lombards who found him there presumed him to be guarding a valuable treasure, but when one of them raised his weapon to strike down Hospice, his arm withered in the air. The other Lombards shrank away, terrified, when Hospice touched the arm and said a prayer. The arm was at once restored to normal and the Lombards fell on their knees and asked to be baptised on the spot.

Saint Hospice continued to live in the tower as a hermit and some remains of the Tower of the Withered Arm – as it came to be known – were visible until recently but were not preserved, and its present whereabouts is uncertain.

Nearby is the 40-foot statue of the Black Virgin. This statue was erected in the 19th century and caused considerable speculation. Black Madonnas have been revered by generations of pilgrims as far back as the pagan tribes of Western Europe and throughout the early days of Christianity. They are thought to be involved with mysterious currents of energy (sometimes called telluric currents). Lines of telluric power have been plotted all over France and include one east–west line which runs directly through the Cap Ferrat area, thus connecting it with the Black Madonna in the church of Les Saintes-Maries-de-la-Mer in Provence.

One thing the peninsula of Cap Ferrat does have is a variety of walks, even if you do have to be careful to avoid trespassing on private property. One such walk is to the old lighthouse, which is 70 metres high. Views from the top are stupendous. Open 9.30 a.m.–12 and 2–7 p.m. in summer, 9.30 a.m.–12 and 2–4 p.m. in winter.

There is a zoological garden, a butterfly house and exotic gardens with over twenty thousand kinds of plant.

One of the sights on the peninsula which should be viewed is the Villa Ephrussi de Rothschild. It was built by the Baroness de Rothschild in 1912 and is an exquisite pink and white structure surrounded by fifteen acres of French and Japanese gardens. It houses an extraordinary collection of 14th- to 18th-century paintings, tapestries, sculpture, furniture, porcelains and wrought-iron work. Many famous artists are represented: Renoir, Sisley and Monet among the painters, a ceiling by Tiepolo, vases from Sèvres, d'Enghien tapestries and Dresden porcelain. Check the times carefully because several changes have been made recently and sometimes the hours for the museum do not coincide with those for the gardens. The latest advised hours are: open every day 2–6 p.m. (except Monday) and 3–7 p.m. in July and August. Closed November.

Fêtes: *February:* St Valentine's Day Masked Ball. *April:* Children's Carnival. *May:* Naval Battle of the Flowers. *June:* Feast of St Jean. *August:* Venetian Festival.

If you go along with the view that the great hotels of the Riviera are landmarks of historical interest, deserving of a visit just as much as a museum, you will certainly want to take a look at the Hôtel Bel Air – a sumptuous palace set in fourteen acres of gardens teeming with exotic flowers and terraces, with glorious views out to sea. Nothing has been spared to achieve the utmost in luxury and the room prices reflect this: 1,600–6,700f per night. Air-conditioning, heated swimming pool, tennis courts, valet parking, impeccable service and a restaurant ranking among the very best – what more could a hotel guest ask?

Well, if the guest asks more down-to-earth prices, there are a few places, but be aware that Cap Ferrat hotels are mainly for recluses, honeymooners or walkers. Tranquillity is the watchword here.

Le Panoramic

(H)M   *av. Albert I   93.76.00.37   Cl. 10/11–28/1   P.   All credit cards*

There is a stunning view of the port from many of the twenty rooms of this smart and very well-run hotel. Prices are from 465–635f (all doubles, with bath, private loggia and TV).

Private parking is available and the hotel is only a few minutes' walk from the sea. No restaurant.

Brise Marine

(HR)M   *av. Jean Mermoz   93.76.04.36   Cl. 1/11–1/2*

A large garden and very pleasing terraces. The rooms are spacious and comfortable, many with sea views, four are air-conditioned. Prices range from 450 to 600f; demi-pension is obligatory in season. M. and Mme Maîtrehenry will make you feel very much at home here.

Looking for inexpensive places to stay on Cap Ferrat is a difficult business. There are very few and they fill up rapidly – probably booked the year before. Two of these are:

La Bastide
(H)S (R)M *av. Albert I   93.01.32.86*

Twelve rooms at 160–230f. Its restaurant is large but always packed, especially at weekends – the food is very good; menus are at 160f.

Bagatelle
(H)S *av. Sauvan   93.01.32.86*

This has rooms at 240–320f, including breakfast.

MAP 4F   **SAINT-JEANNET** 06640 (Alpes-Maritimes). 4 km NE of Vence

---

Take the D 2210 from Vence. There are signs here of over a million years of habitation – first prehistoric man, then Ligurians, Greeks, Celts, Romans, and Goths. All of these lived in the grottoes or used them for storage.

Today it is a busy village, with about 2,000 people, and if chapels are your interest, St-Jeannet is the village for you – it has more than you can see in one day. See particularly the chapels of St Jean-Baptiste, Ste Pétronille, St Bernardin and Notre-Dame, all built between the 15th and 17th centuries.

The village retains its mediaeval aspect and the place de l'Église typifies this with its 17th-century church and the fountain in front.

Fêtes. St-Jeannet is one of the most festival-minded villages in the South of France, and it is rare to visit it without finding a festival either going on or being prepared – *February:* Fête des Bouffets, a pre-Lenten event, with the participants wearing traditional costumes. *May:* Fête des Courcoussin. *20 May:* Fête de St Bernardin-du-Sienne. *Beginning of June:* Fête de Ste Pétronille. *End of June:* Fête de St Jean. *25 June:* Fête de St Éloi – the feast day of the patron saint of blacksmiths. Mules were extremely important to the villages in the past, being the only means of supply and transport, and on this day they are blessed and there are mule races. *13 July*: la Descente du Baou – a torchlight procession down the Baou, the mountain which dominates the village. *Last Sunday in August* (till the Wednesday): Fête de St Jean-Baptiste, the patron saint of the village; a statue of the saint is carried in procession, accompanied by a drum and fife band. *25 November:* Fête de St Jean-Baptiste, the patron saint of the village; a statue of the saint is carried in procession, accompanied by a drum and fife band. *25 November:* Fête de Ste Catherine, the patron saint of young men and women. She was a brilliant scholar who, for converting a group of heathen philosophers, was burned along with them.

Hôtel Sainte-Barbe
(HR)S *93.24.94.38 Cl. Tues.; Feb. AE, V*

There are only six rooms here, but they are quite large and nicely furnished. M. Priori has been running this place long enough to have a regular following, of both visitors to the hotel and locals in the restaurant.

Rooms are 100–140f, or 220–240f for demi-pension. Three substantial courses are served from menus at 80–120f.

An alternative hotel-restaurant is the **Auberge de St-Jeannet** (93.24.90.06), and two other reliable eating-places are the **Chante-Grill** (93.24.90.63) and the cheerful though sometimes noisy **Auberge d'Antoine**.

MAP 4F **SAINT-LAURENT-DU-VAR** 06700 (Alpes-Maritimes). 10 km W of Nice

---

Ⓜ *Sat.*

St Laurent is located on the coast, adjacent to Nice airport. It is notable for three things – its 'Cap 3000' shopping city; its nautical facilities, and its port.

The 'Cap 3000' shopping centre is one of the largest in Europe. Its three levels contain every conceivable kind of shop, store and boutique, and the entire building is spacious, air-conditioned, superbly modern and functional. Parking for 3,500 cars is all around the building, which makes access easy. Among the names represented in the shops are Georges Rech, Charles Jourdan, Louis Féraud, Benetton, Manoukian, Kenzo and Cartier. There are banks, insurers, restaurants, cafés, bars, pharmacies, cleaners, hairdressers, shoe-repairers and an enormous supermarket selling high-quality foods and delicatessen products.

Adjoining the shopping centre are streets of purpose-built stores selling furniture, musical instruments and hi-fi, hotels, car-rentals (half the price of the identical car at the airport) and a petrol station selling at 7 or 8 per cent off the cheapest price you'll see by the roadside.

The nautical facilities provide boats and yachts, water-scooters, water-skis, scuba outfits and everything else marine; you can rent by the hour, day or week (see p. 40). There is a sailing school which caters to all levels.

The port is a fascinating place to walk around, as are all ports. Most of the boats are private but there are few of the larger sizes here, so the mutual sport of boat-people looking at port-strollers and vice-versa is a little less rewarding. The principal attraction of St-Laurent's pleasure port is that it is lined with multi-national restaurants, interspersed with the occasional boutique and yacht-supply store – but mainly restaurants.

This makes it an ideal place to eat if you haven't booked, for you can simply stroll along and pick a place. All look out at the boats, so all have an equally good view. The menus are posted outside so

St-Laurent-du-Var

you can. check prices and offerings and you can have a look at what's on the plates of the people already eating. All have outdoor seating as well as indoor.

Le Moorea
(R)M   *93.31.05.05*

This is a huge place, but even at its busiest (which is always during the season), the service is good. The fish specialities cover every kind of seafood but a particularly good bargain is the three-course meal, of which the main course is the catch of the day, usually pageot (daurade), at 110f. Lobsters, oysters and all shellfish all year round. The coquilles St-Jacques with fresh pasta can be recommended and so can the paella.

Bistro des Halles
(R)M

> Located on a corner, which is unusual here, where all the other
> places are side by side. Tables are far apart which gives a remarkably
> spacious feel. Food is beef, any kind, every kind. Allow 120f.

Yang Tseu Kiang
(R)M   *93.31.92.82*

> The original place in Nice was so popular that this one was
> opened. It serves the same menu, which is superior Chinese cooking.
> The Yang Tseu Kiang is a little pricier than most Oriental
> restaurants but well worth the extra.
>
> The food and the cooking are more to the English and American
> taste than most Oriental restaurants in France. The Dégustation
> Menu at 145f is outstanding value. You may have the Pekinese
> ravioli, then sizzling beef, followed by coquilles St Jacques in
> spicy sauce with rice, and finally an array of exotic fruits. There are,
> however, four other choices for each course. The Gastronomic
> Menu at 175f is an even grander meal. Menus are in English if you
> wish and all the friendly staff speak English. This can be a real
> help in a Chinese restaurant where translations from Chinese into
> French and then into English can have some hilarious and
> misleading results.

La Santana
(R)M   *93.07.02.24*

> Spanish influence on French food. A glass of sangria establishes
> the atmosphere, then the menu at 145f might include dishes such as
> oysters or marinated salmon, followed by duck in green pepper
> sauce, then cheese then dessert. The 190f menu is similar but more
> elaborate. Some unusual specialities appear from time to time on
> the latter such as medallions of lotte in vanilla sauce. A wide range
> of meat dishes is also available and La Santana's own version of
> bouillabaisse may be ordered in advance.

Osaka
(R)M   *93.14.00.11*

> Obviously Japanese, specialities include *neguma* (chicken with
> onions) at 38f, *teba* (chicken wings) at 50f and *camo* (duck) at 50f.
> Charcoal-grilled dishes and meat *en brochette* are featured, while
> complete menus are offered at 73, 90 and 155f.

L'Entrecôte
(R)M

> Open seven days a week. A choice of starters, followed by a large
> T-bone steak is 94f but the best bet in my opinion is the entrecôte
> at 81f.

La Romana
(R)S – M   *93.07.33.36*

> No matter what you fancy or how hungry you are, you will be
> satisfied here. There is a choice of crêpes, pizzas, pastas, salads,
> meat, fish, grills and ices. Simple menus at 59f or, with a T-bone steak
> as the main course, at 90f. The gambas at 95f are a meal in
> themselves.

Mei Hua
(R)S – M   *93.07.31.84*

> Vietnamese and Chinese food. Try the duck with ginger at 56f and
> the scallops with hot sauce at 70f. Lobster is a bargain at 100f, and
> the Peking duck at 260f for two people is excellent.

Borsalino
(R)S – M   *93.07.41.52*

> Italian menus at 60f or 100f. Saltimbocca Romana costs 62f, and
> the veal escalope bocconcini 82f.

Les Jardins d'Agadir
(R)S – M

> Moroccan food, especially the traditional Arab dishes. Seven
> different kinds of couscous ranging from the simplest (Badaoui) at
> 65f to the Royal (which contains lamb and chicken) at 120f. you
> can also choose from six kinds of tadjine at 65f to 85f (containing
> fish or prunes and almonds).

Santa Lucia
(R)S – M   *93.14.00.33*

> A fast grill place, small and busy. There is a Plat du Jour every
> day at 55f, or a three-course meal at 100f, or the same meal based
> on fresh seafood at 140f. Drink wine by the *pichet* here – the
> bottles are priced a little high.

Le Grill de la Mer
(R)S – M   *93.31.03.15*

> Fish specialities, including the day's catch. Menus at 50, 90 and
> 105f.

> There are more restaurants but if you can't find something to please
> you from the list above – and all within a pleasant stroll of a few
> minutes – then you are very hard to please indeed!

Les Trois Sauces
(R)S – M   *93.14.37.37*

A steak house offering every conceivable kind of beef cooked in
every way you can think of. Prices range from 65 to 115f – the latter
is for a *filet mignon*. All dishes accompanied by french fries and a
vegetable.

Le Lotus Bleu
(R)S – M   *93.14.90.02*

An extensive selection of Oriental food here. On the Chinese and
Vietnamese menu, the duck with lychees at 50f, and the pork sautéed
with bamboo shoots at 40f are tasty and good value. On the Thai
menu, try the stuffed crab at 55f, while if you like mild curries, the
Thai curried duck at 52f is very good. There is a choice of Tim
Sum starters.

Palma's
(R)S

Also known as the Palais de la Bière, with beer from twenty
countries as well as cocktails, crêpes and ices.

Sirtaki
R(S)   *93.07.85.41*

A tiny place, serving Greek and Armenian food. The Quelor Koefte
(meatballs in herbs) is 35f and the Dolma (stuffed vine leaves) is 27f.
For the main course, try the kebabs at 58f, moussaka at 59f, or *satsivi*
(chicken with walnuts) at 50f.

Crep's Show
(R)S

Something of an oddity here – a crêperie and a fast-service
Mexican restaurant combined in one. The Mexican dishes are simple
ones such as enchiladas at 40f and chilli con carne at 65f.

Le Marbella
(R)S   *93.07.69.74*

A Spanish flavour, but serving some French dishes too. Tapas to
start in the traditional Spanish style and an authentic paella. Plat du
Jour at 38f and three-course menu at 60f. The light blue and white
décor is fresh and cheerful and very Mediterranean.

La Pierrade
(R)S

Tourist menu at 56f, and a gastronomic menu at 98f. The best bet
is La Pierrade special consisting of loup de mer, salmon, coquilles
St-Jacques and shrimp at 95f.

Le Maldive
(R)S *93.07.30.57*

>   This is a bistro, a cheaper faster version of Le Moorea nearby.
>   Sparkling décor with some eye-catching 'window-view' paintings to
>   convey an impression of size. Menus at 85f.

U Culombu
(R)S *93.31.92.93*

>   Corsican food – not seen too often, though it is only slightly
>   different from French. Salads include a rarely seen seafood one
>   containing squid, scampi and mussels in a light cream sauce
>   flavoured with raspberry at 47f. Where else have you seen a dish
>   like that! Numerous pizzas are offered, including one with squid
>   and one with avocado.
>   Main dishes may be magret de canard, Corsican style, at 90f, or
>   escalope of veal with Roquefort at 75f. Corsican wine at 60f a
>   bottle is an extremely good buy.

MAP 1F   **SAINT-MARTIN-VÉSUBIE** 06450 (Alpes-Maritimes). 65 km N of Nice

---

Ⓜ *Daily*

>   There is a strong Swiss feel to this popular summer mountain resort,
>   which is at 960 metres' altitude. St-Martin is, however, easily accessible
>   from Nice. You drive up the N 202 from the coast, west of Nice
>   airport, then take the D 2565 up the Gorges de la Vésubie, a very
>   thrilling road with the river rushing by and sheer cliffs rising on both
>   sides.
>   The Alpine houses, with wooden balconies, in the village and the
>   chalets scattered in the hills around it add to the Swiss flavour.
>   The village is ringed by peaks, many of them over 3,000 metres high.
>   Water from the local springs is claimed to be purer than that at
>   Évian – taste some for yourself from the fountain in the middle of
>   the village on the Allée de Verdun. The analysis is listed there too.
>   The rue du Docteur-Cagnoli is an unusual sight with a channel
>   down the centre of the street carrying swiftly running water from
>   the melting snows. The Porte Sainte-Anne is the only survivor of the
>   four gates which formerly gave access to the village. By the main
>   square, the place Félix Faure, are the Chapel of the White Penitents
>   and the Chapel of the Black Penitents. Alleys and stairways pass ancient
>   houses and go through dark tunnels in the typically mediaeval
>   setting.
>   The 17th-century Church of the Assumption at the lower end of
>   the village contains many treasures, the most important being the
>   statue of the Madone de Fenestre, carved from Lebanon cedar,
>   according to legend, by Luke the Apostle himself. It is brought out
>   for a pilgrimage twice a year. This goes to the Sanctuary of the
>   Madonna about twelve kilometres east of St-Martin every 15
>   August and 8 September.

It is as a centre of leisure activities that St-Martin is best known. There are nearly a hundred kilometres of sign-posted walks – many of them leading to mountain lakes and peaks. La Boréon, on the north side of the village of St-Martin is the best starting point. There is also downhill skiing in winter from the Colmiane station, eight kilometres from the village, where there is one chair-lift and seven ski-tows, and cross-country skiing, with a refuge hut at La Boréon. For the really adventurous, there is ski touring across the high Alpine route from Lake Geneva to the Mediterranean.

St-Martin's position makes it the most popular place for trips into the National Park of the Mercantour. This covers 270 square miles of gorgeous mountains and valleys, where eagles, kestrels, ptarmigans, ibex, wild sheep, marmots, deer, wild boar and chamois can be seen wild, protected from hunters and guns; dogs, radios, fires and camping are all prohibited. More than 1,500 species of flowers can be seen, so that the mountain's slopes are an unforgettable sight in May and June.

Fêtes. St-Martin is a festival-minded village – *February:* Mardi Gras Carnival and Masked Ball. *Pentecost:* Artisan Fair. *May:* Feast of the Annunciation; procession between the chapels. *June:* Feast of St Jean. *July:* Beer festival at Lac Boréon. *15 August:* Pilgrimage (see above). *8 September:* Pilgrimage (see above). *First Sunday in September:* Fête de la Frairie. *8 December:* Fête de l'Immaculée. *Christmas Day:* Midnight Mass.

Edward's Park Hotel and La Châtaigneraie
(HR)M   *93.03.21.22   Cl. Sept.–Jan.   CB*

The double-barrelled name comes from the fact that this used to be two separate hotels. Now that they are one, they share the same dining-room and are in a wooded park right on the main street and in the centre of the village.

The thirty-five rooms are spread over three storeys, all have bath or shower and some have balconies. It's a little austere but not bad value for 385–440f.

Auberge Saint-Pierre
(HR)M–L   *93.03.30.40   Cl. end Sept.–beginning May   EC, CB*

Almost a kilometre out of St-Martin on the road going south towards Nice. Most visitors prefer it to the other hotels in St-Martin. The twenty-four rooms have bath or shower, and the location on the edge of the valley offers fine mountain views. Prices range from 220–270f – good value for money.

La Treille
(R)S–M   *r. Dr-Cagnoli   93.03.30.85   Cl. Tues. lunch; Wed.*

Since it was taken over recently by a young couple, Patrick and Marie-Rose Prévoteau, La Treille has become an even more popular eating place than before. The terrace has an attractive view and is shaded by vines in the hot weather.

The menu is surprisingly ambitious but the food is very good and the service efficient and smiling.

At midday only, there is a 78f menu, with terrine of deer, leg of duck in orange sauce or rabbit in mustard sauce. You may have cheese or a selection of desserts, though the latter are ordinary.

Menus at 98f, 138f and 178f offer a more extensive range of dishes. If you are undecided about a starter, M. Prévoteau may well recommend the pâté de foie gras which he makes himself according to a recipe from his native south-west. Main courses which will not disappoint include salmon Bellevue and beef en daube.

Provence wines cost at 55f, 75f and 85f a bottle.

MAP 7D   **SAINTE-MAXIME** 83120 (Var). 23 km W of St-Raphael;
61 km W of Cannes

Sainte-Maxime lies on the north side of the gulf, opposite St-Tropez, giving it one significant advantage over its more glamorous and much better known neighbour – it is sheltered from the mistral and so its season lasts all year long, whereas St-Tropez is dead in winter. For this reason, it is not surprising that it is becoming increasingly popular with tourists, as it is also an excellent place to stay, has more hotels, is cheaper, has more local character and is less frenetic.

When the threat of the Barbary pirates had receded at the end of the 18th century, Ste-Maxime sprang up as a fishing village. Its sheltered position, its fine sandy beach, and later the golf course at nearby Beauvallon, made it a great favourite with British visitors, and it made rapid strides from fishing to tourism. Opulent villas were built as more and more people found it an attractive place to live permanently – on the coast but not busy or noisy.

A slender legend attributes the name of the town to the sister of St-Tropez, and just like her brother, the effigy of Ste Maxime is carried through the streets in a Bravade on the nearest Sunday to 15 May. It is very similar to the Bravades in St-Tropez, though not as popular or animated. They are all explained in the Musée des Traditions Locales, in the tower opposite the port. The Musée du Phonographe et de la Musique Mécanique on the road to Le Muy has an extraordinary collection of organs, mechanical pianos, music boxes, etc.

Fêtes – *March*: Mardi Gras. *May*: Ste-Maxime (see above). *Late June*: Feast of St Jean, with fireworks and *farandoles*. *7 August*: Feast of St Donat and Country Fair. *September*: Harvest Fair.

Beau Site
(HR)M   *5 blvd des Cistes   94.96.19.63   Cl. end Sept.–Palm Sun.   All credit cards*

One of the best hotels in the area, with thirty-eight recently renovated rooms, a heated swimming pool, tennis and a terrace with beautiful sea views.

The rooms are cheerful and pleasant, and priced at 250–500f. During the season, demi-pension at 240–395f is obligatory.

Hôtel de la Poste
(HR)M   *7 blvd Frédéric Mistral   94.96.18.33   Cl. 25/10–1/4   All credit cards*

Modern, efficient and good value. Twenty-four bright rooms, priced at 290–500f. Demi-pension is obligatory in season at 300–450f. There is a pool, a garden and a terrace.

Royal Bon Repos
(H)S   *r. Aicard   94.96.08.74   Cl. 15/11–15/3*

Simple but comfortable motel, close to the sea. The twenty-three rooms are only 170–290f and have kitchenettes, as there is no restaurant.

Marie-Louise
(HR)S   *94.96.06.05   Open all year   DC, CB*

Located 2 kilometres out of Sainte-Maxime in Guerre-Vieille. Very reasonable and good value for an overnight stop. There are fourteen rooms at 140–265f, and demi-pension is obligatory in season at 260f. Some of the rooms open out on to the sea.

La Croisette
(H)S–M   *2 blvd des Romarins   94.96.17.75   Cl. 13/10–15/3   All credit cards*

Recently renovated and near the beach. The twenty rooms are value for money at 240–330f.

MAP 4F   **SAINT-PAUL-DE-VENCE (SAINT-PAUL)** PV 06570 (Alpes-Maritimes). 20 km N of Nice; 16 km N of Antibes

---

Extremely popular with tourists, this is a hill-top village surrounded by massive ramparts erected in 1537 when St-Paul was the key fortress in the Var frontier defences against the Duke of Savoy who, from his stronghold at Nice, cast covetous eyes to the west.

Many famous painters have lived and worked here – Renoir, Bonnard, Léger, Braque, Dufy, Matisse, Chagall and Picasso among them. They ate and drank in the Colombe d'Or restaurant and when they were unable to pay their bills – which was often – the owner Paul Roux would accept a painting instead. Soon he had accumulated one of the finest private art collections on the Riviera, and one of the most publicised crimes of the 1960s was committed on the night when twenty of the finest paintings were stolen. None of them was insured; they were recovered and still adorn the walls today.

Movie stars have been another group to patronise the Colombe d'Or. From Dirk Bogarde's autobiography *Snakes and Ladders* comes this passage: 'My table at the Colombe d'Or in St-Paul-de-Vence was just across from hers, summer after summer, year after year. We never spoke nor did we ever recognise each other by nod or by smile. Apart from an occasional slow considering look out of those extraordinary eyes, the years passed in total silence. I was left to worship at a discreet distance over the gigot or the loup de mer.' That was Signoret.

If you think such artistic and name-dropping ambience justifies it, a room here will cost you about 1,000f and a meal about 400f but, to keep matters in perspective, the paintings are probably worth at least thirty million francs.

Another way in which you can appreciate the works of art but minimise the cost is to have a drink at the bar. While looking for the toilet and getting lost doing so, you can see the Léger mural on the veranda where lunch is served, the Braque mosaic and the Calder mobile by the pool, the Miró in the lounge, and the walls of the dining-room adorned with a Matisse, a Picasso and a Utrillo.

The principal reason for going to St-Paul though is to visit the Maeght Foundation, just below the village. Even the most hardened non-museum-goers agree that this is exceptional. The intention was to create 'a museum in nature' where monumental works are integrated with buildings and open spaces. Lawns, woods and mosaic-decorated pools swirl in and out among the airy halls, while giant Giacometti sculptures of metal and stone stalk across the landscape. Most of the great artists of the 20th century are here and periodically there are special exhibitions. The book, catalogue, poster and card shop is an ideal place for gifts, and the films in the free cinema are always enjoyable (check the starting times when you go in the museum). The library contains ten thousand volumes, including catalogues of most of the world's important collections, and there is an etching studio and a ceramics studio. Open in summer 10 a.m.–7 p.m. and in winter 10 a.m.–12.30 and 2.30–6.30 p.m. Parking available.

The village is usually crowded. You will probably approach it on the D 6 from Cagnes-sur-Mer (which passes the Maeght), from which you can spot the towering ramparts, which are very photogenic from this angle.

There are no parking lots and you can't drive through the village. Park at the side of the road along with everyone else and then walk. You enter St-Paul by the Porte de Vence, where you will see the Lacan cannon, captured at the Battle of Cérisoles in 1544. Follow the main street and walk on to the fountain, which is simple but elegant and mainly famous because so many artists have painted it – Winston Churchill among them, for it was one of his favourite subjects. The streets are lined with boutiques and shops and stores of all kinds.

The church of the Conversion of St Paul looks ordinary from the outside but the interior is one of the most beautiful in Provence. The sacristy contains a marvellous collection of silver treasures – crucifixes, statuettes and a tabernacle. There is a holy relic – the shoulder-bone of St George - and a painting, said to be by Tintoretto, of St Catherine.

St-Paul is so touristy that, for a hotel, you're better off going to Vence, which is only four kilometres up the road. If you're determined to stay in St-Paul, though:

La Corbeille
(R)L   *838 rte de la Colle   93.32.80.13*

Cyril Mendjisky was formerly with Jo Rostang at La Bonne Auberge in Antibes. He has now taken over what used to be the Résidence des Oliviers and the sumptuous décor of this ancient villa has been adapted with style and taste. The terrace and the gardens are decorated with metal sculptures and mobiles in keeping with the artistic neighbourhood of St-Paul and above the restaurant is an art gallery – Cyril's father is Serge Mendjisky, a very well-known painter.

Cyril believes in traditional Provençal and Niçois cooking and he has gathered around him a formidable team. Luc Bertoche is the chef, Noël Mantel the chef de cuisine and Frederick Nio the pâtissier. Such an extraordinarily beautiful environment and setting merits food of outstanding quality – and it is. The lunchtime menu at 185f is superb value; with, for example, salade de coquilles St-Jacques or ravioli of lobster with coulis of shellfish, croustillant de rougets with ratatouille, and concluding with kiwi soup with mint and vanilla. The Dégustation Menu at 320f may offer pigeon, loup de mer and ris de veau.

For a remarkable combination of food, cooking, service, art, sculpture, architecture and gardens, La Corbeille is very hard to beat.

Le Hameau
(H)M   *93.32.80.24   Cl. 15/11–15/2   All credit cards*

On the D 7 just south of the village, Le Hameau has fourteen rooms at 300–400f and two suites at 600f. All are very pleasantly furnished and there is a garden and terraces. No restaurant but you can have breakfast.

La Marmite
(R)M   *66 r. Grande   93.32.92.49   Cl. Sun. p.m.; Mon. (except July, Aug. and holidays); Oct. 15–30; Dec. 31–Jan. 15   All credit cards*

The four tables on the terrace have spectacular views of the sea and the mountains, and are always in great demand.

M. Chausse is not swayed by the fact that there are few places serving food at reasonable prices around St-Paul and continues to offer good reliable meals in satisfying quantities. Try the veal escalopes with mustard. Menus at 150 and 200f. The wine list is well-chosen and modestly priced.

MAP 6D   **SAINT-RAPHAËL** 83700 (Var). 43 km W of Cannes; 46 km E of St-
Tropez

Ⓜ *Thurs.*

I like it and I have to say that right up front because a lot of people
don't. Their main objections are its lack of character (whereas I
think it's quiet, uncrowded and leisurely), and its politics – which I
don't think concern the visitor at all.

By no means can all of St-Raphaël's appearance be blamed on
planners or designers – most of the town's charming old buildings
were destroyed in World War II. Since then, both St-Raphaël and
Fréjus have expanded so much that they run right into each other.
There is much more to see in Fréjus but St-Raphaël is preferable as
a place to stay. Much of its charm lies in the enjoyment of a stroll
around the old port and the Pleasure Port, around the Casino and
along the Promenade. It is seldom overcrowded and beaches
stretch eastward from the Promenade.

St-Raphaël first became known just over a century ago when
Alphonse Karr, editor of *Le Figaro* and a notable character in the literary
world of France, made a home there and used to invite his many
friends in Paris to come and visit him. One of those was Charles
Gounod who liked the area so much that he bought a villa in
neighbouring Boulouris, a residential suburb with lush gardens;
it was while he was living there that he composed his opera *Romeo
and Juliet*.

The harbour is quite active and always full of yachts and pleasure
boats, and the quai Albert I is lined with stores and cafés. Just
west of the old port, the Church of the Templars – built in the 12th
century – is one of the sights to see. It is very simple inside, for it
was constructed as much as a fortress as a church, its location near
the water making it vulnerable to barbarian attacks. Its belfry
served as a watchtower and when the villagers heard the bells ring,
it was not a call to service but a warning to take immediate refuge
in the church. At the side of the church is a Roman milestone which
stood on the Via Aurelia, the Roman road now the RN 7.

The Casino is on the north side of the port. It was built on the site
of a Roman villa and adjacent is the recently added Pleasure Port
to accommodate the overflow from the old port.

Worth a visit is the Musée d'Archéologie Sous-Marine on the place
Carnot. The local waters have yielded many treasures to divers and
most of them are displayed here together with graphic illustrations
of underwater techniques. Open 10 a.m.–12 and 3–6 p.m. from
June to September (closed on Tuesdays) and 11 a.m.–12 and 2–
4 p.m. October to May (closed Sundays).

The golf course at Valescure, just north of St-Raphaël, is famous,
having been built in 1891. Piano bars abound here as in other Riviera
resorts. The one at the Coco Club near the marina is the most
popular.

Markets are usually good entertainment. There is a daily food
market on the place de la République and another at place Victor
Hugo, while place Ortolan has a fish market every day.

Fêtes: *May:* Folklore Festival. *July:* Jazz Festival. *August:* Water Festival.

Golf Hôtel de Valescure
(HR)M *av. Pierre Lermite   94.82.40.31   Cl. 15/11–20/12; 7/1–1/2*
All credit cards

> Probably the best of the fully-equipped hotel-restaurants in St-Raphaël. It sits in extensive park-like grounds and the many facilities include golf, tennis, archery and a swimming-pool.
> There are forty rooms at 440–620f. All are large and airy. Some look out over the golf course. Demi-pension is obligatory in season at 430–630f per person.

La Chêneraie
(HR)M *Near the golf course   94.83.65.03   Cl. Sun. p.m.; Mon.; 1/2–15/3   All credit cards*

> The ten rooms are large and decorated with style and taste. There is a view of the mountains or the sea from the rooms and the ambience is quiet and restful, although it is a pity that seminars are sometimes held here.
> Rooms are 250–470f, demi-pension is obligatory in season at 340–420f.
> The restaurant has a high reputation locally and dining in the terrace is delightful in summer. The menu contains a range of reliable favourites; no great surprises but everything is well-prepared. Menus at 180 and 280f.

Le Provençal
(H)S *197 r. de la Garonne   94.95.01.52   Cl. Jan.   V, EC*

> Almost on the old port, Le Provençal offers good hotel value – twenty-eight nicely furnished rooms at 140–250f. The lounge is small but pleasant and although there is no restaurant, breakfast is served at 30f. There is no parking but a municipal lot is only minutes away.

Hôtel France
(H)S *pl. Gallieni   94.95.17.03   Cl. 1/12–3/1   AE*

> Only a block from the port, this very conveniently situated hotel has twenty-eight rooms at 200f. All are comfortable if minimally equipped. There is no restaurant but breakfast is available at 25f and there are numerous places to eat within easy walking distance.

Pastorel
(R)M *54 r. de la Liberté   94.95.02.36   Cl. 15/4–15/5; Sun. p.m.; Mon.   AE, CB*

> The imaginative menus are popular with both tourists and locals in this old house converted into a fine restaurant. Charles Floccia believes in high-quality products, well prepared, and he manages to avoid over-complication even when preparing such dishes as

gratinée of oysters in champagne sauce, filets of rouget with pistou or any of his other specialities, which make full use of the day's catch.

Menus are 145 and 210f; the wine list is extensive but still contains some reasonably priced bottles.

La Voile d'Or
(R)M *1 blvd Gén. de Gaulle 94.95.17.04   Cl. Tues. p.m.; Wed.; 16/11–21/12*
All credit cards

Fresh fish straight out of the Mediterranean go into the seafood specialities served here which many customers insist is the best restaurant in St-Raphaël.

M. Goupil is one of those restaurateurs who make a real effort to please the customer and the dishes are always excellent – well-prepared, nicely served and reasonable in price.

The bourride served St-Raphaël style is a favourite but all the fish is reliable – loup de mer, rouget, pageot, rascasse and langouste. In the summer, you can sit on the tented terrace looking out to sea otherwise the interior dining-room is air-conditioned. Menus at 140f (weekdays only), 185 and 220f.

La Potinière
(HR)M *In Boulouris 5 km east of St-Raphaël 94.95.21.43   Cl. 4/12–20/1*
All credit cards

In a park of trees and flowers, about ten minutes' walk from the sea, this is a large villa with twenty-nine rooms, all modernised and very comfortable. There is a friendly, clubby atmosphere which is aided by the numerous sporting facilities available and the swimming pool.

There is a lovely outdoor restaurant or you can eat by the pool. Menus at 108, 145 and 195f.

MAP 7D   **SAINT-TROPEZ** 93990 (Var). 75 km W of Cannes; 69 km E of Toulon

Ⓜ *Tues., Sat.*

St-Tropez has a longer and more richly tapestried history than most other towns in the South of France and yet, somehow, that seems to be of little concern. People don't come here for history. They come because Brigitte Bardot made it famous. An inconsequential little fishing village in the 1950s, she turned it into one of the world's most celebrated resorts. She didn't do it alone, of course, but she is still here and still making the headlines, though of a different kind.

Meanwhile . . . back in AD 68, a Christian officer in the Roman Army by the name of Torpes was beheaded by the Emperor Nero for refusing to renounce his faith. His headless body was put into a small boat along with a dog and a cockerel and set adrift on the Arno River. The boat was eventually washed ashore and the place was named St Torpes – later to become St-Tropez.

There had been earlier settlements on the site, perhaps Greeks and certainly Romans but the raids of the Saracens left nothing to history. Deserted in the 14th century due to the Black Plague, it was re-built by families from Genoa who were exempted from all taxes and feudal dues other than the defence of the coast. It enjoyed a sort of autonomy until the 18th century when it became the property of the Bailli de Suffren, the greatest admiral in French history. You will see his statue on the waterfront.

The reason why St-Tropez remained isolated from that time until the 1890s was precisely that – it *was* isolated. There were no roads from anywhere to anywhere and when you are fuming in one of the traffic lines trying to get into St-Tropez, you will remember this and appreciate the difficulty of land access before roads were built for cars.

Guy de Maupassant came here in 1888 but he sailed his yacht in, for there was no other way. A few years later, the Neo-Impressionist painter Paul Signac was sailing his yacht down the coast when bad weather forced him into the little fishing port. He loved it at first sight and had a house built there in 1892. He invited his painter friends from Paris to visit him there – Matisse, Bonnard, Dufy, Derain, Seurat and Vlaminck – and the house soon became a small art community.

The reputation of St-Tropez grew from this time on as a Bohemian centre for artists, not just painters but also sculptors, writers and poets. In the 1930s, Colette bought a house there, and Jean Cocteau, Anaïs Nin, and Baroness Orczy, creator of the Scarlet Pimpernel, came to live and work there.

In 1956 came the turning point for St-Tropez. That was the year that Roger Vadim brought his film crew to St-Tropez to make *And God Created Woman*. It starred Brigitte Bardot and made her world-famous. It also co-starred St-Tropez and made it famous. Elton John, Mick Jagger and Françoise Sagan all bought property here and the boom continues.

The population of 6,000 swells to nearly 90,000 during the summer. Where do they put them all? Well, try to get a room in a hotel or a table at a restaurant, try to get a parking place or try to walk along the quay and you'll know. St-Tropez fills up fuller, faster than any place on the Riviera.

You'll still want to see it and so you should. Avoid July and August and then it won't be too bad. Consider staying outside, as the hotels are expensive. Drive in early.

It all sounds like an awful hassle – and it can be. But be assured that it's worth it. St-Tropez's own mayor describes it as 'a dying village' but there's a lot of life left in it yet, and it really is a place where you can enjoy a day or two.

The first thing you have to do is park. Entering the village from the south, the RN 98 runs along the coast. Follow the signs for 'Port Parking'. Inside the huge lot, drive as far north as you can. Walk north until you reach the 'Vieux Port'.

Here is your No. 1 entertainment, the favourite St-Tropez pastime. Those on foot walk around the port looking at the boats and the people on them. The people on the boats look at the people walking by. It's like a very busy zoo with the animals enjoying watching the people just as much as vice-versa.

The extraordinary thing is the amount of activity on the boats. Go to Beaulieu, Monaco, Cannes, St-Laurent, Antibes – their ports have a completely different ambience. Only the occasional boat is occupied – but in St-Tropez there's always dozens of vessels, all with something going on. Maybe they're sipping cocktails, maybe they're getting ready for a meal, maybe they're eating one, maybe they're watching television, maybe they're wrestling with the equipment and maybe they're phoning their broker in London or Bonn. . . .

You'll see flags of all nations – British, German, Italian, Scandinavian, American and even the occasional long-distance sailor from Hong Kong or Australia or the Caribbean or even South America. Boat watching and people watching – they're both great fun and when you've walked around the port of St-Tropez a couple of times, you'll be hooked.

At the far end of the port, walk through the gap in the old wall and past the old watchtower. You will see a rocky bay, almost empty of vessels and in sharp contrast to the bustle of the old port. Just beyond is the fishing port, nearly as quiet.

Then you'll want to walk back around the port – the scene may well have changed by now. You'll also want to stop and watch the portrait painters and the other port artists. Some are painting the harbour, some the distant hills, some are painting boats and others are painting cats. The Mayor recently took the unprecedented action of withdrawing the licence of about a dozen of these painters, saying that their work was sub-standard. Now that the furore over that has died down there is general agreement that improving the quality of the work on show is no bad thing.

As if to emphasise the point, by the time you have strolled back to the end of the port where all the artists are working, you find yourself in front of the museum of l'Annonciade. This is definitely one of those museums you must see. It's open 10 a.m.–12 and 3–7 p.m. in summer and 10 a.m.–12, 2–6 p.m. out of season. Closed on Tuesdays and all November.

Under the leadership of Paul Signac, the group of artists established in the 1890s had prospered. More and more painters came from Paris for the summer and some of the more representative work of these talented visitors was bought by Georges Grammont, a wealthy manufacturer of submarine cables, who lived in St-Tropez.

When Grammont's collection reached a size where his house could no longer contain it, Paul Signac had the idea of establishing a permanent museum of modern art. He and Grammont selected l'Annonciade, a deconsecrated chapel built in 1540 and Grammont's architect, Louis Süe, converted it into one of the finest museums in Europe.

It is a tiny jewel of a museum. Small but exquisitely arranged and beautifully lit, paintings by Matisse, Bonnard, Dufy, Braque, Vuillard adorn the walls. Two Derains are of particular interest – one is of Waterloo Bridge and the other of Westminster Palace. There are bronzes by Despiau and Maillol.

On a moonlit night in July 1961, a van pulled up outside l'Annonciade and fifty-six of the ninety-seven paintings on display at that time were stolen. Not one of them was insured and their value was said to be 8 million francs on the London art market. It was one of the smoothest and most efficient art thefts in the long history of the Riviera, where valuable art treasures are abundant and where crimes are frequent. There is a happy ending in this particular case – all of the paintings were recovered and are back on the walls. Their recovery is another and fascinating story.

Try to time your visit so that it coincides with the time of the Bravades – these are in mid-May and mid-June. They are historical pageants unique to this part of France. They have their origin as far back as 1558 and if you can be there when one is held, it is an unforgettable experience. Every balcony is decked with red and white flowers. All the shop windows are gaily decorated and everywhere are small busts of Tropez, moustached now and chest bulging with medals. A small boat with a dog and a cockerel accompany the bust and sometimes a Tower of Pisa (duly leaning) to commemorate the birthplace of the saint.

On the first day, the Mayor and all the town dignitaries, political and naval, preside over the opening day ceremonies while a hundred men in 18th-century uniforms line up in the Town Square to the sound of fifes, bugles and drums. The large bust of the saint, moustache, helmet, ribbons, medals and all, is brought from the church and carried at the head of the procession.

The banners wave, the bugles blare, the fifes wail and the drums boom out while the musketeers fire volley after deafening volley until the air is thick with smoke. The troops – the Bravadeurs – wear white trousers, blue tunics and red facings with various headgear. Some wear glasses for there is no forced effort at strict accuracy. Many stop for a quick coffee or pastis when they espy friends at a café, as they march by, then have to run to regain their place in the parade.

The whole effect is casual – like St-Tropez itself – yet this in no way diminishes it as a semi-religious, semi-historical re-enactment. There is no drill or discipline, but then there are no tickets, no admission fees, no stands and no seats. The musketeers seem to have an unlimited amount of ammunition, for shots ring out long after the parade is over and into the night.

The bigger Bravade – in mid-May – lasts three days and is in honour of St Torpes himself, while the lesser one – in mid-June – is only one day. The latter is known as the Fête des Espagnols and celebrates the victory of the French over the Spanish who tried to take the town in 1637.

'The loveliest festival in the world,' says one Provençal historian while another has described it as 'a state of mind'. Folk-dancing groups provide peripheral entertainment and small groups of minstrels add further to the song and dance which accompanies the Bravades.

In the town of St-Tropez, the place des Lices is the centre of activity throughout the year. Shops, cafés, boutiques, bars surround it and games of boules contribute their 'clank, clank' to the buzz of conversation and the rattle of cups and glasses.

From the Place, several streets run towards the port, François Sibilli, Clémenceau, Étienne Berny, Charron and all are lined with shops and boutiques. This used to be Greta Garbo's favourite shopping area when she was staying in the South of France and it's an area that's always busy today.

St-Tropez has no beach but roads lead out to the many good sandy beaches which ring the peninsula. Les Graniers beach is the nearest to the town and a little further is the Baie des Canoubiers, the finest yacht anchorage on this part of the coast. Round the headland is Salins beach, very nice but small and usually crowded. Literary visitors come here to see La Maison de la Treille Muscate, where Colette lived from 1923 to 1936. Further south is Tahiti beach which is more famous, and then south of it is Pampelonne beach where the topless fashion originated. This is the longest stretch (over 5 kilometres) of beach around St-Tropez. It is fully equipped with bars and cafés and can supply mattresses, sun umbrellas, bronzing cream and everything else you need to help you either turn brown or stop you turning brown.

L'Escalet beach, round the point, is small and so is La Briande. Being furthest away from St-Tropez, these two are quieter. There are regular bus and minibus services to these beaches from the place des Lices, and many take advantage of these in order to avoid parking problems.

A final word – St-Tropez is the only Riviera resort which faces north. This means that, busy as it is during the summer, it is almost deserted in the winter. Many, if not most, other resorts have some out-of-season activities, but don't rely on St-Tropez from November to March.

Unless you've booked a room in advance, you will have a hard time finding one in summer. Staying outside is a cheaper alternative anyway, but if you really want to be right in the town, these are the hotels to try for.

Hôtel de la Ponche
(HR)M – L *94.97.02.53   Cl. 15/10 – 1/4*

Located just behind the fishing port, this very popular hotel was once a row of fishermen's cottages. Its nineteen air-conditioned rooms cost 500 – 1,000f. At this establishment, run by Mme Barbier, famous people can often be seen, and the restaurant is also very popular. Fish soup, stuffed rascasse and sea bass are three of the seafood specialities you can expect to see on the menus, which are 120 and 160f.

Hôtel des Palmiers
(H)M *94.97.01.61   Open all year*

Also a few minutes from the old port. No restaurant but twenty-three attractively furnished rooms at 250 – 420f and a pleasant patio and garden.

St-Tropez: Hôtel des Palmiers

Hôtel Le Colombier
(H)M *94.97.05.31 Cl. 15/11–1/3*

Thirteen well-furnished and quiet rooms at 300–420f. Large patio for outdoor breakfasts in summer but no restaurant. Only a few minutes from the old port and almost next to the place des Lices.

Hôtel Lou Cagnard
(H)M *94.97.04.24* P. *Open all year*

A long-established favourite in St-Tropez and one of those places that people come back to year after year. Minutes from the old port and from the place des Lices. Nineteen rooms, each for two

St-Tropez: Hôtel Lou Cagnard

people, priced at 220–380f, plus 32f for breakfast. Like most hotels here, no restaurant as there are so many around. Free parking.

Hôtel de la Méditerranée
(HR)S *94.97.00.44   Cl. 15/10–15/3*

A charming little hotel only a few minutes from the old port. Only thirteen rooms, but they're very reasonably priced at 120–360f. The bar is a busy and popular meeting place.

Hôtel des Chimères
(H)S *94.97.02.90   Cl. 1/12–15/2*

A little south of the old port. No restaurant, but quite acceptable rooms at 150–200f. A delightful garden surrounded by trees and plants.

Strolling around the old port and enjoying looking at the boats, the people and the painters will, along with the sea air, make you hungry, especially at lunchtime. The port is lined with cafés and restaurants and none is really cheap but you can sit and eat and watch the people go by – provided you either reserve or stake out a table promptly at noon.

Four restaurants can be personally recommended. These are: **L'Escale**; **Lei Mouscardins**; **La Marine**; and **Le Girelier**. All serve good fresh seafood and all will run to at least 200f because you're paying for the location. Eating in town is better value but less fun. If you opt for the latter . . .

L'Echalote
(R)M   *35 r. Gén. Allard   94.54.83.26   Open all year*

Mme Calderon runs a reliable and pretty little restaurant where you can always count on good food, well-prepared. You can eat either in the garden or in the neat dining-room. The name of the place comes from one of its dinner specialities – boeuf grillé à l'échalote; other dishes include roast leg of lamb and an apple tart which surpasses most. Menus at 135 and 200f and reasonably priced wines.

Lou Revelen
(R)M   *94.97.06.34   Open all year*

Now under new management, this long-established seafood restaurant is making another bid for a place in the St-Tropez firmament. Early indications are promising – fresh pasta, rascasse, sea bass, lobsters. Situated immediately behind the fishing port. Friendly atmosphere and smiling service.

Les Oliviers
(R)M   *94.97.20.13   CB*

From the quay, walk straight up the street next to the Tourist Bureau and you will find Les Oliviers, very popular locally. M. Laugier is a welcoming host and serves unusual dishes such as turbot in fennel. Menus at 100f are extremely good value.

La Frégate
(R)S – M   *94.97.07.08*

Just one street in from the old port and a handy place to get a satisfying three-course meal for 95f.

Outside St-Tropez but still within a short distance is really the best way to enjoy St-Tropez. There are a number of good choices if you wish to pursue this approach.

Le Mas de Chastelas
(HR)L *94.56.09.11   Hotel closed early Oct.–end April. Rest. closed to non-res. at lunch   All credit cards*

I stayed here for many years, year after year. It was always one of the most delightful hotels in France and particularly welcome in the south, where this kind of place is not easy to find. I am pleased to say that it is just as good as ever – a 17th-century farmhouse converted into a luxury hotel, casual but elegant.

It stands in vineyards just west of St-Tropez and about half a kilometre from the sea and the coast road. Famous personalities from screen, TV, politics and the fashion world stay here, and so do folk like you and me. Neither group has affected the easygoing charm of the Mas.

Service is attentive and personal. There are four tennis courts, a large heated swimming pool, a jacuzzi and pleasant walks. There are frequent events – during one stay here, I returned in the afternoon to find at least fifty Rolls-Royces in front. No, they didn't belong to affluent guests, it was a rally of RR owner-drivers. In some places, such a happening might affect the atmosphere but not here.

The thirty-one rooms are priced at 900–1,400f and all are furnished with antiques and all amenities. Many overlook the pool and the terrace.

Meals are an experience – imaginative and delicious such as sardines baked en croute, red mullet lightly browned in the oven and a superb chocolate cake. An à la carte meal will cost 300–400f but it will be a meal to remember.

Hôtel de Trézain
(H)M–L *94.97.70.08   Cl. 11/11–15/3   All credit cards*

A lovely stucco and tile building in true Provence style, about ten minutes south-west of St-Tropez. An excellent and slightly cheaper alternative to the **Mas** (above) as the rooms are 450–650f. There are seventeen and all have tiled floors, views out on to the patio and garden. Rooms and bathrooms are large. All the buildings surround the pool and there are patios.

Chabichou
(R)M–L *av. du Maréchal Foch   94.54.80.00   Cl. 10/10–10/5   A, CB*

Currently *the* place to eat in St-Tropez but who can predict next year?

Michel Rochedy has created a restaurant which probably offers the best food in the area. Some customers think he is trying too hard while others maintain that he is the best chef on the Riviera.

Chabichou is luxurious. All three dining-rooms have a sophisticated décor making considerable use of paintings and mosaics, and the terrace is the place to eat in summer.

Soup of frogs' legs with lentils, thin escalopes of pan-fried cod, tempura of red mullet, and langoustines flavoured with saffron, pigs' trotters St-Tropez style, and roasted apricots with pistachio nuts are some of the items on the menu and the infinite variety of imaginative dishes goes on. You marvel at how any chef can be so creative and so prolific.

You wouldn't expect it to be cheap but 135f for a three-course meal at lunch is incredibly good value. At dinner, the 320f menu, consisting of six courses, is excellent and there is an even more elaborate selection at 420f.

Not a place for everyday eating but if you're looking for a real taste treat and loads of culinary panache, Chabichou, just south of the old town, is the place.

Chez Madeleine
(R)M *rte de Tahiti 94.97.15.74 Cl. Mon. Nov.–Mar. AE, CB*

A very friendly family ambience here, with fresh seafood delicately and simply prepared. Pageot, rouget, loup . . . all the Mediterranean fish, depending on the day's catch. Nothing fancy but good-quality materials attentively cooked and nicely presented. The menu at 140f is very good value indeed and you probably won't need to look past it. Wines are well selected and reasonably priced.

Pat Fenn comments: I found myself miffed that Peter has written so comprehensively about St-Tropez. I had planned on covering it myself and now he has left me with nothing to say! Just as well, since my familiarity with the resort is far more restricted than his, as we would never dream of visiting it in the summer, when I hear appalling tales of day-long traffic jams. Many readers' holidays will of necessity have to be taken then, and it is just as valuable to be warned off as to be directed towards, so Peter's descriptions of the crowds must be individually judged. Is it worth it?

I think it would be a great pity never to visit the unique little town. It's autumn or spring when we go and, rather contrary to Peter's impression, we have often used it to cheer ourselves up when the more remote coastal strip further west has shut up shop, and we seem to be the only customers in the restaurants. St-Trop's animation has always proved a tonic, and the routine of walking round the harbour, speculating about the boats and their owners, before staking a claim at Sénéquier's has always been a treat. You must sit down with a drink for at least an hour in order to justify the price, but when you consider the variety of entertainment from the eclectic paraders-by, all included, it's a bargain.

Fortified, we buy an expensive T-shirt or two, and set out to examine all the menus and the clientèle before deciding where to donate our many francs. Peter has covered the options expertly.

MAP 4E   **SAINT-VALLIER-DE-THIEY** 06460 (Alpes-Maritimes). 12 km W of Grasse

The N 85 from Grass to Castellane (following the route taken by Napoleon returning from Elba) runs right through St-Vallier-de-Thiey and also through an area which probably contains more stone megaliths and Bronze Age relics than anywhere else in the South of France.

The dolmen known as 'Verdoline' is the most impressive of the dolmens, some said to date from 4500 BC. It can be seen just south of the village and has a chamber measuring 2 metres by 1½ metres. A hundred metres away is the 'Druids' Stone', one of the type known as a fairy chimney, where a softer rock has been eroded by time leaving a cylinder of harder rock exposed.

West of St-Vallier-de-Thiey is the Natural Bridge and the Grottes des Goules. Along the road towards St-Cézaire and on the road west into the valley of the Siagne, many tumuli are visible. Maps are available in the village.

Many visitors flee the coastal resorts in high summer to the exhilarating air of St-Vallier's 730-metre altitude, and to enjoy the festivals for which the village has always been known.

1 June: St Jean. *27 July:* Feast of St Christopher, patron saint of travellers, with an open-air Mass and then a blessing of cars. *1 August:* Second-hand Fair. *23–24 August:* Festival of Holiday-Makers (an unusual one!). *29 August–2 September:* Feast of the patron saint of the village, St Constant, with a procession through St-Vallier and folk-dancing. *November:* Feast of St Hubert. *24 December:* Midnight Mass, with a live baby in the crèche.

Le Relais Impérial
(HR)M   *93.42.60.07   Open all year   All credit cards*

A popular favourite for many years. M. et Mme Pasquier cater very well to the needs of locals and visitors alike. Twenty-four rooms have bath and minibar; three other rooms without bath. Pricing is 120–290f. Homely, satisfying meals at 90–170f.

Hôtel Le Préjoly
(HR)M   *93.42.60.86   Cl. Tues.; 19/12–14/1; 9–20/2   All credit cards*

M. Pallanca is a genial host in this hotel set among trees and vegetation. Over half of the twenty rooms have private terraces, with fine views; 150–350f; demi-pension 250–380f (obligatory in season). Basic but adequate menus at 100f weekdays, and 140 or 190f weekends.

Auberge du Thiey
(HR)M   *93.42.63.26   Cl. 1/11–28/2   All credit cards*

Only thirteen rooms here, usually full, since St-Vallier gets a lot of visitors; 150–350f, all with bath. M. Dufrène provides good meals; menus at 80–120f.

La Bonne Auberge
(HR)S   *On the N 85   93.09.61.08   Cl. 15/12–31/1   AE, CB*

A basic and very modestly priced inn for an overnight stay or a
weekend of hunting tumuli and dolmens. Eleven rooms, with shower
and wash-basin, sharing a toilet on each floor. But then the price
is only 110–170f.

MAP 4D   **SEILLANS** 83440 (Var). 31 km NE of Draguignan

Ⓜ *Daily*

When Adam and Eve were dismissed from the Garden of Eden, Eve
took with her a lemon which she promised to give to the most
beautiful place she found in her travels. Seillans was the place.

That's the legend anyway. The past thousand years of Provence
history are better documented. It was the oldest and the largest
of the groups of villages which also includes Bargemon, Callian,
Fayence, Montauroux and Tourrettes. This prominence led to its
being attacked frequently by the Saracens during the period from
the 9th to the 18th centuries and it was this almost perpetual state
of siege which some say gave Seillans its name: the Provençal word
Seilhanso refers to the large pot in which oil is boiled for the
purpose of anointing the heads of attacking soldiers.

Seillans was one of the very few villages which escaped the Black
Plague. Although the nature of contagion was not understood, it
isolated itself from all contact with the inhabitants of other villages
and refused to admit travellers.

The old château sits on a rise, with ancient houses clustered
around it. Three of the original Roman gates into the village
remain in quite good condition. There is the usual attractive square
with an old fountain. The church of St Léger is 11th century (rebuilt
in the 15th) and among its treasures are copper plates, one of which
shows Adam and Eve before their expulsion and fuels the legend
of the lemon.

Two kilometres south-east of the village is the chapel of Notre-
Dame-de-l'Ormeau, built in 1154 for the purpose of housing a
statue of the Virgin found buried to hide it from the Saracens.

Fêtes: 7 July: Feast of Notre-Dame-des-Selves, with boules contests
and a big aioli. *14 July:* Bastille Day. Parades and a torchlight
procession. *15 July:* Feast of Notre-Dame-de-l'Ormeau. This is a
reference to the elm tree under which the statue of the Virgin was
found. *Last Sunday in July*: Fête of St-Cyr. This lasts for four days,
with concerts, folk-dancing, eating and drinking.

Hôtel des Deux Rocs
(HR)M   *pl. Font d'Amont   94.76.87.32   Cl. 16/10–19/3*

A very pleasant little hotel, with fifteen charmingly decorated
rooms, all with bath or shower.

Madame will make you welcome and you will be able to sip an

apéritif or eat in the square by the two rocks which give the hotel its name, or by the fountain.

Food is good and nicely presented. There are set menus at 150 and 180f, and a good choice of à la carte dishes.

MAP 1H   **TENDE** 06430 (Alpes-Maritimes). 83 km NE of Nice; 57 km N of Menton

---

Tende began its life as a Roman fortress and its inhabitants adopted the Christian religion in AD 353. Centuries of struggle followed, with the various Counts of Ventimiglia battling for possession. In the Middle Ages, it was an important stopping point on the highway between Nice and Savoy. Its stormy history only ended as recently as 1947 when it was ceded by Italy to France.

Today Tende is principally important as a place to stay when visiting the Parc des Merveilles, the Forêt de Turini and the Vallée de la Bévéra – all scenic areas where lemon and orange trees grow in profusion and wildlife can exist without fear of the predatory French hunter.

It is also the last major stop before reaching the Col de Tende, the 2,000-metre pass on the road to Turin (there is also a tunnel).

Tende's mediaeval past has largely lost out to its commercial present as a hub of transportation. It's a bit grim and very busy. Should you want to explore, there's a hard climb up the narrow cobbled alley to the 15th-century Cathedral of Notre-Dame-de-l'Assomption. Its bright red bell-tower contrasts strongly with the roofs of the surrounding houses which are made from a local green slate. Further up the hillside is a sliver of stone 20 metres high which is all that remains of the old Lascaris château. The church of St Michel nearby is worth a look. Formerly a convent, it has decorations by a local artist.

The Vallée des Merveilles contains Bronze Age engravings on rocks and rock walls – more than 100,000 of them. They are quite extraordinary and probably date from nearly 2000 BC. The principal groups are animals, geometric figures, weapons and tools (axes, arrowheads and halberds) and human hunters. The biggest concentration is around Mont Bégo, a sacred mountain for many years.

Organised trips can be taken – a guide is essential because the engravings are scattered over an area of twelve square kilometres and most of the locations are over 2,000 metres' altitude. The Réfuge des Merveilles is the best place to start. From there, two trips a day leave every day during July and August.

Because of Tende's focal position on the route of the mule trains, that beast of burden features strongly in the history of the town. The second Sunday in July has seen festivities in its honour ever since the 18th century. Éloi is the patron saint of blacksmiths ever since he astounded the town by cutting off a mule's leg, nailing a shoe to the hoof, then replacing the leg. This is celebrated today by parading teams of mules, all richly caparisoned with embroidered harnesses and jackets and red pompoms and ribbons, attended by muleteers, horsemen and folk dancers.

Among other festivals are: *June:* Spring Fair. *July:* Fête of St-Dalmas-de-Tende (about 4 km S); Fête de Viévola (about 5 km N). *14 July:* Bastille Day. *August:* Feast of the Shepherds (with farandoles – long lines of swaying dancers – and a big polenta meal). *September:* Autumn Fair. *October:* Festival of Chestnuts; Autumn Fair.

Le Cheval Blanc
(H)S   *93.04.62.22   Open all year   No credit cards*

Mme Carletto keeps the prices down in this fifteen-room auberge – 125–180f for a double room, simple but adequate.

Le Miramonti
(HR)S   *93.04.61.82   Open all year*

Only eleven rooms, usually filled. M. and Mme Maubert charge only 110–175f per room, or 150f per person for demi-pension. The simple food in the little dining room is satisfying; menus at 65–130f.

MAP 2E   **TOUËT-SUR-VAR** 06710 (Alpes-Maritimes). 54 km NW of Nice

Take the N 202, which follows the valley of the River Var all the way. Touët-sur-Var is another of the South of France's perched villages – but it is quite unlike any other you may have seen.
It is not a perched village in the same sense as Èze or St-Paul or Montauroux. Built into the side of a nearly vertical rock face, half-way up a mountain, Touët is nothing more than a huddle of houses clinging desperately to the precipitous slope. Many of the extremely ancient houses are crumbling and the atmosphere is positively archaic. Several writers have ascribed a 'Tibetan look' to Touët and its precarious position. This is hard to define, but there is certainly an Oriental slant to the appearance, especially from below.
You will encounter some unusual food specialities here, including ravioli stuffed with squash and covered in chestnut sauce, bread baked over wood fires, and tarts containing Swiss chard. There is a local white wine which is quite good but of very limited production.

Fêtes – *20 January:* Fête de St Sébastien. *20 May:* Village Fair. *August:* Annual Festival.

Touët's fairly remote situation doesn't bring too many visitors, but there is a good hotel-restaurant:

Auberge des Chasseurs
(HR)S   *93.05.71.11   Rest.: lunch only except Fri. and Sat. from June to Oct.*
Cl. Tues.; Feb.   V, DC, EC

Only five rooms, usually filled in season. The restaurant is very
good and very popular. The cooking is simple but the maximum use
is made of local ingredients which are always fresh, and meals
are attractively presented. Menus from 98f.

MAP 4F   **TOURETTE-SUR-LOUP** [PV] 06140 (Alpes-Maritimes). 5 km W of
Vence

The spelling has been a source of controversy. For centuries, the
name of this attractive village was spelled with two 'r's, then in
May 1982 the National Institute of Statistics decided to remove one
of them. The mayor and the town council were furious, the
villagers were scornful and today some use one and some use two.
Map-makers are confused. The three towers which gave it its
name remain aloof from the argument, as they have from most
arguments from the 15th century to date.

Tourette has been called 'The African Village' because of its
micro-climate, which encourages the growth of agave, cactus and
figs. The parallel persists in the tourist months when the narrow
village streets take on the aspect of an Arab bazaar. Artisan shops open
up like sunflowers, offering icons, dolls, ceramics, pottery, metal
sculptures, jewellery, furniture, cloth, cushions, wood carvings and
paintings.

The remarkable thing about Tourette is that it has all this
commerce and yet manages to retain a considerable amount of
charm. The utter mediaevalness of the village is probably
responsible – the incredibly old houses, the narrow winding ways
and the steep climbs. The latter is important to note – you need to
be sure of foot and strong in the lung to cover a lot of Tourette.

Unexpected views sweeping out over the valleys surprise you
everywhere. Try to park in the main square – there are lots of
spaces but they are often filled in the summer.

Tourette is famous for its violets. These grow in great profusion
around the village and are harvested and converted into essences
which go into the great perfume maw of Grasse. In March, violets
are in every window, in every flower pot and on every balcony.
The air is laden with their scent. You will also be able to participate
in the Festival of the Violets which is one of the biggest events of the
year.

Many tourists visit Tourette when going to see the Gorges du
Loup. Roaring torrents of water race down toward the
Mediterranean, leaping over huge rocky barriers and pouring
unchecked over cliffs. The Gorges can be seen from several
vantage points but undoubtedly the best places are near Tourette.
In recent years, the left bank has been made into a driveable road
and this affords spectacular views. The route is clearly signposted
out of the village.

Tourette-sur-Loup

The famous bridge over it – the Pont-du-Loup – is near the hermitage where St Arnoux lived alone for decades in a tiny shelter formed from rocks built into the shape of a cross. He ate only trout from the stream and drank only the stream water.

Still other visitors come here for one of the best restaurants in the neighbourhood and worth a detour. It is:

Le Petit Manoir
(R)M   *93.24.19.19   Cl. Sun. p.m.; Wed. 1/2–1/3; 15/11–15/12   EC, CB*

Very popular with locals who would probably like to keep it to themselves, but enough tourists know about it by now to make it even more popular. Rustic atmosphere, quite simple and small enough to justify the description 'intimate'. In fact, it's downright tiny and booking is essential.

The Gourmand Menu at 120f is the one to go for – first course of fish pieces in a delicious crispy batter rather like a samosa, with a tangy sauce, followed by young rabbit, rolled and stuffed, again in a superb sauce; a portion of broccoli and a patty of potatoes gratinées. The choice of cheese is small but sufficient. Desserts tend to be disappointing – avoid the fruit tarts which can be dry and stodgy, and go for the mousse or the sorbet. Wine needs careful choosing – the reds and the rosés are better than the whites. The wine list is in need of improving and expanding. Despite these criticisms, it is an excellent meal for the money.

Auberge Belles Terrasses
(HR)S   *93.59.30.03*

Fourteen small but perfectly adequate rooms at 200f in this pleasing auberge on the road towards Vence. Alternatively, there is pension at 230f or demi-pension at 195f. Food is carefully cooked from local ingredients.

La Grive Dorée
(HR)S   *93.59.30.05*

This one is in the opposite direction, going from Tourette toward Grasse. La Grive Dorée has eleven rooms at 170–240f; demi-pension is 195–220f, and full pension is 270–300f. Food is good hearty peasant fare and no one goes hungry.

MAP 5B   **TOURTOUR** ꝓᵥ 83690 (Var). 23 km W of Draguignan

Ⓜ   *Tues., Sat.*

The inhabitants of this pretty Var village insist that the name comes from the two towers on their emblem (one of which, the 12th-century Grimaldi Tower, stands on the road to Ampus); other opinion says that it comes from the *tourterelle*, the turtle-dove which used to be prevalent in the area. Yet others say it derives from the Celtic *tur*, meaning 'highest point'.

Whichever origin is the more authentic, Tourtour's description as 'The Village in the Sky' is appropriate. At its altitude of 650 metres, it has magnificent views and is very picturesque. You can walk around it in half an hour.

The usual approach is up from Salernes and Villecroze, but you may also come from Draguignan and through Flayosc. Either way leads through beautiful wooded countryside.

The focal point of the little main street is the two elms, now unfortunately heavily pruned, planted in 1638 to mark the pilgrimage visit of Anne of Austria and Louis XIII to nearby Cotignac.

The 16th-century Château des Raphaëlis is a magnificently feudal bastion at the other end of the main street, now housing the post office and the Mairie. There are sweeping views down the valley from the tiny part next to it and the archway over the end of the street is very photogenic.

The fourteenth of July is a big day, with parades of villagers, veterans and children, complete with bands and banners, and concluding with a tremendous firework display at dusk. Book a table at one of the small restaurants on the main street for a grandstand seat. At the beginning of August, there is a fête with aïoli, and on 15 August, there is soup and anchoïade for everyone.

La Bastide de Tourtour

(HR)L   *94.70.57.30   Hotel closed 1/11–1/3; Rest. closed Tues. lunch*
All credit cards

A magnificent château, in the romantic traditional style, though the hosting of seminars has rubbed off a little of the glamour. The twenty-six rooms are large, airy, attractively-furnished; those on the upper two floors have balconies. There is a heated pool and a tennis court.

M. and Mme Laurent run a fine hotel with good service and it is a shame that the cooking does not match up to it. Meals are unimaginative and disappointing – perhaps the charm of the Bastide itself leads you to expect more. Many guests stroll down into the village to eat.

Rooms are 525–1,260f and demi-pension (unfortunately, obligatory in season) at 575–895f. Menus are 140f (weekday lunch only), 290 and 370f.

Auberge St-Pierre

(HR)M   *94.70.57.17   Cl. Thurs.; 15/11–1/4   No credit cards*

Just outside the village, this old manor-house has been converted into a fifteen-room hotel, in 300 acres of land, where most of the ingredients for the kitchen are raised. There is tennis, and a heated pool overlooked by the dining room. The simple but pleasant rooms are 280–310f; demi-pension 310f. Menus at 160 and 190f use eggs, rabbits, pigeons, fruit, vegetables and herbs, mostly home-produced.

La Petite Auberge

(HR)M   *94.70.57.16   Cl. Tues.; 30/10–15/3   All credit cards*

A pretty Provençal house, with red tiled roof and spectacular views of the Maures mountains. The eleven rooms, at 280–360f, are small and simple; demi-pension, obligatory in season, at 280–390f.

Simplicity is the keyword but there is a pool on the level below the hotel, and a sauna, solarium and tennis. The restaurant is adequate and the service casual.

Hostellerie des Lavandes
(H)M *94.70.57.11 Cl. 1/10–1/1 No credit cards*

> Only just over a kilometre out of Tourtour along the road to
> Ampus, this is a small, pleasant Provençal-style house converted
> into a hotel, with 100 acres of grounds. You can smell the lavender
> from the local fields. Sixteen simple rooms at 235–280f. Pool and
> tennis.

Relais de St-Denis
(R)M *94.70.55.89 Cl. Mon. V, CB*

> Of the several restaurants in the main street, the tiny Relais is the
> best. In summer, the tables outside are very popular with locals and
> visitors, who especially appreciate the excellent soups – fish and
> pistou. Chicken in rosemary and navarin of lamb are very good too,
> and the daube is one of the best in the Var. Menus at 90 and 130f.

MAP 4C   **TRIGANCE** 83840 (Var). 20 km SW of Castellane; 12 km NW of
Comps-sur-Artuby

> The spectacularly handsome mediaeval castle might have been built
> for a film set. It's almost too archetypal – the massive walls, the
> battlements, the sturdy towers and the bravely fluttering flags are
> perfectly assembled to produce a heart-stirring sight. All that is needed
> is a line of armoured knights riding out of the great gates.
>   When the Château de Trigance was built in the 11th century,
> appearance was not of course a consideration. This is one of the
> most formidable fortifications you will ever see. Through the
> centuries, it has suffered all the usual vicissitudes and, by the
> mid-1960s, it was partly ruined. Then Jean-Claude Thomas, a former
> businessman from Paris, bought it, restored it as a hotel and now
> operates it.
>   Trigance itself is only a tiny hamlet. There is a small church, with
> a multi-coloured tiled roof to its tower, but otherwise there are only
> views of the river below and the occasional flock of sheep grazing
> on the hills.
>   The Château *is* Trigance – and it is the hotel.
>   The village is conveniently located for visits to the Lac de
> Sainte-Croix and the Grand Canyon du Verdon, which are about
> 10 kilometres to the west.

Château de Trigance
(HR)M *94.76.91.18 Cl. Wed. o.o.s.; 13/11–20/3 All credit cards*

> All the mediaeval splendour referred to above might make you
> sceptical about the Château's role as a hotel. You need have no fear.
> There are seven rooms, all doubles (some of them four-posters)
> and priced according to size at 450–780f, plus 55f per person for
> breakfast.

There is a large terrace for summer dining and a romantic restaurant with vaulted ceilings. The food is excellent and the service attentive and smiling. The staff speak English. Menus at 180, 240 and 320f, or à la carte.

MAP 4G **LA TURBIE** 06320 (Alpes-Maritimes). 8 km NW of Monaco; 18 km E of Nice

---

Ⓜ *Thurs.*

There is only one reason for a tourist to visit this rather nondescript little town – and that is to see the Trophy of the Alps. It is a pity that a town with such a glorious past should be so ordinary today that it possesses only one feature of interest. Turbia, as it was known, was a busy and prosperous place on the Via Aurelia, the ancient Roman road running from the Forum in Rome to Arles, 800 miles long and built commencing in 241 BC.

For the Roman soldier, Turbia was a very important town, marking the frontier into Gaul. In the year 6 BC the Roman senate ordered the building of a huge monument to mark the location and commemorate the victories of the Emperor Augustus over the forty-four tribes of southern Gaul and the final conquest.

It was a magnificent structure and the awe of all who saw it. Even today it is extremely impressive, despite the damage done to it over the centuries. The Lords of Èze and the Genoese carried away tens of tons of it to decorate palaces and shrines, St Honorat tried to have it dismantled because many superstitious locals went there to worship, the French tried to blow it up, and all over the south there are walls, villas, garages and cowsheds that contain parts of it – including Nice's cathedral, whose high altar is made of a block of its stone. Lightning has struck it several times and earthquakes have shaken it.

This extraordinary capacity for survival and seeming indestructibility have added to the legends and myths surrounding it. It is believed to be haunted, it is said to have had a speaking oracle, and troubadours have sung of its efficacy in marriage counselling.

It still stands, quite out of place so close to the fun-loving Riviera. There is little you can do there other than photograph it and be amazed at its size. A small adjacent museum and model show how it looked when it was completed. These are open May to September 9 a.m.–12.30 and 2–7.30 p.m.; October to April 9 a.m.– 12 and 2–5 p.m.

Hôtel Napoleon
(HR)M *av. de la Victoire 93.41.00.54 Hotel closed 19/2–18/3; Rest. closed Tues. o.o.s. All credit cards*

Very centrally located, right on the main street through town, just a short walk away from the Trophy of the Alps and on the corner leading down to Monaco.

La Turbie: A corner of the old town

This is a well-run small hotel with twenty-four rooms, all with bath, at 250–300f; demi-pension is available at 300f per person.
Good menus in the restaurant from 99f.

MAP 2F   **UTELLE** PV 06450 (Alpes-Maritimes). 45 km NW of Nice

Take the N 202 north from Nice airport, then the D 2565 east, to run through the scenic Gorges de la Vésubie to St-Jean-la-Rivière;

from here the D 32 winds its tedious, snake-like way up and up, west to the perched village of Utelle.

Two centuries ago it was an important village, with a sizeable population, due to its strategic position overlooking the vital mule-train routes up the valley. Today it has less than 400 people, but its altitude of 800 metres is still commanding.

Enter the village through the old Portal gate and go into the square, with its 11th-century church of St Véran. The beautifully carved wooden door depicts events from the life of the saint. The interior of the church is extremely rich and very impressive and sufficient reason in itself to visit Utelle. It blazes with powerful, primitive colours and gold, accented by the black columns. The sacristy contains many religious relics and paintings.

The Sanctuary of the Madonna of Utelle is worth a visit too, but only for the resolute, for it's nine kilometres from the village and the climb takes over two hours. According to legend, in the year 850 two Portuguese sailors in a storm-tossed ship off the coast prayed to the Virgin for rescue and were rewarded with a supernatural glow which they followed to safety. It appeared over the mountain above Utelle and in gratitude the sailors built a chapel here, rebuilt in 1806 as the Sanctuary. There is a viewing platform with spectacular views. The Sanctuary contains one painting which is the only survivor of a dozen left here by Georges Lascaris, Count of Tende, in the 16th century.

If you are in Utelle on 16 April, you will be able to witness an unusual ritual. It is performed by the villagers to commemorate an incident in 1450 when most of the men of the village went off to help defend the neighbouring villages of Peille and Lucéram against the Saracens. The wives pined for their husbands for an unrecorded period of time, then consoled themselves with the few remaining bachelors.

When the husbands returned, they were understandably piqued and challenged the bachelors to a trial of strength. This involved lifting a huge billet of wood weighing 80 kilos and called in Provençal a *capoun*. The billet has remained a symbol of power ever since and a contest is held every year between the married men and the bachelors for possession of the *capoun*. Wine is drunk at intervals during the contest and must be supplied by the most recently married man in the village. Drum and fife bands play loud accompaniments.

Other fêtes include: *Easter Monday, Whit Monday, 15 August, 8 September:* pilgrimages to the Sanctuary. *16 August:* Fête de St Roch, with music and dancing, and general jollity.

Hôtel Bellevue
(HR)S   *93.03.17.19   Cl. Wed. o.o.s.   No credit cards*

M. Martinon has seventeen rooms at 160–200f in this pleasant village auberge. Ten of the rooms have baths. Demi-pension is available at 220f. The cooking is good country fare, with an emphasis on local products, and there are numerous fish dishes. Menus at 75 to 130f.

MAP 4E   **VALBONNE** 06560 (Alpes-Maritimes). 10 km E of Grasse; 13 km N of Cannes

Ⓜ *Tues., Fri.*

Any village with a choice of twenty-four places to eat obviously gets a lot of tourists – and there is no question about Valbonne's popularity. The locals are frequent customers too though, and you will hear plenty of English spoken, as the surrounding area has homes belonging to numbers of British, Dutch, Americans and Scandinavians.

Valbonne is very unusual in that the streets of the village are laid out like a grid. Don't think that this means modern town planning – the streets are narrow, cobbled and lined with ancient houses. Valbonne's origins are prehistoric. Bronze Age relics have been found and Roman remains are still being found. It was occupied by the Romans at the end of the 2nd century and, with the spread of Christianity during the 4th and 5th centuries, several monasteries and chapels here established here.

The church you can visit today is on the southern edge of the village. It is in daily use and was built as a Chalaisian abbey (a Benedictine order) by Olivier, Bishop of Antibes. It is simply but very attractively decorated, the principal feature being the set of 16 panels from the 16th century, depicting the life of Christ. (In contrast to the age of the church, the pews are individually heated!)

Next to the church is the Salle du St-Esprit, now used by the progressive Mairie as the Espace d'Art Contemporain. Paintings and sculpture by local artists are on exhibition and the display changes frequently. Admission free. Behind the War Memorial is the Moulin des Artisans, once a glass-blowing centre but now an exhibition hall of glassware, ceramics and paintings.

The River Brague runs past all these and, a couple of hundred metres further along, goes past La Pierre du Diable which shows clearly the imprint of a horse's hoof and a clear indication of how high the horse must have jumped with the Devil on his back!

In the centre of the village is the place des Arcades bounded by thirteen Roman arches and containing two large elm trees nearly three hundred years old. There are outdoor cafés and restaurants all around the square, which is the village meeting place. Pottie Annie's on the south side of the square is an unusual shop selling very decorative presents and the bakery is irresistible to most visitors. The surrounding streets have small boutiques selling artisans' wares. The English Reading Centre on rue Aléxis Julien in the heart of the village is a bookshop selling all kinds of fiction and non-fiction in English and renting English-language videos; open Tuesday to Saturday, 9.30 a.m. to 12.30 and 2.30 to 7 p.m.

A curiosity of Valbonne is the Servan grape. This is a table grape, white and of exceptional quality, but its unique characteristic is that it remains fresh right through the winter. The vine branches bearing the fruit are plunged into water and then hung out in lofts and barns with a southern exposure. It is harvested from mid-October to the end of November and is sold fresh from Christmas to Easter. There is a Fête du Raisin on the first Sunday in

February every year (the Feast of St Blaise) with folk-dancing in the square and wine-tasting. The fame of the Servan grape has become such that the modest crop (from small local vineyards only) is in great demand and inevitably expensive, but you should certainly try to taste it.

Other festivals – *mid-August*: Fête de St Roch. *September*: 'Art in the Streets'.

Auberge Provençal
(HR)S *pl. des Arcades   93.42.01.03   Open all year   All credit cards*

Right in the centre of the village and overlooking the place des Arcades, so you can expect it to be a little noisy in the evenings. There are nineteen simple auberge rooms, ten with bath, priced at 120–220f.

This is a popular place to eat, especially in summer, when the tables and umbrellas are spread out over one corner of the square. The food is good and satisfying. The 75f menu might offer a buffet of crudités, coquelon de loup or calamars with lobster bisque sauce, then hot goat's-cheese salad and dessert. On the 95f menu frogs' legs Provençale is one of the first-course choices, then escalope of salmon with herb butter, or pepper steak, followed by the hot goat's-cheese salad and dessert.

La Chandellerie
(R)M *r. de la Mairie   93.42.03.66   Cl. Tues.; Wed.*

Right in the old village, M. Sauvan's establishment offers excellent Provençal cooking, and is rightly one of the most popular restaurants around. There are only 30 seats, so booking is highly advisable.

The menus are 85f – soupe au pistou/mixed peppers Niçoises, and daube/calamars Niçoises, for instance, followed by cheese and dessert – or 130f, with scampi/stuffed mussels and rabbit Provençale/filet de St-Pierre in saffron sauce, for example, plus cheese and pud of course.

A bottle of Provence wine costs 38 to 58f. The service is friendly and always helpful.

Le Bistro
(R)M *11 r. Fontaine   93.42.05.59*

Since Roger Moore and Elizabeth Taylor ate here, the fame of Raymond Purgato's little restaurant, right in the heart of old Valbonne village, has spread. (Both of the last occasions when I ate here, Richard Attenborough was at the next table.) Le Bistro is unquestionably good value for money and in a very cosy atmosphere.

Cosy means it's small – about twenty seats, plus a couple of tables outside in the summer (in the narrow street where pedestrians more than two abreast might sweep your wineglass off the table).

The menu at 150f is popular; it offers, for instance, stuffed mussels with garlic butter and chives, or snails followed by breast of duck in red berries, or fish of the day *en papillote*. Pear Charlotte or Chocolate Marquise finally for dessert.

The Gastronomic Menu at 245f features Périgourdin pâté, coquilles St-Jacques, gambas en brochette or beef Stroganoff, followed by sorbet cassis in champagne.

La Brouette
(R)M   *r. Aléxis Julien*   *93.42.06.25*

M. Bichon has a devoted following in his little restaurant with only thirty seats. The food is French traditional and menus at 95, 130 and 180f are all excellent value: straightforward cooking, well prepared. The service is friendly and helpful, and you will thoroughly enjoy a meal here.

Valbonne: La Brouette

> **Le Cadran Solaire**
(R)M   *4 r. Girard   93.42.13.30   Cl. Wed.; Thurs.; 1/12–28/2*

M. Dardis has only 30 places in his small restaurant on a narrow
street in the old village, and they are usually all filled.

This is the place to try a bouillabaisse (a) without spending a
fortune (it's a dish you might not even like), and (b) without it
being obligatory for more than one person to order the dish – here,
the 120f mini-bouillabaisse is not just a ragbag of whatever is
cheapest in the market, but includes classy specimens like monkfish
and St-Pierre. The scampi flambéd with Pernod is special too, as is the
best hot apple tart for miles around. Good menu at 110f.

MAP 5F   **VALLAURIS** 06220 (Alpes-Maritimes). 7 km W of Antibes

---

Ⓜ   *Sun.*

Famous for its pottery and its association with Picasso, Vallauris
really doesn't have much else to offer. It's a dusty everyday sort of
town, with 20,000 inhabitants going about their everyday business.

The Gauls dug out the local clay for making bricks and cooking
utensils – fragments of these are still found from time to time.
Waves of Barbarian and Saracen invasions ruined the town and then
the Plague in the 14th century virtually destroyed it. As with other
communities in the region, it was then re-populated with seventy
families from Albisola – today the Italian equivalent of Vallauris,
just across the border and the best and cheapest place to buy pots.

From that time on, pottery production continued to flourish in
Vallauris. One reason for the quality of the products was said to be the
firing of the clay with the local pine wood. The products themselves
all had a practical purpose, usually connected with cooking. It was
in 1859 that the artistic possibilities began to be realised, and glazing
with colours turned out decorative plaques and badges for houses,
walls and gates. Still, the output was small, the market local only
and the methods primitive.

It was during a beach party at Golfe-Juan in 1946 that it was
suggested to Picasso that he should try his hand at pottery. The
nearest place was the village of Vallauris and he went there and met
Suzanne and Georges Ramié. In their Madoura workshop, he
decorated some red clay plates with drawings of fish and eels. Losing
interest fast, as he did not find the form or the materials challenging,
Picasso returned to his painting.

Soon however, his work had filled the Antibes Museum and his
restless creative energy demanded new outlets. Still not convinced that
ceramics was a direction that he wanted to pursue, but lacking an
alternative, Picasso went back to Vallauris and set about
redesigning their pots and amphorae into more original shapes. He
changed the forms, the values and the techniques and went to
talk to an English chemist at a factory in Golfe-Juan who had original
ideas on glaze materials.

Gradually a new art form developed out of all this and Picasso became more and more fascinated with the possibilities. In one afternoon, he would decorate an entire week's ceramic production.

A whole industry arose, using electric kilns, modern mechanical equipment and more efficient techniques, and it was Picasso's idea to bring in white clay from Provins as a contrast to the dark red local material.

Today, ceramics is still a thriving business and Vallauris is a living monument to Picasso and to pottery – but not, alas, to good taste. The main street is lined with shops selling the most garish stuff, but you can visit the Madoura workshop where Picasso worked with Georges Ramié. It still has the sole rights to use Picasso's name. Open 9.30 a.m.–12.30 and 2.30–6 p.m., Monday to Friday.

Nevertheless, the revival of Vallauris as a community was due to Picasso alone and as Jean Casson says: 'With the prodigality of his imagination, with his love of craft, of creating, his deeply ingrained sense of being a man of the people and of the soil, he produced a mass of plates, pots, all kinds and shapes of objects, a countless fantastic treasure.' His immense productivity can be judged by the fact that hardly a museum of repute throughout the world does not have some of the output of those prodigious years.

The Musée Municipal in the castle shows many of the ceramics made by Picasso at the Madoura workshop, although it was recently the victim of yet another of the daring art robberies for which the French Riviera is famous and over sixty of the best works disappeared. At the time of writing, they have not yet been recovered.

On display here too are the works of the painter Alberto Magnelli and of the local family of ceramicists, Massier. Open 10 a.m.–12 and 2–6 p.m., closed Tuesdays.

The vestibule of the chapel of the Château has Picasso's celebrated fresco *War and Peace*. It was painted on wood and covers 125 square metres. Critics have treated it harshly. This building also goes under the name of 'Musée National Picasso' and is open every day 10 a.m.–12 and 2–6 p.m. in summer and 10 a.m.–12 and 2–5 p.m. in winter. Small charge.

In the shady square at the top of the main street is Picasso's famous bronze 'Man with a Sheep'. It depicts a naked bearded man carrying in his arms a struggling sheep. When he offered it to the town of Vallauris, he suggested that children could climb on it and dogs could water it. The town council were sceptical until Picasso assured them that it did indeed look like a man with a sheep. Now you can see for yourself.

Vallauris's Annual Fair is on 11 November, and there are two local fêtes, on 26 July, and on 29 August.

It is unlikely that you will want to stay in Vallauris. If you want to stay in the area, you will do much better to use a hotel in Golfe-Juan. Being there at lunchtime however may prompt you to look for a restaurant in Vallauris. In that case . . .

La Gousse d'Ail

(R)M   *11b av. de Grasse   93.64.10.71   Cl. Mon. p.m. 1/10–30/6; Tues.; 13/11–20/12   CB*

A long-established favourite which has shrugged off all competition for a couple of decades. Menus are 105, 150 and 200f and all are excellent value for money in this country-style restaurant.

The medallions of lotte with crab and the leek fondue are popular specialities. The salmon in sorrel sauce is a dish frequently encountered in the South of France but there is nothing routine about the way it is prepared here. Occasional touches of the Italian influence make themselves known, as for instance in the veal piccata with mushrooms.

➤ Le Manuscrit

(R)M   *chemin Lintier   93.64.56.56   Cl. Sun. p.m.; Mon. & Tues.*

It's in a residential area and not easy to find but customers come up from the coast and down from the hills to eat here. The reason is the authentic French country cooking, although the down-to-earth prices and the charming atmosphere with rough stone walls and tiled floors are two bonuses.

There are only two menus and no carte. At 90f, you could choose from several starters – fillets of herring with potatoes cooked in olive oil, or maybe mousseline of fish in sherry sauce. For the main course there is trout poached in champagne, or fricassée of salmon with Nantais sauce.

At 160f, the snails in pastry with garlic cream make an exotic starter; of wider appeal is a very generous portion of smoked salmon. For the main course, the Marmite du Pêcheur (like a seafood stew) is famous, or there is the cassoulette of sweetbreads with cream.

One indication of genuine country cooking is the absence of desserts – so if you have a sweet tooth, be warned that both the menus conclude with just cheese.

MAP 1F   **VENANSON** [PV] 06450 (Alpes-Maritimes). 64 km NW of Nice; 5 km S of St-Martin-Vésubie

---

You can spot Venanson long before you get there. Approaching St-Martin (D 31) up the Vésubie valley, you see Venanson perched impossibly high up on the far side of the valley, hanging precariously on to the edge of a rocky shelf, off which it seems about to slide at any moment.

There's not a lot to see in the village itself, which derives its name from *Venatio*, meaning hunting ground, for the whole area teemed with game in past centuries. It is 1,164 metres high, looking down on St-Martin, far below its lofty parapets. It was St-Martin's look-out point, and the plague which virtually destroyed Venanson's population in the 15th century vitally affected the security of St-Martin. Venanson never really recovered and its population today is less than one hundred.

The chapel of St Sébastien was built during the plague and has some vividly coloured frescos – much more attractive than you might expect from the rather drab exterior of the building. The nearby church of St Michel is 17th century.

There are a number of hikes possible from the village, which attract outdoor enthusiasts: to Les Granges, where there are traditional dwellings; to Rigons (3 km); and to Le Libaret (7 km). Trails also lead up to La Maluna Forest, to Mont Tournairet (over 2,000 metres high) and to La Colmiane Pass.

Fêtes: *late July:* annual pilgrimage. *Mid-August:* village fête with costumes, and singing and dancing to drum and fife bands.

There is a popular bar-restaurant-pizzeria which has rooms, recently under new management, which is making itself a very good place to stay if you wish to tour the area:

La Bella Vista
(HR)S   *pl. St-Jean   93.03.25.11   CB*

Challenging the hotels in St-Martin, La Bella Vista has six rooms, simple but sufficient, at 120f, or 200f for full pension. The young couple, M. and Mme Michel Baccarini, who have recently taken it over, are exerting real efforts to make it attractive, with a prettily decorated dining room and fresh flowers on the tables every day.

Provençal specialities are emerging from the kitchen, and the locals are patronising it even more than before. The menus at 90f and 120f offer a choice of two starters, a plat garni, plus cheese, plus dessert.

MAP 4F   **VENCE** 06140 (Alpes-Maritimes). 25 km W of Nice

Ⓜ *Daily*

The first place to head for in Vence is the old town. This is a walled city-within-a-city. To reach it, you have to go through the outer city, the shops and houses that have sprung up since the Middle Ages to surround the old town like a cocoon and provide thoroughfares for those in transit.

Vence's old town is satisfyingly mediaeval – a maze of tiny narrow streets. It is small – you can walk every street in it in less than an hour – although you will probably want to take longer, stopping to take photographs or browse in the antique shops or eat and drink in the innumerable cafés, bistros, pizzerias, bars and restaurants. The houses are ancient and a great many are in the process of being restored – generally in good taste, maintaining the outer façade but installing surprisingly sophisticated interiors, for Vence is a desirable place to live and property values run high.

You will see the old cathedral, right in the heart of the old town.

It was built in the 10th century on the site of a Roman temple dedicated to the god Mars. Inside is the tomb of St Véran, one of the patron saints of Vence and Bishop here during the 5th century.

Entry to the old town is only through one of the original Roman portals, and inside life is busy and bustling with the markets selling flowers, fruit, vegetables, fish, poultry, meat, eggs just as they have always done. It's modern merchandising in a mediaeval environment. The shops selling wood-carvings, basketwork and other touristic gewgaws obtrude slightly but not enough to ruin the whole effect.

The place Godeau, the place Clémenceau, the place Surian and the place du Peyra are the centres around which almost all of the restaurants and cafés are centred. Adjacent to the place du Peyra and just outside the city wall is the Château, built about 1450. It contains the Musée Carzou and houses the work of that prolific French painter and local resident. Open every day but Monday.

The main market, open every day on the rue du Marché, is particularly colourful. The place Surian also has a daily market, which sells only locally produced goods. Chez Moraldo at No. 28 offers nougat which is made while you watch – with nuts, vanilla, honey, raspberry, chocolate, coffee or covered with chocolate. The time to be there is 11 a.m. every Wednesday and Saturday. All the nougat is on sale of course, and though it's expensive, you won't taste better in your life.

Also on the rue du Marché, M. Barbier's Au Poivre d'Âne at No. 12 is a boutique with a superb selection of cheeses, salads, tarts, pies and wines. Below is a small restaurant serving meals at 120f.

On the road to St-Jeannet, north-east of Vence, you will find the Chapelle du Rosaire. It is on the avenue Henri Matisse, because the great painter was nursed by the Dominican nuns when seriously ill and in return, on his recovery, he designed this chapel for them. He dedicated five out of the last seven years of his life to this project.

The figure of St Dominic you will see there was painted first as a study while Matisse was still bed-ridden, using his paintbrush tied to the end of a stick as his hands were too shaky. Earlier in his career, Matisse had been an earnest disciple of Paul Signac's pointillism technique and he now reverted to this method as being particularly appropriate to the ceramic murals for the chapel.

The building is, in fact, an extraordinarily moving example of one man's dedication, for everything in it is of Matisse's design, from the candlesticks to the windows. Matisse designed, while Auguste Perret, an engineer famous for his ingenious employment of reinforced concrete, supervised the actual construction. The full-length windows are simply done, using only three colours – yellow, blue and green – in order to allow the maximum passage of light and subtly illuminate the interior of the chapel. The black and white drawings of St Dominic and of the Virgin and Child, as well as the Stations of the Cross, are stark in their simplicity.

Open Tuesdays and Thursdays, 10–11.30 a.m. and 2.30–5.30 p.m.

Vence is an excellent base for visits in the region and prices are more reasonable than on the coast.

Le Mas de Vence
(HR)M *93.58.06.16 AE, V, DC, EC*

On the D 236 coming out of Vence heading south. Recently built, but in the Provençal style, the forty-one rooms here, 305–390f, are well-equipped and run; demi-pension is also available at 340f and full pension at 445f. All rooms now have bath or shower and TV. There is a large pool.

La Roseraie
(HR)M *av. Henri Giraud 93.58.02.20 Cl. Jan. AE, V, EC*

Just on the edge of town going north-west this two-star hotel has twelve rooms at 260–380f and a pool. It has taken Josette and Maurice Ganier a few years to get the place the way they want it and it is an extremely pleasant stop for either one or several nights. In the summer, you can eat in the garden or by candlelight on the terrace. Cooking has a south-west France character, with dishes like confits, foie gras. Salmon and breast of duck are two of the entrées to be found on the menus, which are 110, 170 and 260f.

Diana
(H)M *93.58.28.56 Open all year AE, V, DC, EC*

A few minutes west of the old walled town, the Diana is modern and has twenty-five small but beautifully designed and furnished rooms at 275–300f. There is no restaurant but every room has a small kitchen, of which the daily cleaning and washing-up is part of the service. There is a garden and a terrace, two breakfast rooms and a library (with some English books). Garage underground.

La Closerie des Genets
(HR)M *93.58.33.25 Open all year AE, V, EC*

Across the street from the city walls, but down a short cul-de-sac so it's tranquil but still well located. The nine rooms are priced at 120–265f, or demi-pension at 210–375f. The cooking is versatile and imaginative, menus range from 100 to 250f. The game specialities are very popular. The staff speak English and there is a garden and a terrace. Lack of parking is a problem but as long as you don't leave anything in the car and you remember to set the alarm, you can use the municipal lot two minutes away in the place Grand Jardin.

Auberge des Seigneurs
(HR)S *93.58.06.05 Cl. Sun. p.m.; Mon.; 15/10–1/12 AE, V, DC*

If you want to be right in the old town, this is the place. The eight rooms are named after the painters who have stayed here – Modigliani, Dufy, Bonnard, Soutine, Renoir, etc. They are priced at 220–240f. It's all casual, arty and good fun. Meals are 150–170f.

La Victoire
(HR)S   *93.58.61.30   CB*

> Just outside the old walls and facing the Tourist Bureau and the
> main parking area. Busy and noisy with traffic and pedestrians, but
> if you don't mind these, this two-star hotel is good value at 200–240f
> for the fifteen rooms, twelve of which have showers.
>
> The brasserie downstairs serves food all day – the plat du jour
> may be daube à la Provençale or roast beef at 45f. Service is slow
> but the patio where you can eat and watch the world of Vence go by
> is pleasant.

La Lubiane
(HR)S   *93.58.01.10   Cl. 1/11–1/2*

> Walking distance from the old town so it's fairly quiet. Rooms are
> 140–225f, or full pension at 230–310f. There are two terraces for
> meals, one outdoors and one glassed in. Menus are simple at 80 and
> 90f.

➤Château des Arômes
(R)L   *rte de Grasse   93.58.70.24   Cl. Sun p.m.; Mon.; 8/1–mid-Feb.   AE, CB*

> You won't see many more dramatic châteaux in the South of
> France than this one and you won't eat better food in any château.
>
> Lube and Gérard Mosiniak run a most unusual restaurant – under
> the vaulted stone arches of this 11th-century château which has
> also been the traditional home of the Bishops of Vence. The huge
> iron lanterns, the candlesticks and the massive tapestries
> complete the thoroughly mediaeval atmosphere.
>
> Nothing mediaeval about the cooking, though. Gérard Mosiniak
> brought modern expertise with him from London. The cuisine is
> basically nouvelle cuisine but don't be concerned about going
> hungry. The intention of the cooking here is to make the maximum
> use of flavours and tastes. As many as forty different flavouring
> media may be used in a meal. The arômes in the name of the château
> are the essences of nutmeg, truffles, garlic and tarragon, for instance,
> and fruits used with them may include kiwi, orange, cranberry
> and lemon. The presentation is so superb that you will want to
> photograph it before you eat it.
>
> There is a lunch menu weekdays at 180f, but in the evening the
> menus are 240, 280 and 330f and there is a vegetarian meal at
> 220f. The 240f menu offers choices such as raviolis stuffed with
> oxtail, and veal with a delicate and delicious sauce blending so
> many indefinable flavours that I gave up trying to identify any of
> them; followed by lobster salad with artichokes and mangetouts
> in walnut oil and sherry vinegar dressing; then a main course of
> mignons of pork with wild mushrooms and cinnamon sauce, or
> rack of lamb with thyme and lemon and tiny vegetables or rolled
> stuffed guinea-hen; followed by hot goat's cheese, with a wide
> choice of delicious desserts to finish. At 240f this is unquestionably
> excellent value for money.

Vence: Château des Arômes

Service is smooth and efficient and everyone speaks impeccable English. The wine list is lengthy and there is a very good selection of quality wines between 100 and 200f. It is hard to put a value on the atmosphere which is an undoubted plus.

In the adjacent vaulted chambers are displays of paintings and sculpture and a perfume museum. The latter contains more than forty pieces of ancient equipment for the processing of perfumes and liqueurs. Allow some time either before or after the meal for appreciating this. In summer, you can eat on the terrace by the huge fountain, with a sweeping view of the countryside.

La Farigoule
(R)M   *93.58.01.27   Cl. Fri. o.o.s.; mid-Nov.–mid-Dec.*

A restaurant very popular with the locals. It's on a flower-decked street and a minute outside the city walls. Mme Gastaud serves a 100f menu of three courses, where the main course may well be a choice of duck, quail, rabbit, guinea-fowl or daube – all country fare. Other menus at 120 and 130f recommended too.

There is a terrace and a garden. This is one of those places where you can always be sure of a very good meal at a reasonable price.

While browing inside the walls of the old town, you may be seduced by the ambience and want to eat there. This is no problem for there is a restaurant everywhere you look. The Italian influence is obvious and pizzerias abound. If you should want something more, try some of these:

Au Coin de Feu. Three-course meals at 85 or 130f. Adequate fare, not strong on imagination but good portions.

L'Oranger. Vaulted caverns dating from the 13th century, dinner by candlelight. Permanent sculpture exhibition. The menu at 90f is good value but even better is the Dégustation which is a number of courses, each a small portion. For 130f, you might have: gratin of crab, then rack of lamb grilled with Provençal potatoes, then fillet of veal with five sauces, then potato gratin à la crème, followed by farmstyle salad with goat's cheese, and then a choice of pastries.

Le Pêcheur de Soleil. Needs mentioning even if it is a pizza house because it serves no less than 220 kinds of pizza. Also available are charcoal grills. About 50f a person.

Le Feelings. A slightly weird mixture – a piano bar with jazz ambience and Mexican food. About 120f.

Le Grenouille. Just behind the Mairie and serving Greek specialities at 100–150f.

Auberge des Templiers
(R)M   *93.58.06.05   V, EC*

Just outside the walls, run by an ex-Vergé sommelier, Patrice Lopez. Specialises in fish of the day; the lobster at 155f is a bargain. Menus at 100, 185 and 280f.

MAP 2F   **VILLARS-SUR-VAR** PV 06710 (Alpes-Maritimes). 47 km N of Nice

Drive north on the N 202 from Nice and when you reach Villars-sur-Var you must – as in so many perched villages – park as near as you can to the square and walk from there. Villars has the tiny alleys, the haphazard arrangement of passageways and staircases and the mediaeval air you expect in such an ancient village.

The church of St Jean-Baptiste, on the square, is the first sight to see. It was built in 1520 in baroque style and carefully restored so that today it is very close to what must have been its original appearance.

The altarpiece and the wooden statue of John the Baptist are particularly deserving of study.

Climb up from the square, under stone archways, through a maze of cobbled streets, to the ruins of the Château Grimaldi, built by the Grimaldi family in the 15th century. It fell into decline when Annibal Grimaldi was executed for treason.

Villars-sur-Var claims to have the most northerly vineyard of all the wines carrying the appellation 'Côte-de-Provence'. The wine is of exceptionally good quality and is prized all over France but as there is little land available for cultivation, the volume produced is small, so here is a unique opportunity to taste it. Many of the older houses still have their own cellars and wine-producing equipment.

The Fête des Vendanges is a very exuberant celebration and takes place at the time of the grape harvest. Due to Villars's altitude and northerly position, this can vary considerably so it may be the latter half of September or the first half of October. The Feast of St John the Baptist is celebrated every 24 June with particular fervour as he is the patron saint of the village, and there is a big pilgrimage procession.

Villars has nothing recommendable in the way of hotels or restaurants. Touët-sur-Var and Puget-Théniers, 27 kilometres continuing west along the N 202, are probably the nearest locations.

MAP 5B **VILLECROZE** 83690 (Var). 5 km E of Salernes; 20 km W of Draguignan

---

Not many Var villages have remained quite unspoilt and yet not fallen into decay. Villecroze has managed this – it is tiny but still personable.

The grottoes in the public park are one of the first sights to see. The charming young English lady who conducts the tour will tell you the history of the grottoes – used for grain storage by the Roman army, as a refuge during the days of religious persecution and later as free housing. In massive chambers and caverns are spectacular stalactites and stalagmites. The name of the village comes from *ville creusée*, the hollow town.

The old part of Villecroze, within the walls, is mediaeval, with winding cobbled stairways, sharp turns, stone arches, ancient houses and gurgling basins for the communal wash. Most of the houses have modern interiors but from the outside there is no difficulty in accepting them as more than five hundred years old.

The village square is unremarkable, though it takes on some colour on market day. The church adjoining the square is ordinary too. Opposite is the bar and café, Les Cascades, a lively meeting place for the locals who still call it by its former name of Chez Édouard.

The music centre may be finished by the time this appears in print – concert halls, accommodation and classrooms for music students, all the funds donated by Mme Schlumberger of the wealthy multinational company (she lives nearby). September has traditionally

been the month of musical concerts, with performances given by
students from several countries. From now on, these will be in
this new music centre. Admission is free and the standard is very
high. A sad note is that to build the music centre it was necessary
to tear down Le Vieux Moulin, a landmark among local hostelries
and run so well for so many years by Mme Gillin.

The vineyard of St-Jean-de-Villecroze is about two kilometres out
of Villecroze on the road to Draguignan. You really should visit it
and taste the wine – one of the best in Provence. Rescued from
oblivion by an American, Al Hirsch, it was brought into the front
rank of Var vineyards with the installation of modern equipment and
a lot of hard work. You can buy wine from the vats or by the bottle.
The Syrah and Cabernet wines are exceptionally good and all the
wines are natural, i.e. grown without the use of synthetic
fertilisers, insecticide or fungicide sprays.

The Grand Hôtel and the Petit Hôtel are barely so-so – you will fare
better for rooms by going to Tourtour (about four kilometres). There
is, however, one restaurant of note in Villecroze:

La Marmite du Colombier
(R)M   *Cl. Tues.   V, CB*

On the road leaving Villecroze, heading towards Draguignan. It is
rustic inside and quite small but the covered terrace is large and
usually full in summer.

Cooking is good and reliable. The pâtés are excellent as is the
chicken in tarragon sauce. Menus at 120 and 160f with local wines
of good quality and reasonably priced.

MAP 4G   **VILLEFRANCHE-SUR-MER** 06230 (Alpes-Maritimes). 6 km E of Nice

---

(M)   *Sun.*

Don't miss the opportunity to see Villefranche, one of the most
charming and picturesque towns on the Côte d'Azur.

Turn off the Basse Corniche and follow the winding road down
towards the sea. Instead of turnng right to the port (it's a dead-end
and there's not much to see), turn left at the sign 'Vieille Ville' (the
old town).

This is one of the spookiest entrances to a town you will ever see
– the road goes between Cyclopean rock walls. These are part of
the magnificent battlemented and turretted Citadelle de St-Elme built
by the Duke of Savoy in 1537. When you emerge, you can drive down
along the waterfront or park and walk. In summer, you may have no
choice but to park. If you drive all the way along the waterfront,
you will come to more parking at the far end, but it is a two-lane
road only and there is no exit so Villefranche seethes with slow
traffic. The earlier you go the better, and I can assure you it's worth
it.

Along the waterfront is one of the most painted and photographed
sections of the Riviera. You will probably recognise the Hôtel

Villefranche-sur-Mer

Welcome from a score of pictures, and the exceptionally mild
micro-climate, even for the Riviera, encourages rich and luxuriant
vegetation. Past the Hôtel Welcome is a long line of restaurants, all
looking out at the harbour and most with outside terraces.
Menu-checking is the local equivalent of window-shopping.

Villefranche was founded in the second century BC and named
Olivula by the Romans, but Charles II of Anjou, Count of Provence, gave
it its present name in 1293 when establishing it as a 'free port'. He
considered that its exposed position made it virtually impossible to
defend in those days.

Indefensible against barbarian raids it may have been, but after
the Duke of Savoy built the Citadel the town changed hands

between Savoy and the French several times. Today sees a new role for the 200-foot-deep harbour and one of the finest anchorages on the coast, for it is one of the headquarters of the US Sixth Fleet in the Mediterranean.

When strolling on the quay, turn up one of the ancient stone stairways – on the rue de l'Église or the rue de May – and walk through the rue Obscure, covered for some of its length, as it runs under the houses like an Oriental souk. For centuries, it has served as a shelter for the villagers when the town came under naval bombardment, and the vaulted arches, massive weathered beams and darkness alleviated only by elaborate wrought-iron lanterns, transport you back immediately to the street's 14th-century origins.

At the far end of the horseshoe-shaped bay, at the Pointe du Rube is a small promontory with popular (but shingle) beaches. At the entrance to the tiny fishing port is the 14th-century chapel of St Pierre which used to be the storage for the nets of the local fishermen. In 1957, it was converted back into a chapel and Jean Cocteau, then a local resident, decorated it with scenes from the life of St Peter. It is open 9.30 a.m. – 12 and 2–6 p.m. every day except Friday; the small fee goes to the fishermen's charity fund.

There is an open-air cinema inside the Citadel and two art museums. The more important of these is now known as the Goetz-Boumeester Museum and contains work by Picasso and Miró and has frequent exhibitions of other work. The Musée Volti has works in bronze, copper and clay by the local sculptor, Volti. Both are open every day from June to September 10 a.m. – 12 and 2–5 p.m., but closed on Sunday morning and Tuesday.

Fêtes: *30 June* and *1 July:* Festival of the Fishermen. *July* (dates vary): Folklore International; Open Air Ballet. *July* and *August:* Arts Festival in the Citadel. *29 September:* Fête Patronale.

There are also a great many additional events from April to December – check the local Syndicat d'Initiative.

Hôtel Welcome
(HR)M   *1 quai Courbet   93.76.76.93   Cl. 25/11–18/12   All credit cards*

This ancient convent, dating from the 17th century, has been a hotel for over a hundred years and remains a prominent feature of the famous view of the waterfront at Villefranche. Painters and writers have stayed here, and M. and Mme Gérard Galbois-Sabatier ensure that the hotel lives up to its name.

The 32 rooms are priced at 430–780f per person for demi-pension and all the rooms are air-conditioned. Those on the lower floors are larger but a little noisier; all are very comfortably furnished.

Its Saint-Pierre Restaurant is famous in its own right. The terrace looks out across the harbour and though it is not cheap, the quality is excellent.

The bourride is one of the best on the Riviera, and the loup de mer and scampi in saffron cream are local favourites. Set menus are 170, 270 and 480f.

Hôtel Provençal
(HR)S – M   *av. Maréchal Joffre   93.01.71.42   CB*

A good choice if you don't want to be right on the busy waterfront.
Only 150 metres away, a five-storey building, with charming
turretted rooms on the top floor and balconies on others. Calm
and peaceful atmosphere.

The fifty rooms are all pleasant, especially the twenty-five that
have sea views. All have bath or shower, and there is a lift. Rooms
are 200–380f, or you get a good deal on demi-pension at 250–350f
out of season and 285–410f in season. The restaurant, with patio
for the summer, is patronised by non-residents – a good sign of
quality. Menus at 65 and 115f, or there are numerous pasta
specialities at 35–48f; the paella, at 48f, is a favourite.

Hôtel Vauban
(H)M   *11 av. Gén. de Gaulle   93.01.71.20   Cl. 15/11–15/2*

Located on the road leading into the town of Villefranche, so only
walking distance from the port.

The gardens and patio, filled with flowers and statuary, are
delightful. The hotel is quiet and there are views of the harbour.

The twelve rooms are priced at 180–520f but there is a charge of
68f for breakfast, which is a little excessive.

La Mère Germaine
(R)M – L   *quai Courbet   93.01.71.39   Cl. 14/12–24/12; Wed. 1/10–30/4   AE, V*

The biggest and the most expensive of the many restaurants along
the waterfront but everyone who has eaten here says it was a superb
meal.

The food is dominantly fish, and the bouillabaisse at 250 or 400f
is a feast in itself. Scampis in garlic come cheaper at 175f, but
langoustes Thermidor will set you back 415f. There is a good-value
set menu at 170f, which is based on the day's fish catch.

Le Dauphin
(R)M   *3 quai Courbet   93.01.75.13   Open all year   CB*

Another very good bet for excellent seafood at reasonable prices,
also on the waterfront with views of the harbour.

The menu at 90f is for the not-excessively-hungry, with, for
example, fish soup or avocado vinaigrette, stuffed sardines or
moules marinières, and cheese or dessert. At 135f you can have
snails, grilled fish, salad and dessert.

There is a menu at 300f but I don't know anyone who has had the
appetite to tackle it.

La Frégate
(R)M *quai Courbet   93.01.71.31   Cl. Mon.   V, CB*

A very popular seafood restaurant, also on the waterfront, very busy in summer. The patterned whitewashed walls and the pastel tablecloths give it a calm, pleasing atmosphere and there is an enormous outside terrace which also gets full during the season.
Seafood only, and the menu at 115f is exceptionally good value.

Don Camillo
(R)S *pl. du Marché   Open all year   V, CB*

Always busy and popular, this café-restaurant is on the square as you approach the waterfront area. It is a good place to eat when you don't want a full meal. The sole meunière and the grilled salmon are each 50f, and there are lots of different pizzas ranging from 35 to 65f.
Half-bottles of wine are an unbeatable 20f.

Wines and spirits by John Doxat

AN INTRODUCTION TO FRENCH WINES

Bonne cuisine et bons vins, c'est le paradis sur terre. (Good cooking
and good wines, that is earthly paradise.)

King Henri IV

French food positively invites accompaniment by wine, albeit only a
couple of glasses because one is driving on after lunch. At dinner one
can usually be self-indulgent. Then wine becomes more than a sensory
pleasure: with some rich regional meals it is almost imperative
digestively. Civilised drinking of wine inhibits the speedy eating that is
the cause of much Anglo-Saxon dyspepsia.

The most basic French wine generically is *vin ordinaire*, and very
ordinary indeed it can be. The term is seldom used nowadays: *vin de
table* is a fancier description – simple blended wine of no particular
provenance. *Vins de table* often come under brand-names, such as
those of the ubiquitous Nicolas stores (Vieux Ceps, etc.) – and highly
reliable they are. Only personal experience can lead you to your
preference: in a take-away situation I would never buy the absolute
cheapest just to save a franc or so.

Nearly every restaurant has its house wines. Many an owner, even of
a chain of establishments, takes pride in those he has chosen to signify
as *vins de la maison*, *vin du patron* or similar listing. In a wine-rich
area, house wines (in carafe or bottle) are likely to be *vins de pays*, one
step up from *vins de table*, since this label indicated that they come
from a distinct certificated area and only that area, though they may be
a blend (thus sometimes an improvement) of several wines.

Ever since they invented the useful, if frequently confusing,
Appellation d'Origine Contrôlée (AC) the French have created
qualitative sub-divisions. An AC wine, whose label will give you a
good deal of information, will usually be costlier – but not necessarily
better – than one that is a VDQS. To avoid excessive use of French, I
translate that as 'designated (regional) wine of superior quality'. A
newer, marginally lesser category is VQPRD: 'quality wine from a
specified district'.

Hundreds of wines bear AC descriptions: you require knowledge
and/or a wine guide to find your way around. The intention of the AC
laws was to protect consumers and ensure wine was not falsely
labelled – and also to prevent over-production, without noticeable
reduction of the 'EEC wine lake'. Only wines of reasonable standards
should achieve AC status: new ones are being regularly admitted to
the list, and the hand of politics as much as the expertise of the taster
can be suspected in some instances. Thus AC covers some
unimportant wines as well as the rarest, vastly expensive vintages.

Advice? In wine regions, drink local wines. Do not hesitate to ask the
opinion of patron or wine-waiter: they are not all venal, and most folk
are flattered by being consulted. By all means refer to a vintage chart,
when considering top class wines, but it cannot be an infallible guide:
it has no bearing on blended wines.

OUTLINE OF FRENCH WINE REGIONS

Bordeaux

Divided into a score of districts, and sub-divided into very many *communes* (parishes). The big district names are Médoc, St. Emilion, Pomerol, Graves and Sauternes. Prices for the great reds (châteaux Pérus, Mouton-Rothschild, etc.) or the finest sweet whites (especially the miraculous Yquem) have become stratospheric. Yet château in itself means little and the classification of various rankings of châteaux is not easily understood. Some tiny vineyards are entitled to be called château, which has led to disputes about what have been dubbed 'phantom châteaux'. Visitors are advised, unless wine-wise, to stick to the simpler designations.

Bourgogne (Burgundy)

Topographically a large region, stretching from Chablis (on the east end of the Loire), noted for its steely dry whites, to Lyons. It is particularly associated with fairly powerful red wines and very dry whites, which tend to acidity except for the costlier styles. Almost to Bordeaux excesses, the prices for really top Burgundies have gone through the roof. For value, stick to simpler local wines.

Technically Burgundies, but often separately listed, are the Beaujolais wines. The young red Beaujolais (not necessarily the over-publicised *nouveau*) are delicious, mildly chilled. There are several rather neglected Beaujolais wines (Moulin-à-Vent, Morgon, St. Amour, for instance) that improve for several years: they represent good value as a rule. The Mâconnais and Chalonnais also produce sound Burgundies (red and white) that are usually priced within reason.

Rhône

Continuation south of Burgundy. The Rhône is particularly associated with very robust reds, notably Châteauneuf-du-Pape; also Tavel, to my mind the finest of all still *rosé* wines. Lirac *rosé* is nearly as good. Hermitage and Gigondas are names to respect for reds, whites and *rosés*. Rhône has well earned its modern reputation – no longer Burgundy's poorer brother. From the extreme south comes the newly 'smart' dessert *vin doux naturel*, ultra-sweet Muscat des Beaumes-de-Venise, once despised by British wine-drinkers. There are fashions in wine just like anything else.

Alsace

Producer of attractive, light white wines, mostly medium-dry, widely used as carafe wines in middle-range French restaurants. Alsace wines are not greatly appreciated overseas and thus remain comparatively inexpensive for their quality; they are well placed to compete with popular German varieties. Alsace wines are designated by grape – principally Sylvaner for lightest styles and, the widespread and reliable Riesling for a large part of the total, and Gerwürtztraminer for slightly fruitier wines.

Loire

Prolific producer of very reliable, if rarely great, white wines, notably Muscadet, Sancerre, Anjou (its *rosé* is famous), Vouvray (sparkling and semi-sparkling), and Saumur (particularly its 'champagne styles'). Touraine makes excellent whites and also reds of some distinction – Bourgueil and Chinon. It used to be widely believed – a rumour put out by rivals? – that Loire wines 'did not travel'; nonsense. They are a successful export.

Champagne

So important is Champagne that, alone of French wines, it carries no AC: its name is sufficient guarantee. (It shares this distinction with the brandies Cognac and Armagnac.) Vintage Champagnes from the *grandes marques* – a limited number of 'great brands' – tend to be as expensive in France as in Britain. You can find unknown brands of high quality (often off-shoots of *grandes marques*) at attractive prices, especially in the Champagne country itself. However, you need information to discover these, and there are true Champagnes for the home market that are *doux* (sweet) or *demi-sec* (medium sweet) that are pleasing to few non-French tastes. Champagne is very closely controlled as to region, quantities, grape types, and is made only by secondary fermentation in the bottle. From 1993, it is prohibited (under EEC law) to state that other wines are made by the 'champagne method' – even if they are.

Minor regions, very briefly

Jura – Virtually known outside France. Try local speciality wines such as *vin jaune* if in the region.

Jurançon – Remote area; sound, unimportant white wines, sweet styles being the better.

Cahors – Noted for its powerful *vin de pays* 'black wine', darkest red made.

Gaillac – Little known; once celebrated for dessert wines.

Savoy – Good enough table wines for local consumption. Best product of the region is delicious Chambéry vermouth: as an aperitif, do try the well distributed Chambéryzette, a unique vermouth with a hint of wild strawberries.

Bergerac – Attractive basic reds; also sweet Monbazillac, relished in France but not easily obtained outside: aged examples can be superb.

Provence – Large wine region of immense antiquity. Many and varied *vins de pays* of little distinction, usually on the sweet side, inexpensive and totally drinkable.

Midi – Stretches from Marseilles to the Spanish border. Outstandingly prolific contributor to the 'EEC wine lake' and producer of some 80 per cent of French *vins de table*, white and red. Sweet whites dominate, and there is major production of *vins doux naturels* (fortified sugary wines).

Corsica – Roughish wines of more antiquity than breeding, but by all means drink local reds – and try the wine-based aperitif Cap Corse – if visiting this remarkable island.

Paris – Yes, there is a vineyard – in Montmartre! Don't ask for a bottle: the tiny production is sold by auction, for charity, to rich collectors of curiosities.

HINTS ON SPIRITS

The great French spirit is brandy. Cognac, commercially the leader, must come from the closely controlled region of that name. Of various quality designations, the commonest is VSOP (very special old pale): it will be a cognac worth drinking neat. Remember, *champagne* in a cognac connotation has absolutely no connection with the wine. It is a topographical term, *grande champagne* being the most prestigious cognac area: *fine champagne* is a blend of brandy from the two top cognac sub-divisions.

Armagnac has become better known lately outside France, and rightly so. As a brandy it has a much longer history than cognac: some connoisseurs rate old armagnac (the quality designations are roughly similar) above cognac.

Be cautious of French brandy without a cognac or armagnac title, regardless of how many meaningless 'stars' the label carries or even the magic word 'Napoléon' (which has no legal significance).

Little appreciated in Britain is the splendid 'apple brandy', Calvados, mainly associated with Normandy but also made in Brittany and the Marne. The best is *Calvados du Pays d'Auge*. Do take well-aged Calvados, but avoid any suspiciously cheap.

Contrary to popular belief, true Calvados is not distilled from cider – but an inferior imitation is: French cider (*cidre*) is excellent.

Though most French proprietary aperitifs, like Dubonnet, are fairly low in alcohol, the extremely popular Pernod/Ricard *pastis*-style brands are highly spirituous. *Eau-de-vie* is the generic term for all spirits, but colloquially tends to refer to local, often rough, distillates. Exceptions are the better *alcohols blancs* (white spirits), which are not inexpensive, made from fresh fruits and not sweetened as *crèmes* are.

Liqueurs

Numerous travellers deem it worth allocating their allowance to bring back some of the famous French liqueurs (Bénédictine, Chartreuse, Cointreau, and so on) which are so costly in Britain. Compare 'duty free' prices with those in stores, which can vary markedly. There is a plethora of regional liqueurs, and numerous sickly *crèmes*, interesting to taste locally. The only *crème* generally meriting serious consideration as a liqueur is *crème de menthe* (preferably Cusenier), though the newish *crème de Grand Marnier* has been successful. *Crème de cassis* has a special function: see *Kir* in alphabetical list.

Wine glossary by John Doxat

Abricotine – Generic apricot liqueur. Look for known brand-names.

Alcool blanc – Spirit distilled from fruit (not wine); not to be confused with fruit-flavoured cordials.

Aligoté – Burgundy wine (from grape of same name); light and dry.

Anis – Aniseed; much used in aperitifs of Pernod type.

Apéritif – Any drink taken as an appetiser (literally 'opener'). France has a huge range of proprietary aperitifs.

Appellation (d'Origine) Contrôlée – AC; see An Introduction to French Wines.

Armagnac – Superb brandy of the Gascon country, now achieving something of a rediscovery. See Hints on Spirits.

Barsac – Sweet Bordeaux wine (officially part of Sauternes); wide range from excellent to sickly boring.

Basserau – Sparkling red Burgundy; unusual if nothing else.

Beaune – Prestigious Burgundy name (red), the best very costly.

Blanc de Blancs – White wine from white grapes only. White wine is often made from black grapes, skins being removed before fermentation – as this is.

Blanc de Noirs – See immediately above: these are essentially type descriptions; some prestige accrues to *Blanc de Blancs*.

Bordeaux – See An Introduction to French Wines.

Bourgogne – Burgundy, see An Introduction to French Wines.

Brut – Very dry; particularly with good Champagne.

Cabernet – Noble grape, especially Cabernet-Sauvignon. Just its name on a label denotes a sound red wine.

Cacao – Cocoa; usually as *crème de cacao*.

Calvados – Apple brandy; see Hints on Spirits.

Cassis – Blackcurrant; *crème de cassis* widely favoured, notably in Kir (q.v.).

Cave – Cellar.

Cépage – Indication of grape variety; e.g. *cépage Sauvignon*.

Chai – Ground-level wine store, exclusively used in Cognac, frequently also in Bordeaux.

Champagne – See An Introduction to French Wines.

Clairet – Unimportant little-known Bordeaux wine, but probably origin of English word Claret (red Bordeaux).

Clos – Principally Burgundian word for vineyard enclosed, or formerly protected, by a wall.

Cognac – see Hints on Spirits.

Côte – Vineyard on a slope; no particular quality significance.

Coteaux(x) – Hillside(s); much the same as *côte*.

Crème – Sweet, mildly alcoholic cordials of many flavours. Not rated as true liqueurs, but one exception is *crème de menthe* (mint). See also *cassis*.

Crémant – Sparkling wine, without lasting champagne-style effervescence.

Cru – Literally 'growth'. Somewhat complicated term. *Grand cru* only meaningful if allied to good name. *Grand cru classé* (officially classified great wine) covers greatest wines, but not all *cru classé* is *grand*.

Cuve close – Sealed vat; describes production of sparkling wine by bulk secondary fermentation as opposed to bottle fermentation of 'champagne method'.

Cuvée – Wine from one vat, unblended. Another confusing word; *cuvée spéciale* can have more than its literal meaning.

Demi-sec – Translates as 'medium dry'; in practice means sweet.

Domaine – Mainly Burgundian word; broadly equivalent to château.

Doux – Very sweet.

Eau-de-vie – Generic term for all distilled spirits.

Frappé – Drink served on finely crushed ice.

Glacé – Iced by immersion of bottle, or other refrigeration.

Goût – Taste. In some regions also describes rough local spirit.

Haut – 'High'; denotes upper part of wine district. Not necessarily a mark of quality, though Haut-Medoc produces notably better wines than its lower areas

Izarra – Ancient, Armagnac-based Basque liqueur.

Kir – Excellent, now very popular aperitif: very dry chilled white wine (properly *Bourgogne Aligoté*) with a teaspoon of *crème de cassis* (q.v.) added. Kir Royale employs champagne.

Liqueur – originally *liqueur de dessert*, denoting post-prandial digestive use. Always sweet, so to speak of a 'liqueur Cognac' is absurd.

Litre – 1.7 pints; 5 litres equals 1.1 gallons.

Méthode Champenoise – Wine made by the champagne method.

Marc – Usually roughish brandy distilled from wine residue, though a few *Marcs* (pronounced 'mar') – notably *Marc de Bourgogne* – have some status.

Marque – Brand or company name.

Mise – As in *mise en bouteilles au château* (bottled at the château) or . . . *dans nos caves* (in our own cellars), etc.

Moelleux – On the sweet side.

Mousseux – Semi-technical term for sparkling; applies to the greatest champagne and to artificially carbonated rubbish.

Nouveau – New wine, particularly Beaujolais; made for drinking within a few months of harvest.

Pastis – General description, once more specific, for strong anis/liquorice-flavoured aperitifs originating in Marseilles; Ricard is a prime example.

Pétillant – Gently effervescent; sometimes translated as 'prickly' or 'crackling'.

Pineau – Unfermented grape juice fortified with grape spirit. Made in many regions: *Pineau des Charantes* (Cognac area) is best known. Well chilled, an attractive aperitif.

Porto – Portwine. The French are very big consumers, often using it (chilled) as an aperitif.

Primeur – Basically the same as *nouveau*. However, much fine Bordeaux and Burgundy is sold *'en primeur'* for long maturing by buyer.

Rosé – 'Pink wine'. Made by leaving skins of black grapes briefly in contact with juice; also by addition of red wine to white.

Sauvignon – Splendid white grape.

Sec – 'Dry', but wines thus marked will be sweetish. *Extra sec* may actually mean what it says.

Sirop – Syrup; akin to non-alcoholic *crème*.

Vermout – Vermouth.

Vin de Xérès – 'Vin de 'ereth'; sherry.

Glossary of cooking terms and dishes

(It would take another book to list comprehensively French cooking terms and dishes, but here are the ones most likely to be encountered)

Aigre-doux	bittersweet	*Braisé*	braised
Aiguillette	thin slice (aiguille – needle)	*Brandade*	dried salt cod pounded into
Aile	wing	*(de morue)*	a mousse
Aïoli	garlic mayonnaise	*Broche*	spit
Allemande (à l')	German style, i.e.: with	*Brochette*	skewer
	sausages and sauerkraut	*Brouillade*	stew, using oil
Amuses-gueule	appetisers	*Brouillé*	scrambled
Anglaise (à l')	plain boiled. Crème	*Brulé*	burnt, i.e. crème brulée
	Anglaise – egg and cream		
	sauce		
Andouille	large boiling sausage	*Campagne*	country style
Andouillettes	ditto but made from smaller	*Cannelle*	cinnamon
	intestines, usually served	*Carbonade*	braised in beer
	hot after grilling	*Cardinal*	red-coloured sauce, i.e.
Anis	aniseed		with lobster or in pâtisserie
Argenteuil	with asparagus		with redcurrant
Assiette Anglaise	plate of cold meats	*Cassolette or*	small pan
		cassoulette	
Baba au Rhum	yeast-based sponge	*Cassoulet*	rich stew with goose, pork
	macerated in rum		and haricot beans
Baguette	long thin loaf	*Cervelas*	pork garlic sausage
Ballotine	boned, stuffed and rolled	*Cervelles*	brains
	meat or poultry, usually	*Chantilly*	whipped sweetened cream
	cold	*Charcuterie*	cold pork-butcher's meats
Béarnaise	sauce made from egg yolks,	*Charlotte*	mould, as dessert lined
	butter, tarragon, wine,		with spongefingers, as
	shallots		savoury lined with
Beurre Blanc	sauce from Nantes, with		vegetable
	butter, reduction of shallot-	*Chasseur*	with mushrooms, shallots,
	flavoured vinegar or wine		wine
Béchamel	white sauce flavoured with	*Chausson*	pastry turnover
	infusion of herbs	*Chemise*	covering, i.e. pastry
Beignets	fritters	*Chiffonade*	thinly-cut, i.e. lettuce
Bercy	sauce with white wine and	*Choron*	tomato Béarnaise
	shallots	*Choucroute*	Alsatian stew with
Beurre noir	browned butter		sauerkraut and sausages
Bigarade	with oranges	*Civet*	stew
Billy By	mussel soup	*Clafoutis*	batter desert, usually with
Bisque	creamy shellfish soup		cherries
Blanquette	stew with thick white	*Clamart*	with peas
	creamy sauce, usually veal	*Cocotte*	covered casserole
Boeuf à la mode	braised beef	*Compôte*	cooked fruit
Bombe	ice cream mould	*Concassé*	i.e. tomatoes concassées –
Bonne femme	with root vegetables		skinned, chopped, juice
Bordelais	Bordeaux-style, with red or		extracted
	white wine, marrow bone	*Confit*	preserved
	fat	*Confiture*	jam
Bouchée	mouthful, i.e. vol au vent	*Consommé*	clear soup
Boudin	sausage or black pudding	*Coque (à la)*	i.e. oeufs – boiled eggs
Bourride	thick fish soup	*Cou*	neck

Coulis	juice, puree (of vegetables or fruit)
Court-bouillon	aromatic liquor for cooking meat, fish, vegetables
Couscous	N. African dish with millet, chicken, vegetable variations
Crapaudine	involving fowl, particularly pigeon, trussed
Crécy	with carrots
Crême Pâtissière	thick custard filling
Crêpe	pancake
Crépinette	little flat sausage, encased in caul
Croque Monsieur	toasted cheese and ham sandwich
Croustade	pastry or baked bread shell
Croûte	pastry crust
Croûton	cube of fried or toasted bread
Cru	raw
Crudités	raw vegetables
Demi-glâce	basic brown sauce
Doria	with cucumber
Emincé	thinly sliced
Entremets	sweets
Etuvé	stewed, i.e. vegetables in butter
Farci	stuffed
Fines herbes	parsley, thyme, bayleaf
Feuillété	leaves of flaky pastry
Flamande	Flemish style, with beer
Flambé	flamed in spirit
Flamiche	flan
Florentine	with spinach
Flute	thinnest bread loaf
Foie gras	goose liver
Fondu	melted
Fond (d'artichaut)	heart (of artichoke)
Forestière	with mushrooms, bacon and potatoes
Four (au)	baked in the oven
Fourré	stuffed, usually sweets
Fricandeau	veal, usually topside
Frais, fraiche	fresh and cool
Frangipane	almond creme patisserie
Fricadelle	Swedish meat ball
Fricassée	(usually of veal) in creamy sauce
Frit	fried
Frites	chips
Friture	assorted small fish, fried in batter

Froid	cold
Fumé	smoked
Galatine	loaf-shaped chopped meat, fish or vegetable, set in natural jelly
Galette	Breton pancake, flat cake
Garbure	thick country soup
Garni	garnished, usually with vegetables
Gaufre	waffle
Gelée	aspic
Gésier	gizzard
Gibier	game
Gigôt	leg
Glacé	iced
Gougère	choux pastry, large base
Goujons	fried strips, usually of fish
Graine	seed
Gratin	baked dish of vegetables cooked in cream and eggs
Gratinée	browned under grill
Grêcque (à la)	cold vegetables served in oil
Grenouilles	frogs; cuisses de grenouille – frogs' legs
Grillé	grilled
Gros sel	coarse salt
Hachis	minced or chopped
Hericot	slow cooked stew
Hochepot	hotpot
Hollandaise	sauce with egg, butter, lemon
Hongroise	Hungarian, i.e. spiced with paprika
Hors d'oeuvre	assorted starters
Huile	oil
Île flottante	floating island – soft meringue on egg custard sauce
Indienne	Indian, i.e. with hot spices
Jambon	ham
Jardinière	from the garden, i.e. with vegetables
Jarret	shin, i.e. jarret de veau
Julienne	matchstick vegetables
Jus	natural juice
Lait	milk
Langue	tongue
Lard	bacon
Longe	loin
Macedoine	diced fruits or vegetables
Madeleine	small sponge cake

Magret	breast (of duck)
Maïs	sweetcorn
Maître d'hôtel	sauce with butter, lemon, parsley
Marchand de vin	sauce with red wine, shallot
Marengo	sauce with tomatoes, olive oil, white wine
Marinière	seamen's style, i.e. moules marinières (mussels in white wine)
Marmite	deep casserole
Matelote	fish stew, i.e. of eel
Médaillon	round slice
Mélange	mixture
Meunière	sauce with butter, lemon
Miel	honey
Mille feuille	flaky pastry, lit. 1,000 leaves
Mirepoix	cubed carrot, onion etc. used for sauces
Moëlle	beef marrow
Mornay	cheese sauce
Mouclade	mussel stew
Mousseline	Hollandaise sauce, lightened with egg white
Moutarde	mustard
Nage (à la)	poached in flavoured liquor (fish)
Nature	plain
Navarin (d'agneau)	stew of lamb with spring vegetables
Noisette	nut-brown, burned butter
Noix de veau	nut of veal (leg)
Normande	Normandy style, with cream, apple, cider, Calvados
Nouilles	noodles
Os	bone
Paillettes	straws (of pastry)
Panaché	mixed
Panade	flour crust
Papillote (en)	cooked in paper case
Parmentier	with potatoes
Pâté	paste, of meat or fish
Pâte	pastry
Pâte brisée	rich short crust pastry
Pâtisserie	pastries
Paupiettes	paper-thin slice
Pavé	thick slice
Paysan	country style
Perigueux	with truffles
Persillade	chopped parsley and garlic topping
Petits fours	tiny cakes, sweetmeats
Petit pain	bread roll
Piperade	peppers, onions, tomatoes in scrambled egg

Poché	poached
Poëlé	fried
Poitrine	breast
Poivre	pepper
Pommade	paste
Potage	thick soup
Pot-au-four	broth with meat and vegetables
Potée	country soup with cabbage
Pralines	caramelised almonds
Primeurs	young veg
Printanièr(e)	garnished with early vegetables
Profiteroles	choux pastry balls
Provençale	with garlic, tomatoes, olive oil, peppers
Purée	mashed and sieved
Quenelle	pounded fish or meat, bound with egg, poached
Queue	tail
Quiche	pastry flan, i.e. quiche Lorraine – egg, bacon, cream
Râble	saddle, i.e. rable de lièvre
Ragout	stew
Ramequin	little pot
Rapé	grated
Ratatouille	provencale stew of onions, garlic, peppers, tomatoes
Ravigote	highly seasoned white sauce
Rémoulade	mayonnaise with gherkins, capers, herbs and shallot
Rillettes	potted shredded meat, usually fat pork or goose
Riz	rice
Robert	sauce with mustard, vinegar, onion
Roquefort	ewe's milk blue cheese
Rossini	garnished with foie gras and truffle
Rôti	roast
Rouelle	nugget
Rouille	hot garlicky sauce for soupe de poisson
Roulade	roll
Roux	sauce base – flour and butter
Sabayon	sweet fluffy sauce, with eggs and wine
Safran	saffron
Sagou	sago
St.-Germain	with peas
Salade niçoise	with tunny, anchovies, tomatoes, beans, black olives

Salé	salted
Salmis	dish of game or fowl, with red wine
Sang	blood
Santé	lit. healthy, i.e. with spinach and potato
Salpicon	meat, fowl, vegetables, chopped fine, bound with sauce and used as fillings
Saucisse	fresh sausage
Saucisson	dried sausage
Sauté	cooked in fat in open pan
Sauvage	wild
Savarin	ring of yeast sponge, soaked in syrup and liquor
Sel	salt
Selle	saddle
Selon	according to, i.e. selon grosseur (according to size)
Smitane	with sour cream, white wine, onion
Soissons	with dried white beans
Sorbet	water ice
Soubise	with creamed onions
Soufflé	puffed, i.e. mixed with egg white and baked
Sucre	sugar (Sucré – sugared)
Suprême	fillet of poultry breast or fish
Tartare	raw minced beef, flavoured with onion etc. and bound with raw egg
Tartare (sauce)	mayonnaise with capers, herbs, onions

Tarte Tatin	upside-down apple pie
Terrine	pottery dish/baked minced, chopped meat, veg., chicken, fish or fruit
Thé	tea
Tiède	luke warm
Timbale	steamed mould
Tisane	infusion
Tourte	pie
Tranche	thick slice
Truffes	truffles
Tuile	tile, i.e. thin biscuit
Vacherin	meringue confection
Vallée d'Auge	with cream, apple, Calvados
Vapeur (au)	steamed
Velouté	white sauce, bouillon-flavoured
Véronique	with grapes
Vert(e)	green, i.e. sauce verte with herbs
Vessie	pig's bladder
Vichyssoise	chilled creamy leek and potato soup
Vierge	prime olive oil
Vinaigre	vinegar (lit. bitter wine)
Vinaigrette	wine vinegar and oil dressing
Volaille	poultry
Vol-au-vent	puff pastry case
Xérès	sherry
Yaourt	yoghurt

FISH – Les Poissons, SHELLFISH – Les Coquillages

Aiglefin	haddock – also Églefin	*Langouste*	crawfish
Alose	shad	*Langoustine*	Dublin Bay prawn
Anchois	anchovy	*Lieu*	ling
Anguille	eel	*Limand*	lemon sole
Araignée de mer	spider crab	*Lotte de mer*	monkfish
Bar	sea bass	*Loup de mer*	sea bass
Barbue	brill	*Maquereau*	mackerel
Baudroie	monkfish, anglerfish	*Merlan*	whiting
Belon	oyster – flat shelled	*Mérou*	grouper
Bigorneau	winkle	*Morue*	salt cod
Blanchaille	whitebait	*Moule*	mussel
Brochet	pike	*Muge, mulet*	grey mullet
Cabillaud	cod	*Murène*	moray eel
Calmar	squid	*Nonat*	tiny fish similar to
Carrelet	plaice		whitebait
Chapon de mer	scorpion fish	*Ombre*	grayling
Claire	oyster	*Orade*	gilt-headed bream
Clovisse	large clam	*Oursin*	sea urchin
Colin	hake	*Pageot*	sea bream
Congre	conger eel	*Palourde*	clam
Coques	cockles	*Perche*	perch
Coquille	scallop	*Petoncle*	small scallop
St. Jacques		*Plie*	plaice
Crabe	crab	*Portugaise*	oyster
Crevette grise	shrimp	*Poulpe*	octopus
Crevette rose	prawn	*Praire*	small clam
Daurade	sea bream	*Raie*	skate
Donzelle or Girelle	a brightly coloured eel-	*Rascasse*	scorpion-fish
	like Mediterranean fish	*Rouget*	red mullet
Écrevisse	crayfish	*St. Pierre*	John Dory
Encornet	cuttlefish, squid	*Sauclet*	sand smelt
Éperlan	smelt	*Saumon*	salmon
Espadon	swordfish	*Saumonette*	rock salmon
Etrille	baby crab	*Scipion*	cuttlefish
Favouille	spider crab	*Seiche*	squid
Fiecas	conger eel	*Sole*	sole
Flétan	halibut	*Soupion*	inkfish
Fruits de mer	seafood	*Sourdon*	cockle
Gamba	large prawn	*Thon*	tunny
Grondin	red gurnet	*Tortue*	turtle
Hareng	herring	*Tourteau*	large crab
Homard	lobster	*Truite*	trout
Huitre	oyster	*Turbot*	turbot
Julienne	ling	*Turbotin*	chicken turbot
Laitance	soft herring roe	*Vernis*	clam
Lamproie	lamprey	*Violet*	soft-shelled shellfish

FRUITS – Les fruits, VEGETABLES – Les légumes, NUTS – Les noix
HERBS – Les herbes, SPICES – Les épices

Ail	garlic	*Groseille à maquereau*	gooseberry
Algue	seaweed	*Groseille noire*	blackcurrant
Amande	almond	*Groseille rouge*	redcurrant
Ananas	pineapple	*Haricot*	dried white bean
Aneth	dill	*Haricot vert*	French bean
Abricot	apricot	*Laitue*	lettuce
Arachide	peanut	*Mandarine*	tangerine, mandarin
Artichaut	globe artichoke	*Mangetout*	sugar pea
Asperge	asparagus	*Marron*	chestnut
Avocat	avocado	*Menthe*	mint
Banane	banana	*Mirabelle*	tiny gold plum
Basilic	basil	*Morille*	dark brown crinkly
Betterave	beetroot		edible fungus
Blette	Swiss chard	*Mûre*	blackberry
Brugnon	nectarine	*Muscade*	nutmeg
Cassis	blackcurrant	*Myrtille*	bilberry, blueberry
Céleri	celery	*Navet*	turnip
Céleri-rave	celeriac	*Noisette*	hazelnut
Cèpe	edible fungus	*Oignon*	onion
Cerfeuil	chervil	*Oseille*	sorrel
Cérise	cherry	*Palmier*	palm
Champignon	mushroom	*Pamplemousse*	grapefruit
Chanterelle	edible fungus	*Panais*	parsnip
Chatâigne	chestnut	*Passe-Pierre*	seaweed
Chicorée	endive	*Pastèque*	water melon
Chou	cabbage	*Pêche*	peach
Choufleur	cauliflower	*Persil*	parsley
Choux de Bruxelles	Brussels sprout	*Petit pois*	pea
Ciboulette	chive	*Piment doux*	sweet pepper
Citron	lemon	*Pissenlit*	dandelion
Citron vert	lime	*Pistache*	pistachio
Coing	quince	*Pleurote*	edible fungi
Concombre	cucumber	*Poire*	pear
Coriandre	coriander	*Poireau*	leek
Cornichon	gherkin	*Poivre*	pepper
Courge	marrow, pumpkin	*Poivron*	green, red and yellow
Courgette	courgette		peppers
Cresson	watercress	*Pomme*	apple
Échalotte	shallot	*Pomme-de-terre*	potato
Endive	chicory	*Prune*	plum
Épinard	spinach	*Pruneau*	prune
Escarole	salad leaves	*Quetsch*	small dark plum
Estragon	tarragon	*Radis*	radish
Fenouil	fennel	*Raifort*	horseradish
Fève	broad bean	*Raisin*	grape
Flageolet	small green bean	*Reine Claude*	greengage
Fraise	strawberry	*Romarin*	rosemary
Framboise	raspberry	*Safran*	saffron
Genièvre	juniper	*Salisifis*	salsify
Gingembre	ginger	*Thym*	thyme
Girofle	clove	*Tilleul*	lime blossom
Girolle	edible fungus	*Tomate*	tomato
Granade	pomegranate	*Topinambour*	Jerusalem artichoke
Griotte	bitter red cherry	*Truffe*	truffle

MEAT – Les Viandes

Le Boeuf	Beef	*Jambon cru*	raw smoked ham
Charolais	is the best	*Porcelet*	suckling pig
Chateaubriand	double fillet steak		
Contrefilet	sirloin	*Le Veau*	Veal
Entrecôte	rib steak	*Escalope*	thin slice cut from fillet
Faux Filet	sirloin steak		
Filet	fillet		
L'Agneau	Lamb	*Les Abats*	Offal
Pré-Salé	is the best	*Foie*	liver
Carré	neck cutlets	*Foie gras*	goose liver
Côte	chump chop	*Cervelles*	brains
Epaule	shoulder	*Langue*	tongue
Gigot	leg	*Ris*	sweetbreads
		Rognons	kidneys
Le Porc	Pork	*Tripes*	tripe
Jambon	ham		

POULTRY– Volaille, GAME – Gibier

Abatis	giblets	*Lièvre*	hare
Bécasse	woodcock	*Oie*	goose
Bécassine	snipe	*Perdreau*	partridge
Caille	quail	*Pigeon*	pigeon
Canard	duck	*Pintade*	guineafowl
Caneton	duckling	*Pluvier*	plover
Chapon	capon	*Poularde*	chicken (boiling)
Chevreuil	roe deer	*Poulet*	chicken (roasting)
Dinde	young hen turkey	*Poussin*	spring chicken
Dindon	turkey	*Sanglier*	wild boar
Dindonneau	young turkey	*Sarcelle*	teal
Faisan	pheasant	*Venaison*	venison
Grive	thrush		

Notes

Other French Entrée Guides

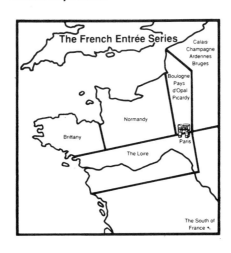

'She doesn't care what she says.' *Observer*

'Well worth looking through for anyone wondering where to spend the first (or last) night of a holiday in France.' *Country Life*

'Makes you want to drive down to Dover and onto a cross-Channel ferry right away.' *Sunday Telegraph*

'An excellent, evocative but crisp little guide to the neglected North of France.' *Good Book Guide*

'. . . a very objective and highly readable book for visitors to the three ports of Calais, Le Havre, Cherbourg and their environs.' *Autosport*

'Can there be an auberge or dockside café that Ms Fenn has failed to report on?' *Books and Bookmen*

'Patricia Fenn's immensely reliable guides to the places to eat and sleep need no recommendation to anyone who has used them.' *Evening Standard*

'Time and again she has got to good places and chefs before the news reached Michelin or Gault-et-Millau.' *Guardian*

'Lively, humorous and above all immensely readable.' *Country Life*

'Makes you want to dash across on the ferry immediately.' *Good Housekeeping*

In preparation:
FRENCH ENTRÉE 11 Paris
ENTREE TO MALTA
ENTREE TO ALGARVE
ENTREE TO MAJORCA   and many others.

Also published by Quiller Press

– two companions to French Entrée to help you enjoy your holiday more.

LEGAL BEAGLE GOES TO FRANCE

Bill Thomas £3.95

All you need to deal with problems involving the law in France – accidents, houses, travel – even births and deaths. Includes: legal and customs formalities; daily life in France; eating, sleeping and drinking; en route; getting around without a car; renting a gîte and buying a house.

CONTINENTAL MOTORING GUIDE

Paul Youden £3.95

A concise and highly illustrated full-colour guide for motorists. Gives essential facts on continental road signs and regulations, as well as tips to make your drive more enjoyable right from the time you leave the ferry.

SPAIN BY CAR

Norman Renouf £7.95

The essential guide to food and accommodation for all motorists in Spain. Objective information and photographs of over 650 hotels, guest houses, motels and hostels along the main roads.

WALES – A GOOD EATING GUIDE

Roger Thomas   £5.95

A guide for tourists and locals alike, to nearly 300 restaurants and shops recommended for typically Welsh food. Inside information on where to eat in Wales, with a map and 40 line drawings.

INVITATION TO DEVON

Joy David   £6.95

Places to visit, eat and sleep throughout the county, by a devoted Devonian. With over 100 line drawings.

EVERYBODY'S HISTORIC LONDON

Jonathan Kiek   £4.95

Historian and teacher Jonathan Kiek's award-winning guide to London is now in its fourth edition. 60 photographs, maps and plans complement background history and up-to-date practical information.

EVERYBODY'S HISTORIC ENGLAND

Jonathan Kiek   £4.95

Much-praised combination of popular history and carefully thought-out tours of the whole of England – required reading for all travellers who enjoy our national heritage.

Please order from your bookshop or, in case of difficulty, write with payment to:
Quiller Press, 46 Lillie Road, London SW6 1TN.